VOICES of the CONFEDERATION

By
Don Elkins and Carla L. Rueckert

L/L Research
Louisville, Kentucky
© 2016

Voices of the Confederation

Copyright © 2016 L/L Research

All rights reserved. No part of this book may be reproduced or used in any form or by any means—graphic, electronic or mechanical, including photocopying or information storage and retrieval systems—without written permission from the copyright holder.

ISBN: 978-0-945007-08-1

Published by L/L Research
Box 5195
Louisville, Kentucky 40255-0195, USA
www.llresearch.org

Cover credit: Michele Matossian, www.lightweaver.com

Table of Contents

Introduction by Don Elkins 5
Carla L. Rueckert's Editor's Preface (1975) 22
Carla L. Rueckert's Editor's Preface (2009) 24
Chapter 1: The UFOs 28
    Their Presence 28
    Their Elusiveness 36
    Why the UFOs Don't Land 39
    The Early Contactees 46
    The Confederation's Mission 46
Chapter 2: Channels And Channeling 53
    The Function of Channels 53
    Channeling 63
    Graded Groups 67
    Being a Channel 68
Chapter 3: The Channeling Experience 84
    Interviews with Developing Channels 86
Chapter 4: About Specific Information 98
Chapter 5: Cycles 103
    The Concept of Cycles 103
    The Concept of Vibration 114
Chapter 6: Entering the Silence 120
    Meditation 120
    Desire 130
    Seeking 137
    Service to others 146
    Language 157
Chapter 7: The Original Creation 160
    The Original Creation 160
    The Concept of All-Consciousness 165
    Healing 166
    Jesus 166
    Love 169

Light 175
The Creator's Law 177
Truth 179
Unity 183
Confidence 191
Space Travel 193

Chapter 8: The World in Which We Live 195
The Physical Illusion 195
The Physical Illusion II: 207
Dream/Reality 209
Channeling Selections 210
Evil 212
Lack and Limitation 214
The Antichrist 216
Satan 217
Death 218
Wealth 221
Time 223
Sleep 224
Sex 227
Drugs 229

Chapter 9: The Place of the Intellect 232
The Intellect 232
Free Will 237
The Mind 239

Chapter 10: Complete Messages 244

Introduction by Don Elkins

It was a cold, clear evening in February, 1963. There were fifteen people sitting in Hal Price's living room, although they were hard to count in the darkness. The house was situated in middle class, suburban normalcy in one of the small cities around Louisville, Kentucky. But inside the dark room, the fifteen people were acting somewhat oddly.

If you looked closely, the faint light that filtered through the fabric of the closed curtain was sufficient to reveal that a few of the people there were opening and closing their mouths, and occasionally one of them would rapidly move his tongue, making a clicking sound with his mouth.

Then one of those present began to speak in a strange, extremely forced manner. "Greetings in the love and the light of the Infinite Creator," he blurted.

Another person asked, "Are you nearby?"

In the same strained voice, the first speaker suggested that if the person who asked would come outside, they would show him the craft. First all fifteen people went outside for the craft, but they saw nothing but a clear and starry sky. The people went back inside and resumed their former posture.

Again the speaker with the strained voice suggested that if the one who had asked where the craft was would come outside, this person would be shown their craft. The questioner immediately left the group. When he got outside he waited for no more than twenty seconds. Then he saw an orange-ish light, which crossed the sky until it came to rest over his head. It then changed colors, from orange through blue to white. It remained fixed for a few seconds, larger than Venus, but smaller than the moon. Then it disappeared.

Introduction

I was one of the fifteen who were at that meeting in February, 1963. I did not see that UFO. However, careful questioning of the man who saw it convinced me that the phenomenon was within the limits for definite classification as an "unidentified" object. I have, however, seen two other UFOs, and have pursued numerous allegations of contact with UFOs since that time.

This volume is intended to put before you some of the data I have gathered.

I met Hal Price in 1962. He was a design engineer and had recently been transferred from Detroit to Louisville. Mr. Price told me that he'd been in a group of people in Detroit who had received regular telepathic communications from flying saucer pilots. I was somewhat skeptical about his claim until I read some of the messages that had been received in Detroit. The general content of the material was identical to that which I personally had been receiving since 1952.

My own telepathic contact had induced me to investigate paranormal phenomena in general deeply, and to conduct several hundred experiments studying extrasensory ability, in particular under hypnosis.

The important factor that I had overlooked in my research was being demonstrated by the Detroit group. It was possible to convert telepathic impressions directly into language and then speak, just as if the telepath were acting as a radio receiver.

I immediately planned an experiment using Mr. Price as an instructor of technique. I had no trouble at all finding volunteers for the experiment. At that time I was teaching at the Speed Scientific School, a College of the University of Louisville, and I had more than enough interested students available for a study group. We had close to one hundred people in the experiment before a year was up, and over a dozen had been extremely faithful members. These students

Introduction

made up the preponderance of the group. However, a couple of dozen volunteers from other areas were also involved.

How to conduct such an unorthodox experiment could have been a difficult question. However, we had previous instructions given to us by the Detroit group. This data was, of course, only alleged to be from the aliens in the flying saucers, but since we were attempting to talk to them, we decided to take their alleged advice as to how to do so.

The information given us by the Detroit Group was simple. Our instructions were to sit, as a group, quietly, in the dark, in an upright position, with the spine as vertical as possible and then to think of nothing. These were very simple instructions: sit up straight and think of nothing. Many found them difficult to follow, at first. It took some practice to find the knack of it.

One or two nights each week for the next two months, we sat in the dark together with our eyes closed, thinking of nothing, or as near to nothing as possible. We awaited results, but no results had yet transpired. We felt a bit subdued about the experiment until a member of the Detroit Group came to us for a visit. He joined us in our meeting and spoke to us, telepathically "channeling" the alleged thoughts of a UFOnaut, who assured us that if we continued our meetings, we would have success in receiving their thoughts.

We felt cheered by this encouragement, and continued our meetings as before. Within a few weeks, results began to manifest themselves. An unusual phenomenon which we came to call "conditioning" began occurring to almost every member of the group. As we sat in the darkened room, eyes closed, letting our minds run down, we found, one by one, that our mouth and tongue muscles were being exercised. The exercise would often be abrupt, almost painful, with the mouth flying open vehemently, or the tongue flopping and gyrating so quickly that it made popping and flapping sounds.

Introduction

If this had happened to only one person, it would simply have been very funny, and indeed it was sometimes difficult not to laugh, as we all sat around making these strange sounds, but this happened to all but one of the most faithful members of the group.

It was several weeks before the "conditioning" period began to give way to the breakthrough of speaking. Participants in the group slowly began to find their mouths forming words, instead of unintelligible sounds and silent movements. They began to speak one word at a time, involuntarily. This progress was always quite slow initially, but in time, practice seemed to make perfect, and the channel would become more and more fluent, less and less controlled and jerky in his delivery. In the messages herein printed, you will find the alleged UFOnauts' own explanation of the various types of channeling.

The data we received and the results we were and are getting bring us up against the problem of data evaluation. I had originally intended to design a system of experimentation with controlled boundaries so that material of a scientifically evidential nature could be produced, but before the first month of the experiment had ended, I had begun to realize that this phenomenon would not lend itself to rigorous analytical control. The basic phenomenon of telepathic contact could not even be adequately researched. Had we been able to show concrete evidence of telepathy, it would still have been very difficult to prove evidentially from where the contact emanated.

Of one thing we were certain: we would have an abundance of data. All but one of the original group had manifested the same syndrome of conditioning and, subsequently, speaking, and their messages from the alleged UFOnauts had begun to collect. This material was amazingly self-consistent, and coincided in content and in style with messages received from

Introduction

the same alleged source at places all over the continent. Indeed, this pile of messages has continued to grow until now I can offer you, in this book, only a small part of the material we have in our files.

It seemed rather an exaggeration of scientific caution to declare that all of the people who exhibited the conditioning and speaking syndrome were suffering from identical forms of mental aberration. Since the original group was studied, many others have developed, and the process is always the same: sometimes much accelerated as compared with our early experience, but it is always the same general syndrome and process.

We have gone ahead in securing in-depth data, which we present to you for your own evaluation. I have spent many an hour reflecting on what this experiment has produced, and what scientific or non-scientific questions could be said to find an answer from within this material, and I have concluded that because of the nature of the material received, there are no systems of evaluation extant which can be used to judge this body of data. The system of evaluation that may emerge for this in the future will, I believe, have its principle keys within this data itself.

I base this rather presumptuous and logically dubious assertion on a thought I have found stated well by Thomas Goudge, a Canadian philosopher of science. Goudge is considering the problems of evaluation of new scientific advances, and he writes,

"Roughly I would say that a necessary condition of scientific advance is that allowance must be made for a) genuinely new empirical observations and b) new explanation schemes."[1]

---

[1] Sagan, Carl, and Thornton Page. *Ufo's - A Scientific Debate*. Ithaca, Cornell U.P., c1972, p.38.

Introduction

Goudge goes on to point out that he feels that the scientific establishment's view of UFO phenomena is that UFOs are either not scientific data or else are misinterpretations of natural objects; and that he finds this type of judgmental approach to "reject a necessary condition of scientific advance."[2]

Having reasoned that I could not possibly arrange a scientifically evidential experiment, and aware that I lacked the ability to formulate the new explanation scheme, which Goudge postulates as necessary for evaluating new information, I had the choice of either being overcome with a sense of futility, or carrying on with the data-gathering as best as possible.

A great deal of this data have now been accumulated, and I feel at this point that I can take a position on UFOs. The position is perhaps best stated as being one of direct disagreement with the Condon Committee's statement of summary after the completion of their one-year, half-million dollar research program for the investigation of UFOs. Dr. Condon wrote: "Our general conclusion is that nothing has come from the study of UFO's in the past 21 year that has added to scientific knowledge."[3]

As you may well guess before I say it, my position is that there is little possibility of gaining material that could add to scientific knowledge <u>as we now know it</u>. The only type of activity which I can readily perceive as having evidential value would be some maneuver on command by a visible UFO, a specified physical contact, or an actual visitation from an alien being. Although such events have been reported, there is still

---

[2] Ibid.
[3] Condon. Edward U. *Scientific Studies Of Unidentified Flying Objects*. New York, Dutton, 1969, p. 1.

Introduction

no method of reproducing this phenomenon at will. The UFOs are everlastingly elusive.

This elusive quality is worth noting. From the beginning, UFO sightings and contacts have been highly colored by obscure details and tantalizing mysteries. This shroud of mystery might be very much intended by the UFOnauts; might, in fact, be an integral part of the phenomena. In these messages we find many references to the UFOnauts' motives for their creating this shroud of mystery.

Perhaps the non-evidential quality of the telepathy syndrome is one of the keys which will eventually unlock the explanation scheme of a new understanding of science. At any rate, this sort of thinking was what led us on to further data-gathering, long after we had become fully aware that there was no hope of securing evidence in the current scientific sense.

Reports of telepathic contact with UFOnauts had begun coming in as early as 1952, with George Adamski's claimed contact. In the early fifties, Adamski was joined by a prominent anthropologist, George Hunt Williamson, who also claimed initial contact with UFOnauts using both telepathy and radio-telegraphy. George Van Tassel claimed telepathic contact with the UFO occupants at this time, and drew such an interested crowd in response to his published claims that a "space" convention, which he held at his desert airport, was the subject for an article in a national magazine. Major Wayne Ahoe attended one of these conventions, also reporting UFO contact, including telepathic communications. Major Ahoe has lectured on the UFO phenomenon unceasingly since that time. Daniel Fry claimed that he was taken on board a UFO at White Sands, New Mexico, and many other individuals made similar contact claims.

So, when I began to investigate the phenomenon in earnest, two things were abundantly clear: 1) that UFO contact was

Introduction

allegedly possible, and 2) that the scientific establishment in general grouped these contact reports under the headings of doubtful lunacies, frauds, or material from cultist groups.

It was not hard to see why the scientific community would be sorely tempted to classify all UFO contacts in a lump under cultist claims because of the metaphysical or religious orientation of most of the messages which were allegedly received from the extraterrestrial sources. On the surface, such contacts seemed like highly imaginative science fiction stories, or like the creations of fanatic cultist groups seeking frantically for their new Messiah.

But what the scientific community chose to overlook was the independence of many of the claims from each other claim of contact, and the extreme degree of consistency in the content of the messages. This independence was a fact in my own group: the participants did not know when they started what their goal was or what they should expect to happen to them. The messages which they eventually produced were extremely consistent in content with other alleged UFO messages.

In 1963, 1964, and 1965 I made a point of visiting several groups claiming telepathic contact with UFOnauts. I met with groups in Ohio, Florida, Michigan, Pennsylvania, Illinois, and California. Since that time I have not found it helpful further to visit other groups, but I have heard of increasing numbers of functioning groups around the country, in Canada, England and elsewhere in the world. And, in addition to the growing number of voluntary contacts, one can come across many sincerely told stories of involuntary contact, which is sometimes frightening to the unprepared individual.

An example of this which has been fairly well documented Is Herbert Schirmer's story. Schirmer, a highway patrolman in the Midwest, reported sighting a flying saucer during a routine patrol. The Condon Committee heard of this and put

Introduction

him through age-regression hypnosis, a medically approved therapy for inducing remembrance of traumatic experiences. Under hypnosis, Schirmer recounted contact with the UFOnauts themselves, rather than a simple sighting of a flying saucer. Repeated testing of Schirmer's memory only proved that Schirmer believed very sincerely that his story of contact with extraterrestrials was true. The Condon Committee people could not shake his faith in what he remembered of the UFOnauts.

In a book called *Gods And Devils From Outer Space*, Herb Schirmer's story is told rather fully, and one of the investigating reporters, who seemed well versed in this area, offered a list of general observations regarding the UFO contactees. Among his points was this one concerning the way the contactee allegedly receives his messages from the UFOnauts:

"While he is being interviewed or questioned, the contactee often seems to be listening to another "voice" or presence in the room. Often there are pauses in his conversation which last as long as forty-five seconds to a minute. After this pause, the answer to a query is given with great lucidity. In interview session wherein the contactee has been hypnotically regressed to the time of contact, he begins his entranced recreation of the experience in "normal" hypnotic voice trance patterns. When he reaches the time when the "message" was relayed to him (usually after the mental and physical examination), his voice and manner change, even under hypnotic trance and he recites, rather than recalls, the dogma which saucer people have relayed to him."[4]

I recognized this description of the contactee's manner when speaking as a messenger for alleged UFOnauts as being similar

---

[4] Norman, Eric, *Gods And Devils From Outer Space*. Lancer, N.Y., 1973, pp. 161-2.

to the style of speaking used by all the "telepathic receivers" that I had investigated.

Another extremely apt description of this telepathic contact is found in John Fuller's book, *Interrupted Journey*. Included in this volume is a great deal of directly transcribed and quoted material from the file of Betty and Barney Hill. They had gone to a psychiatrist with an anxiety problem. The Doctor had performed age-regression hypnosis on both of them and uncovered an alleged contact with the space people. This book is an excellent one. Let us look at how Barney Hill describes his contact with the space man in this volume:

"**Doctor:** Did the men speak to you?

Barney: Only the one I thought was the leader.

Doctor: The one you thought was the leader in the space ship?

Barney: Yes.

Doctor: What kind of language did he use?

Barney: He did not speak by word. I was told what to do by his thoughts making my thoughts understand. And I could hear him. And I could not understand in that I <u>could</u> understand him. And I was told that I would not be harmed.

Doctor: Was this some kind of mental telepathy?

Barney: I am not familiar with this term.

Doctor: Mental telepathy is being able to understand someone else's thoughts or having your thoughts understood by someone else.

Barney: I could understand his thoughts."[5]

---

[5] Fuller, John, *Interrupted Journey*, New York, Dial, 1966, pp. 201-2.

Introduction

The most important single UFO contactee report I have seen to date is Andrija Puharich's book, *Uri: A Journal Of The Mystery Of Uri Geller (Garden City, Doubleday, 1974)*. Dr. Puharich, a widely respected researcher into paranormal phenomena such as telepathy, psychic healing and the Kahuna priestly tradition, reports in this volume on a UFO contact story that is most informative and exciting. If you seek out only one book on the physical aspects of contactee phenomena, seek out *Uri*, by all means!

What impressed me in my researching through the data these groups have collected, and through the books published by the more careful of the researchers, was the feeling that I had a puzzle in my hands, and that the pieces were all beginning to fit. I can now say for sure that the puzzles lies outside the boundaries of contemporary orthodox science.

Three things have especially impressed me about all this data. One, as I have said, is the extremely high degree of correlation of the material of one group or individual with other groups and sources. Identifications of alleged extraterrestrial sources often match, and the style and content of the messages matches in almost every case.

Considerable effort has been put forward in the past twenty years by various organizations in an attempt to ascertain information as to what UFOs are and why they are here. Over seventy books have been published on the subject in the U.S., and pamphlets and magazine articles have proliferated. The Air Force Projects "Grunge" and "Blue Book" were aimed at finding out whether we needed to protect our skies from these UFO "invaders". Canada has run two such projects, named "Second Storey" and "Magnet". The National Investigations Committee for Aerial Phenomena, with a very large network of volunteer investigators, presented a lengthy report on the subject to Congress in 1964.

Introduction

In 1966 the Condon Committee was formed, backed by a half-million dollar government appropriation. Its mission was the investigation of the possible scientific value of UFO-related phenomena. The report of that Committee seems to support the actuality of UFOs by its sheer bulk, even though its conclusion refutes the possibility of advancing science through their study.

Another interesting volume, John Fuller's *Aliens In Our Skies*, contains several eminent scientists' opinions of UFO's, as presented to the House Committee on Science and Aeronautics in 1968. In 1969, the American Association for the Advancement of Science held a two-day debate on UFO's during its annual meeting. The list of published works is too long to annotate. If you wish to delve into the background material on UFOs, please consult the bibliography at the end of this volume for specific references.

What many clergy and religious lay people are associating the UFO sightings with is the Day of Judgment, or Armageddon. Many people who believe in UFOs at all believe this interpretation of their meaning. I think the reason is that the truth is somewhere in the area of religion or metaphysics, rather than in science as we know it. Perhaps the concept of Armageddon is far different from the real reason they are here; still, that concept is at least born of a religious or moral impulse, and I suggest that this religious impulse may be another one of the keys that unlocks the explanation system for a new understanding of science and of the world.

It is apparent that as far as the general scientific community is concerned, the idea that UFOnauts could be contacting people on this planet with messages of a religious or metaphysical nature is simply beneath notice. The late Dr. James E. McDonald, of the University of Arizona, included in a list of possible explanations for UFOs the notion that such objects could be "space ships bringing messengers of terrestrial

Introduction

salvation and occult truth," but, he stated, he only listed that hypothesis in order to keep his list scientifically complete. He felt that this hypothesis could not be true.[6] And this attitude of ridicule is standard among most scientists, in spite of comments from within their own ranks by men who are more open-minded.

In 1967, Professor Hermann Oberth spoke on the subject of extraterrestrial cultures, and suggested that scientists "should tackle problems that may seem fantastic at first. Scholars behave like stuffed geese who refuse to digest anything else. They simply reject new ideas as nonsense."[7]

And again, there is the persuasive parable drawn by Dr. McDonald, the same man whom we earlier quoted as finding the messages of the UFOs ridiculous. In fact, the parable becomes just that much more persuasive as we see Dr. McDonald caught in the same trap which he himself describes so well. I quote from *Aliens In The Skies*. Mr. McDonald is speaking to members of Congress:

"There is a very real ridicule lid that has not been contrived by any group, it has just evolved the way the whole problem has unfolded. This is not entirely new in science. It has occurred before.

"I am sure a number here at the speakers' table are familiar with an interesting chapter in science years ago when meteorites, out of which NASA and many scientists around the world, get a very large amount of useful scientific information, were scorned and scoffed as unreal. It was regarded as nonsense that peasants were telling stories about stones falling out of the sky. The efforts of a few scientists to take a look at the problem and to get some initial data simply

---

[6] Fuller, John, *Aliens In Our Skies*. New York, Putnam, 1969, p. 91.
[7] Daniken, Erich, *Chariots Of The Gods?* New York, Putnam, 1967, p. 143.

were ignored until a very unusual but very real event occurred, in northern France, a meteorite shower. So they sent an eminent academician out to have a look at what these people were talking about, and by golly, the peasants appeared to be right. Everybody in the village, the prefect of police, the local administrators, all the peasants, had seen stones fall out of the sky, and for the first time the French Academy deigned to take a look at the problem. Meteorites were born.

"Here we now face a very similar situation in science. We have tended to ignore it because we didn't think it made sense. It definitely defies any explanation, and hence the situation has evolved where we can't get going because we aren't already going."[8]

So, here we are with a real "meteor shower" happening to us. Reports of UFO sightings and contacts are perhaps several thousand times more common than the reports of meteors in the France of the eighteenth century. Over half of the population of the United States, according to a recent poll, believes in the reality of UFOs. We know nothing of the UFOs, except what they allegedly have told us in the contactee's messages. Indeed, we know nothing about the phenomena connected with telepathy. We have been able to prove that the phenomena exist: that thought can be sent and received with no physical aid. But that is all we have been able to do. We have no rational idea of how telepathy works.

In the middle 1930's, Dr. J. B. Rhine of Duke University was able to show conclusively that thought transference between individuals could be achieved and apparently did not diminish with increasing distance of separation. Some of his best results were achieved at a distance of separation of experimental subjects of over 200 miles.

---

[8] Fuller, Aliens In Our Skies, pp. 6-8.

Introduction

And American hypnotist, Stanley V. Mitchell, discovered in 1964 that, while an elderly subject of his was under hypnosis, she could respond to his instructions although she did not understand English. Mitchell, reports the authors of *Psychic Discoveries Behind The Iron Curtain*, became very interested in this phenomenon. From that book:

"Intrigued, he questioned the old woman. She said she could easily understand him under hypnosis. 'But when you don't hypnotize, all you say is cha cha cha.'"[9]

This gives us an indication that language may be no barrier to the transference of thought by telepathy. But to date, there has been no answer to the "why" or "how" of telepathy.

It would seem that our only choice is to try to consider without bias all reports concerning UFOs, even if they seem to be of an unacceptable nature by our standards. We choose this standpoint not because it has any special virtue but because it has the least amount of presupposition involved that can be consistent with doing anything in the world of physical science. This means that there is a correspondingly higher possibility that a part of the data we have thusly gathered may be of use to us in unlocking the new concept of the nature of the universe that may lie within the data we have gathered.

One question very central to this enquiry is, if the UFOs are real, why don't they just land and talk to us in person? I have already mentioned to you that the shroud of mystery surrounding the UFO phenomena is one of its significant attributes. My investigations have led me to suspect that the UFOnauts wish us to remain free either to believe or to

---

[9] Ostrander, Sheila, and Lynn Schroeder, *Psychic Discoveries Behind The Iron Curtain*: Englewood Cliffs, Prentice-Hall, c1970, p. 110.

disbelieve in them and in their message. This sentiment is spelled out in the alleged messages received telepathically.

Let us draw a parallel between a very advanced culture compared to ours and our culture compared to one much less advanced. I have a friend whose father was a missionary to a remote tribe in the New Guinea interior. His was the first white skin they had ever seen. They thought of him as a God, and it took him most of his life to win some of them to Christianity. It is interesting to note that they were very much afraid of him, and many of the older tribe members remained terrified of him all their lives.

It is ego-deflating to compare ourselves with such a culture, but perhaps the comparison is apt. Our technology has only been growing and snowballing for a century. Progress seems to accelerate exponentially, and the next century may see many times the progress we have already won.

The UFOnauts may come from a culture very, very advanced in comparison with ours. We are aware that the impact of an advanced culture on a primitive one is profound and irreversible. The UFOnauts might be quite reluctant to disturb our culture to the extent which they would necessarily achieve by proving their existence definitively to the world's population.

There is another point, too. Regardless of our technological advances, our social-humanistic advances have been almost non-existent, on the average, for centuries. We seem unable to do without warfare, crime, social unrest, mass hypocrisy and selfishness. It is possible that there is a "Stone Age" culture here, too, which science has overlooked simply because the latter qualities are not tangible, and cannot be evidentially tested with physical parameters.

At any rate, we have been contacted, so it would seem, and in this rather unusual and quite unexpected way. If one accepts the hypothesis that there is some direction behind the vast amount of data which has already been sent to Earth telepathically by the UFOnauts, then one must accept the connected hypothesis that this method of contact achieves the desired result better than any other means of contact which they have available.

What result do the UFOnauts wish to obtain from sending these messages to us? Perhaps they simply want us to read them, listen to them, and think about them. Perhaps in time we will all find that the new explanation scheme which this body of telepathic messages suggests exists. Perhaps these messages are not so significant philosophically. What they certainly are, no matter what their origin, is a strong and simplistic ethic, or way of life, which puts forth a realizable goal in life, and an easily achievable plan for day-to-day living.

You may take the data at either level. Make your own decision as to the value of this material. That is what the UFOnauts suggest, anyway!

Carla L. Rueckert's Editor's Preface (1975)

For six years, I have been assisting Don Elkins in his research, and I have been involved in meditation groups for twelve years. When Don and I decided to compile a volume of these messages, I was given the task of selecting and editing enough messages to make one volume.

These messages are almost always preserved in magnetic tape form.[10] We had hundreds of tapes to choose from, dating back to about 1962, from the Louisville group alone; the supply from other groups went to volumes of printed material, heretofore unpublished, and many other tapes.[11]

At the time we decided to prepare this volume, we had just begun a new "class" or meditation group. All of the participants were just being introduced to the Confederation message; none were channeling as yet. So, faced with the great mountain of old manna, we chose simply to use the new material, as the group developed. Therefore the messages in this book are all selected from transcriptions of channeling sessions collected during the period from December 18, 1973 to May 19, 1974. Even within this limitation, we were forced to omit about half the messages in order to keep this volume a reasonable length.

The subject arrangement of the first part of the book is intended to make it easier for you to get into the messages.

---

[10] To examine the archives of our channeled material, please go to http://www.llresearch.org/transcripts/transcripts_toc_year.aspx. However, in the years that have passed since this Preface was written, we have lost some of the audio-cassettes of the channelings in this volume, because we taped newer meditation sessions over the older ones.

[11] Many of these older tapes have been lost.

Editor's Preface

Go ahead and sample the book, under a subject of special interest to you. See how the answer strikes you. Then, explore at will. The last chapter is a selection of messages which are given just as they were received by the Louisville Group, complete with greetings, closing farewells, and changes in subject. This completeness makes the messages a bit more difficult to get used to, which is why the subject classification precedes it.

Many thanks to Elaine Flaherty, who helped with the typing, to the group members who gave interviews, and most of all to the members of the Confederation, who are the real authors of this book.

Carla L. Rueckert

Carla L. Rueckert's Editor's Preface (2009)

Thirty-four years have passed since I wrote the words above. I finished tidying up this manuscript then and we sent it out to various publishers, collecting rejection notes. So we tucked the material away in our archives and moved on. We took a whole new tack and wrote a book about the UFO phenomena, *Secrets of the UFO*, which we published in 1976. This unique and quite cogent volume is still in print and available from L/L Research.

In that thirty-four years, much has occurred here at L/L Research. In the later 1970s, Elkins and I tried three times to create a screenplay from our novel, *The Crucifixion of Esmerelda Sweetwater*, which we had co-written in 1969 and 1970. We got as far as interesting a Hollywood producer working with James Coburn, who we hoped at the time could play a starring role in the film version of *Esmerelda*. So did he, but I never created a screenplay that satisfied the producer.

In 1971 and early 1972, Elkins' and my work took a wonderfully screwy turn when we contracted with a producer of southern drive-in movies, Lee S. Jones, Jr., to make a genre film. Our reasoning was that if we wanted to break into the film business successfully, we had better learn the business. Elkins and I were told by Jones that any script would be fine as long as it contained sex and violence. Given these parameters, we came up with a screenplay about aliens who were trying, in a particularly ineffectual and haphazard way, to take over Earth.

One of the good guys was a magician named Aph. This character's lines were lifted almost without exception from some of the murkier sections of *Oahspe*. The film's working

Editor's Preface

title, *The Hidan of Maukbeiangjow*, was also taken from that august volume. Another good guy, Aph's apprentice, Prudence, used a psychic self-defense ritual taken from Dion Fortune's eponymous book, *Psychic Self-Defense*. There was sex; there was violence; above all there was humor and a hodge-podge of metaphysics.

Another unexpected turn occurred the day before filming was begun. We had rented the equipment, dressed the set and hired the crew. We had cast an actress who had played topless roles previously as our sex object. However, when she arrived and took a good look at the script, she quit. "I am a movie star, not a comedienne," she huffed on her way out of town.

At this point, I was deep in creating the shooting script, something our producer-director had neglected to do. At dinner that night, I got food poisoning, and finished the shooting script, the continuity and properties tables, and so forth overnight while trotting repeatedly to the bathroom to be ill. So when we heard that our topless actress had quit, I was in a daze. Elkins quickly outfitted me with a cheap blonde wig, oversized sunglasses and ill-fitting, white go-go boots that were nearly the death of me when we filmed a chase scene in a local park shortly after a rainfall. And I was a star.

Fortunately, I knew the lines, having written them. Unfortunately, I never had time to rehearse them even once, and it bothers me to this day that I had no time to do a halfway good job with the part. However, the show went on. During the several days in which my scenes were filmed, I was seldom clothed fully, since I was set secretary and in charge of continuity and special effects, and had many duties to fulfill between takes. It was a unique experience to play the topless role, and perhaps it even added to the film's humor that my top was definitely of modest proportions.

The film came out in the summer of 1972, under the title, *The Girl Snatchers*. It had a short run at the drive-in theaters for which it was made. It is still available, though out of print, in video-cassette form, put out by "Le Bad Cinema." As far as I know, the movie has exactly one fan, Scott Hutchins. And I thank him!

In the middle and later 1970s, Elkins and I kept creating screenplays and being unable to sell them. Our archives files are full of them! In 1975, we were advisors on a film called *The Force Beyond*, which Elkins quickly renamed *The Farce Beyond* when he saw the rough cut.

A dramatic documentary script we created in 1978 was taken up by a group of producers who had it stolen from them. Four steals after them it came out as a work of pure fiction titled *Hangar 18*.

In 1981, we stopped trying to break into the film business. Our research group began receiving messages from those of the Ra group, and those were published, first under the title, *The Law of One*, in 8 ½ x 11" format, and then under the title, *The Ra Material*, in quality paperback format. This material quickly became popular amongst those who enjoy channeling. Since it covers the same material as the *Voices of the Gods* manuscript had covered, it did not occur to us, then or in the years since, to resurrect this present volume.

Earlier this year, Ian Jaffray suggested that we gather the archives of channeling work done by L/L Research, which by now total over 1,500 sessions, into printed volumes. In the process of preparing these eighteen volumes of our collected channeling, the *Voices of the Gods* manuscript was rediscovered. It did not fit into the archives volumes, since the material it used, from the period of my learning to channel from Don in 1974 and 1975, had been changed from whole transcripts into material sorted by subject. And we had lost some of the original tapes by taping over them, and lost the transcripts I had typed by cutting them up to make the *Voices* manuscript.

Editor's Preface

So we decided to publish this volume separately, under the title, *Voices of the Confederation*. It is the single largest remaining repository of Don Elkins' channeling. He did not like to channel, and was forced into doing so only in order to teach me how to do it. I was the single original Louisville Group member who did not learn to channel in 1962. I agreed to do so in 1974 because our group had run out of channels. After 1975, there are few instances of his channeling except as part of a large circle. So this book is valuable in that it preserves his work. His channeling "voice" is unique and has the characteristic of coming in many short sentences, rather than in my much more periphrastic, long-sentenced style. As you read through these pages, you will be able to tell our styles apart easily!

There were several places in the original manuscript where I had neglected to find a good quotation for a given subject, or to make a comment on it. I have now filled in those blanks. Since the choice of what quotation to use is always intuitive, this could be the longest-running case of editorial whimsy in existence!

Thanks go to Gary Bean, who resurrected this manuscript, and to Ian Jaffray, who has produced it for printing as a labor of love.[12] We hope that you will enjoy this material and find it useful in your seeking.

Carla L. Rueckert
Louisville, Kentucky
August 17, 2009

---

[12] And thanks to Michele Matossian for the beautiful cover art.

Chapter 1: The UFOs

Their Presence

> "We have a bogey at 10 o'clock high"
> —Frank Borman
>
> "Behold a fairer time is with you than any men have dreamed of; behold there is a gladness again in the heavens when a host not of Earth is seen of all shepherds."
> —From *The Golden Scriptures*

Comment

This book investigates telepathic contacts, not visual or physical ones. We have not found any attempts made by these extraterrestrial sources to prove their presence. They are interested in teaching, in a free and open atmosphere.

The information in this section, then, deals more with their motives in being here than with any other aspect.

Since the telepathic contact is conceptual in many instances, the wording of the messages will vary slightly with different receivers. The title, "Confederation of Planets in the Service of the Infinite Creator," for instance, is as close an approximation as our language will provide to fit the idea, or concept, of their society.

Channeling Selections

January 8, 1974
We of the Confederation of Planets in the Service of the Infinite Creator are here now. Now is an important time. It is time, my friends, for your people to be awakened. It is time for them to understand what is happening. They have slept for a long enough time. We are going to accomplish this, with

help. We will be seen much more often in your skies in the coming years. Many questions will be asked.

January 10, 1974

I am in a craft, high above you. I am aware of your thoughts, even though I am quite some distance above. I am, at this time, in a craft which is capable of interplanetary flight. This craft has been seen by some of your people. It will shortly be seen by more of them. It may shortly be seen by yourselves, if you look for it. The time is closely approaching now when we must be seen much, much more by the people of this planet. The time is now closely approaching when we must create a high degree of inquisitiveness among your people.

They are quite inquisitive at the present, but they are not yet seeking. This is what we intend to do: we intend to provide a stimulus for them, to increase their seeking. The larger percentage of your people, although interested in our craft, are not sufficiently interested to seek an answer to what they see. This we intend to alleviate by stimulating a more intense interest.

January 12, 1974

We, the Confederation of Planets in the Service of the Infinite Creator, are waiting to meet as many of the people of your planet as would wish to meet us. The reaction of the people of your planet is quite varied [as] to their realization of our presence. Some of them seem convinced that we are here now. Some of them do not believe in us at all. That is exactly the condition for which we have striven. It is a condition which will produce a maximum effort on the part of the individual to seek: to seek the truth of our existence, or of our nonexistence. This seeking will lead him upon other ideas. These ideas have been presented in many forms in your literature in the past many hundreds of years.

Chapter 1: The UFOs

In his seeking he will, if things are correctly progressing, discover certain truths that have been available throughout all time. He will also, if he is fortunate, come in contact with some of the material that we make available through channels such as this one to the peoples of your planet.

This condition of questioning, seeking and thinking about things is precisely the condition that we have attempted to generate by our rather nebulous contact. It is always much more satisfactory if the individual finds something out by his own efforts than it is if he is taught a principle. The mental activity required for the individual to seek out and find the basic truths of the creation allows him time to reflect and examine with his own point of view each one of the propositions offered to him. This results in an understanding of the propositions that surpasses any understanding that he could achieve if these propositions were made to him in a relatively short period of time.

This, of course, would have been necessary if we had landed upon your surface and directly communicated with the people of your planet. The ways of the Confederation in establishing contact with a planet that has no knowledge of their presence, or the galactic Confederation, or any of our peoples, is now quite standardized. For this reason, we have chosen to limit our contacts severely. There is, however, only a certain amount of time available to make and establish a contact which will disseminate to as many of your people as possible the truth of this infinite creation, and the true workings of man in it.

We will, therefore, be much more in evidence in your skies in the very near future. As I have stated earlier, many, many more of your people are ready for the truth that we bring than were ready a few years ago. We therefore increase our activity, in hopes that it will increase the seeking of individuals in an attempt to understand us. We must emphasize that this understanding can come only through an effort put forth by the individual to do so. Without this, there will be very little progress in his development of understanding.

January 13, 1974
I am speaking to you from a craft known to you as an otevana. It is a very, very large craft compared to your standards. It is several miles in length. We have been aboard this craft here above your planet for some numbers of years. It is like a world in itself, and is used for intergalactic travel. Aboard this craft we have all of the facilities that you have in your world, plus many others.

February 11, 1974
At this time I occupy a craft that you know as a flying saucer. It is a small craft, approximately thirty feet in diameter, and is capable of landing at any point upon your surface. I am aware of this instrument's feeling of skepticism towards message such as this one. I am going to suggest that he totally relax and clear his mind of thoughts. In this way, I will be able to use him as an instrument in relaying this message.

I and my brothers in the Confederation of Planets in the Service of the Infinite Creator are in your atmosphere, and we are also around your planet outside your atmosphere. We are constantly keeping your planet under surveillance. We are constantly ready to serve in any way that we can.

February 17, 1974
I am Hatonn. I greet you in the love and in the light of our infinite Creator. It is a very great privilege to be with you this evening. It is a very great privilege to be with you at all times. We of the Confederation of Planets in the Service of the Infinite Creator are here to serve you. This is sometimes difficult. We have attempted to contact the people of this planet through many different ways. We have not always been successful. There have been, in some instances,

misunderstandings about our contacts. There have been, in some cases, misrepresentations, through no fault of the contactee, of what we would bring to the people of this planet.

We are attempting to bring to you one thing. We have attempted to do this in many ways, but still we have but one thing to bring to you at this time. We are bringing to you love. This is all that is necessary, for when you are able to receive this love, with it will come the understanding that many of you now seek.

March 24, 1974
We have attempted throughout what you would consider ancient times on your planet to bring to mankind, to those who would desire it, the knowledge, the knowledge that is necessary for experiencing all of the infinite experiences created by our Creator. Some of those who dwell upon this planet in the past have accepted these teachings and have benefited from them; benefited far beyond anything that could be imagined by those who are not experiencing the benefits. We have attempted for many of your years to bring to all of those who desire the teachings, the very simple teachings that allow you to know all. However, these teachings have not been understood very well.

May 19, 1974
Questioner: What level are you on? Have you been on our level? Will we attain your level? How far are you from the final destination?

We shall attempt to answer this question. Through our experiences within this creation, we have found that there exists an infinite experience, which is to be experienced by all entities. We of the Confederation of Planets in the Service of the Infinite Creator have experienced the type of physical illusion which you now find yourselves experiencing. This

Chapter 1: The UFOs

illusion that you are presently in is culminating in what we call its present cycle. The entity asking this question is truly aware of that which he considers the second coming of the master teacher, Jesus.

These times truly are here, and these times are within the will of the Creator, the times for graduation into a higher spiritual awareness for those who would desire it.

We have experienced this same, shall we say, trial; and we sought the truth of creation through meditation. We attained a higher rate of vibration within our spiritual being through this meditation, and evolved to a greater awareness than that which can be attained within this illusion.

We of the Confederation are truly aware of the difficulties which you encounter, for as we have stated, we also have experienced your physical illusion. Our, as you say, level of existence is one which you would consider spiritual. It is much more highly evolved than that which you are presently in, yet the question of the attainment of the ultimate source, or shall we say, union with the Creator, to us, at this time, [is something] we cannot answer. For we have not evolved into realms higher than the one we presently occupy.

Yet we are truly aware of their existence, for in our travels throughout this creation, we have come upon experiences and entities who were able to avail to us truths of even a higher awareness. And they have availed to us the thought of infinite levels of awareness on the path to total union with the Creator. There is much within this creation that we do not comprehend, as there is much that you do not comprehend. Yet we have experienced your present existence, and do have the understanding and realization of a higher awareness.

We do not claim to be an ultimate source of information. We are capable of committing error. And I would like to say that, in your experiences, if you encounter any entity who exclaims that he can commit no error, you should truly know that this entity has erred in that judgment, for only the Creator can function without error. And it is our mission at this time to aid the peoples of your planet in seeking the union with the Creator from within through meditation.

Questioner: What is life like on your planet, as compared to our life?

Life on our planet at one time was much like that upon Planet Earth. However, at this time our entire population of sentient beings has developed a singular desire. This desire began as a simple seeking for understanding, and has developed into a completely unitary and combined ability of each brother of the planet known as Hatonn. The combination is so strong that we are able to do many, many things. Feeling and being as one, we are now seeking as one, and as our seeking has led us forward, we have found our way to be pointed directly at service, ever-expanding service, service to all parts of the creation.

And as our service has been needed, whereas before we were not capable of discovering the means to perform this service, we became able to perform the service that we came to see as our service.

In this manner, we have developed abilities which you may call miraculous. We have the ability to transcend what you know as time and space. We have access in a conscious manner to knowledge to which you have access only during meditation, in a subconscious manner. The freedoms which we enjoy, my friends, are there because we have begun to see that we are all one. Realization is all that is between Planet Earth and the planet Hatonn.

On your planet, as on our planet, each blade of grass is alive with the knowledge of the Creator. The winds sing his praises. Trees shout for joy in the creation of our infinite Father. If you are not able to see the Creator, my friends, it is a matter

Chapter 1: The UFOs

of seeking, and seeking, and continued seeking. And then, my friends, you will begin to realize, and to understand, that the creation of the Father is all around you.

Planet Earth, my friends, is indeed a lovely planet. It will soon be vibrating in a vibratory manner which is far more associated with realization of the Father's creation. Begin to realize, and move with your planet as we moved with ours. There is only that which is in your mind, within your consciousness, and within your faith, between the pain, the lack, and the limitation which you experience and the complete freedom which in our vibration we experience.

We invite you to join us, my friends. Seek and ye shall find.

Are there further questions?

Questioner: The service you perform with Earth -- does this same service extend to other planets? If so, can you give us some idea of how many, and their levels of consciousness?

We have aided many other planets within the same general vibratory level. The aid is given to this level by us because we are, shall we say, at the next level of awareness, and are best able to communicate to those people who wish to enter into understanding which we share.

We have dealt with many planets which are beginning a new phase of vibration. We have aided many a graduating class, and we have done so successfully. We have also failed, not once, but several times. It is completely possible for us to fail, because we wish to fail if it be the will of the people of the planet we are attempting to aid.

We come because we feel the desire that brings us here. And we give what aid we can to those who wish it. Our thoughts are available to all who desire them. However, we attempt to do this in such a way that no individual is ever in a position where he cannot accept or deny our thinking as he so pleases. Those who are vibrating within the level that will appreciate

Chapter 1: The UFOs

the information that we give surely recognize that which is truth.

At the present time, we are far behind where we had hoped to be at this point while helping Planet Earth. We had hoped to have been much more successful at reaching the people of this planet. It is possible that there will be a smaller graduation then we had hoped.

However, my friends, it is our greatest pleasure to be working with those of you, however many or however few, who are seeking. It is only necessary to seek, and the spiritual path shall roll behind you, and open before you. And what you desire shall be yours.

Their Elusiveness

> "Give help, without obligation. Lead without dominating. This is the Mystic Virtue."
> —Tao Te Ching

Comment

If you've read much of the UFO literature, you're already aware pragmatically that UFOs are often seen and not seen in patterns that seem to have some plan or meaning. One person may see a UFO which another cannot see at all.

According to the following messages, there is a plan or purpose to these sightings. There is a definite reason for this elusive quality.

Channeling Selections

January 6, 1974

We of the Confederation are here, as I have said, in great numbers. We are allowing your people to see us. At present we are allowing more of your peoples to see us. You can see us, as this instrument has. I will appear to you in the very near

Chapter 1: The UFOs

future. I will be seen in your skies. It is only necessary that you continue in your seeking. You see, my friends, it is truly written that, in order to find, you must seek. That is the scheme of things at this time. All of our efforts have be directed toward fulfilling this simple phrase: "Seek and ye shall find." Why do you think we have been so elusive? This was wisdom, my friends, that it is necessary to seek in order to find. You will understand this wisdom, if you think about it. It is a very old and tried system of producing an increase in the awareness of an individual, for only he himself can produce this increase in awareness. We cannot impress it upon him. But he can very easily increase his awareness many, many-fold. But the seeking is necessary.

We of the Confederation of Planets in the Service of the Infinite Creator are preparing to launch a new attack upon your planet, an attack of love. If one is to attack with love, it is necessary that it be done with utmost care. The only possibility, if one is to attack with love, is that the ones attacked desire that they be attacked. More and more of the people of your planet have become aware of this attack. More and more of them are now welcoming this attack. For this reason, it is possible to accelerate our program.

Many of those that are at this time aware of some form of attack are not welcoming it. This results in our limitations. It is necessary that we do not in any way infringe upon those of your planet who do not desire the attack. Therefore, we must remain a mystery, a mystery that can be rejected by those who wish to reject our presence. We must, however, bring to more and more of those of your people who wish to accept us the truth and understanding that they deserve. That is theirs. That is all man's. For this was given to him by his Creator. We are merely agents, acting in a way to bring that which is desired to those who desire it.

Chapter 1: The UFOs

I am aware that many of the people of your planet consider that we have wasted too much time in our attempts to awaken the slumbering population of your planet. We would greatly prefer to act much, much more rapidly, but the speed and the degree of our activities must be regulated, not by us, but by you. The acceptance of us by the total population of this planet is the only governing principle that controls our activities.

We will, very shortly, increase these activities. More and more of our craft will be seen by the people of your planet. This can be done because they are beginning to accept us. We will do this, in order that their curiosity will be stimulated. This curiosity will then lead them to seeking the truth of our presence. This truth is what they desire, even though they do not consciously realize it.

February 17, 1974
One question which is asked many times is, "Why don't these brothers from space meet us face to face? Why don't they bring a craft down where we can get a close look?"

My friends, one of the problems which we have encountered in contacting your peoples is what I should call an overreaction, either based upon fear or a semblance of what you might even call worship. Neither one of these attitudes is necessary or even desirable, my friends. Realize that when you have reached a maturity in your development that will allow you to meet us casually, as an equal -- I should say, as a friend—when all of you can greet us in this way, then our meeting of face-to-face contact will be more possible, I shall say.

Chapter 1: The UFOs

Why the UFOs Don't Land

> "Hey, Mister Spaceman,
> Won't you please take me along?
> I won't do anything wrong!
> Hey, Mister Spaceman,
> Won't you please take me along for a ride?"
> —The Byrds

Comment

"Why don't they land?" Perhaps this is the most often asked question with regard to UFOs, which may explain why a fair portion of many of their messages to us is devoted to dealing with this question.

Channeling Selections

December 18, 1973

Do not be dismayed if your ideas are totally rejected by some, for this is to be expected. And this is the major reason that we cannot come among you, for it would be a direct violation of one of the laws of which I earlier spoke. Due to their conditions, it is necessary for those of you who would help us, who are on the surface of your planet, to help us. We request that you meditate. This is all that is necessary. This is all the help that we need. Because, if you meditate, then you will know what to do.

January 4, 1974

Yes, my friends, the Confederation of Planets in His Service is here to serve you. They orbit your planet in their craft. They come in swarms, by millions and millions they come, from all of creation. They come to you at this time to serve you. Will you not let them serve you? For they are here, now. If you will look, you will see them, for they will show themselves to those of you who would wish to know them. They would greet you openly, but they cannot, for most of the people of your planet have so willed it. It is already known the exact reactions that would occur if a direct meeting were to take place at this time. For this reason it is very necessary that you continue in more active service. It is very necessary that more and more of your peoples learn the truth. Only this will bring about a condition which will enable direct contact to take place.

January 7, 1974
We of the Confederation of Planets in the Service of Our Infinite Creator are here to contact you now. We must emphasize this: we are here to do this. This is our purpose. We must, however, make this contact very, very carefully, in a predetermined way. That is what is happening in this room at this instant. There can be no variation from this technique at this time. We have had many experiences in contacting peoples. It has always been found that it must be done with extreme caution. There are grave consequences when an alien society is impressed directly upon another society, especially when technological separation is as vast as is ours.

Your people would not understand us at all. They would not accept us for what we are. We could not walk among them and be accepted, and this is what we wish to do: be accepted. For, my friends, we are all exactly the same. We could not speak directly to your people and have them gain benefit from our teachings, for they would feel that they must accept, without question, what we say. This is of no benefit, my friends. You are here, at this time, as we are where we are, primarily to seek, to seek in our own way that which is the path back toward the Creator of us all. An interruption that is too great in this personal seeking is not a very good thing. For this reason, we are unable to directly contact your people. We must provide them, however, with that which they need. And this we are doing to the best of our ability.

Chapter 1: The UFOs

January 8, 1974
We of the Confederation of Planets in the Service of the Infinite Creator are here to serve you. It is a great privilege, yet we must remain aloof. This is our understanding of proper service, for in serving your fellow man, it is necessary that you serve his exact wants and needs. You cannot determine for him what these are. Therefore, if his wants and needs lie outside the limits of your ability or your desire to serve, it is best that you remain aloof, as we. There are, however, many, many of your people, who desire exactly our service. We are hindered by those who do not desire our service. For this reason it is impossible at this time to come among you. For this reason it is necessary at this time to act through instruments such as this one.

January 25, 1974
We would prefer to land upon your surface and greet you openly, but we are aware of certain principles in this creation that do not allow for such a direct infringement.

February 2, 1974
It is necessary that if an individual is to make progress in a spiritual sense, it be a result of an inner-directed seeking of his own, rather than an outer-directed commandment given to him by an organization of a religious or other nature. For this reason, it is necessary that we do not make ourselves too generally known and accepted by the people of your planet. If we were to do this, then the inner direction of their seeking would be for the most part lost. This is the basic reason for the conditions that you experience in your present physical environment. These conditions have been selected by yourselves and by others, and they are a natural consequence of the creation, so as to act upon the consciousness of the individuals and create an atmosphere which will produce the inner-directed seeking for truth of which I spoke.

Chapter 1: The UFOs

Unfortunately, many of the people of this planet at this time are so involved in activities that are of an extremely transient and unimportant nature that they do not have opportunities for experiencing the growth of an awareness that is necessary in order to accomplish the seeking that they actually desire.

We of the Confederation of Planets in the Service of the Infinite Creator have attempted to balance between too much exposure of our craft to the people of this planet and too little exposure. If we were to become too much a common phenomenon, so that our presence was beyond question, then we would eliminate, at least in part, a large interest in seeking for spiritual truth. This may seem to be a strange or unusual point of view, but we have observed this in the past, and since the basic reason for the physical isolation of a people such as yourselves is to cause an inner-directed seeking, then it is evident to us that we should follow, as closely as possible, this plan.

Our craft and our people have visited this planet many, many times in the past. This was done only after the civilization that we visited was ready to accept us. This was done only after the civilization had reached a satisfactory level of inner-directed seeking of the truth of the creation, and therefore it was displaying the principles of love and brotherhood that are the product of this seeking.

We are at this time forced by conditions over which we have no control to visit the civilizations of your world, even though they have not reached a state of spiritual awareness satisfactorily high enough for our contact. We are aware that some of the people of this planet are, however, already sufficiently aware of their spiritual nature and are sufficiently demonstrating the love and brotherhood that is necessary for our contact. This presents a problem. The problem is that we must approach a part of the peoples of this planet without distressing the rest.

Chapter 1: The UFOs

We are attempting to do this. It is necessary that the evidence of our visits and our communications be of such a nature that it can be rejected or accepted by anyone who is exposed to it. There will be, unfortunately, a degree of infringement upon those people of this planet who do not wish to accept our contact. This is an unfortunate condition, but it is one with which we must deal, since at this time it is necessary that those of the people of this planet who are seeking truth be given truth.

It will not be necessary to prove to these people that what we are giving them is truth, for if an individual has reached an understanding of truth through the inner-directed seeking of which I spoke, then he will recognize this truth when it is given to him. It is therefore only necessary that we, by some means that will not disturb those not seeking our contact, give to the rest of the people of your planet that which they seek in a form that is suitable.

This, then, is our service: to lend a helping hand up the ladder of spiritual evolution to that part of the people of this planet at this particular time, a time that is unique in the history of this planet, a time that must be dealt with in a more direct and forceful way than previous times and experiences in the history of this planet. We are extremely privileged in being able to offer this service to those who seek it. And our service is largely given to then through the process of their daily meditation. If they are to avail themselves of this service, it is necessary that they do so through meditation.

February 9, 1974
We cannot come directly to you, land upon your surface and speak with you. For it would do no good. We must provide a spark, a clue, something for a start, a start of seeking, seeking that results in finding the truth that is within you.

This, my friends, is the only way to help the people of your planet. For they must help themselves. They must find the truth that is within them. They must initiate the seeking. All that we can do is to provide a stimulus for their own initiation of this seeking.

February 18, 1974
We of the Confederation of Planets in the Service of the Infinite Creator avail ourselves of this knowledge through meditation. For this reason, we do not come among your people, giving them our services directly, for we are aware of detrimental effects upon them in doing this. Our service is aimed at what they actually desire. What they actually desire is an ability to realize truth. In order to give to them this ability, it is necessary that we bring about a condition to cause within them a personal seeking of service and a personal seeking of knowledge of the truth of the creation. Only through this process may they understand the truth that is within them. It is something that cannot be too effectively given to them in an intellectual manner.

May 14, 1974
Questioner: Hatonn, can you give us a specific reason why we can't meet you face to face?

I am Hatonn. I am with the instrument. I will meet you face to face on the day you enter the kingdom of heaven. You may do this at any time. It is doubtful that you will do it while in the body. If you do achieve this state, then whether you are in the body or not, you will be able to speak with me instantly on any level you desire. At that point you will recognize me as your brother. I am afraid that one cannot fulfill the burden of influencing one or any of your people by appearing within your vibration while your consciousness is as it is now.

Chapter 1: The UFOs

February 23, 1974
In the future, when the conditions have manifested of which we speak, and many of the people upon this planet have initiated seeking, there will be groups of people who, having initiated seeking and having been educated by channels such as this one and channels of other groups, will then be in a state of understanding sufficiently enlightened so that they may meet with us directly. We will at that time provide direct and physical aid to these people. There are many, many more of us than you could imagine, waiting to act in this fashion, in the service of the Creator, for that is how we label ourselves. And this service at this time will include a direct service to those groups of people who are desiring our service. It will be necessary, however, that these groups be somewhat isolated from groups or individuals who do not desire our service. This will be done in many ways. And these will be made apparent to you at a later time, for you do not at this time have an understanding of the many, many ways in which we can serve you.

February 25, 1974
We are striving and doing our utmost to help your people and to make them aware of the situation they are in, but they are not paying attention. We can only do so much. The more attention your people pay, the more that we can do. It is a simple matter of direct free will. If the population of a planet asks for our services then we may give them freely; if only a portion of that population asks, then we must limit our services. If none of the population asks for our services, we are unable to give any of our services. For this reason, you find us in a state of hiding, you might say, at this time. For far too few of the people of this planet have asked for our services. Consequently, we must act through instruments such as this one to speak to you and tell you of the problems that now exist for us and for you and for the rest of the population of your planet.

Chapter 1: The UFOs

The Early Contactees

> "We find it hard to believe what lies beyond our understanding."
> —La Rochefoucauld

Comment

When this manuscript was cobbled together in 1975, I did not comment here. In 2009, I would comment that the early contactees did a credible job of reporting what they saw. Before the ridicule lid came down, a good bit of solid information was offered. I recall, for instance, as a child, reading an interview with Betty and Barney Hill in a national magazine that was not at all sensationalized. Rather, it was sympathetic to the couple and thoughtful in considering the story's implications. In the late '70s, the ridicule lid was dropped by the government and all hope of a calm and searching conversation on this topic was lost.

Channeling Selection

January 13, 1974
The early contactees, as they are known, were not too successful. They were unable to approach the people of your planet through the channels of communications on your planet, with our messages as much as we would have liked for them to. The reason for this was that the people of your planet could not understand such a form of contact, and they were not prepared to accept messages of the nature that we were able to give them. However, we are now in the position to give them much more.

The Confederation's Mission

> "Now behold, ye have taken a great work upon yourselves; which is to raise up these little ones according to your highest light."
> —Oahspe

Chapter 1: The UFOs

Comment

They are here to teach us, but only if we wish to learn. It is a very soft sell!

Channeling Selections

January 8, 1974

Your fellow man cries out in many ways, for many things. He is seeking, but for the most part he does not know what he seeks. Shortly, he will seek your service. Prepare yourself now, for there is very little time remaining.

January 10, 1974

We have spent considerable time studying the people of this planet, and we have found that there are a reasonably large number of them that can join us in the peace and the love of our Creator's infinite creation.

For this reason, we are here now. If there were none of your people ready for this we would have no task. We would be incapable of arousing people that do not wish to join us in this love and light to do so. It is not possible for us to do this, my friends. It is only possible that the individual do this. Each of you must arouse himself to a state of seeking that which we hold out to you as the only worthwhile objective in the creation; that is, the love and the light of the Creation itself. We of the Confederation are very, very privileged to be here to do this at this time. It is something that we have desired for a long time. We have waited impatiently to be here and to help you, for this a service that gives us much, much pleasure.

We are aware that it is very difficult for you who have been, shall I say, stuck on the surface of your planet for quite some time to encompass in your minds fully the grandeur and the magnitude of this project. But it is possible for you to do this, my friends. The only thing that is necessary is for you to avail yourself to this knowledge through meditation.

Chapter 1: The UFOs

We are speaking of something that is so much beyond anything that you have previously experienced that you would find no comparison. There will be certain problems for you, but if you will keep foremost in your mind that the objective which we share is to bring truth to a people who are for the most part totally unaware of this truth, then, my friends, we will be triumphant, and we will, working together, accomplish a satisfactory culmination in the great scheme of our Father's creation.

December 18, 1973
It is our plan to alert as many of these people as possible, so that when it becomes obvious, to your leaders and to your scientists, that we are real, and we are what they suspect that we might be, there will be a sufficient number of awakened entities on your planet for some form of communication to take place between those who are already awake, and those who are lightly slumbering in the future. For, as time passes, those who are in the depths of slumber now will begin to awake. Those whom you cannot contact at all now will begin to awaken. It will be a self-generating process, so that large numbers of your people will be given the truth. It is a very, very big task.

It will be up to you, and those like you, to help us in carrying this out. We have said before that we would very much like to land upon your surface and contact your peoples directly but we have explained that this is not at all feasible.

January 21, 1974
We of the Confederation of Planets in the Service of the Infinite Creator are here for the purpose of speaking with you and giving you directly our thoughts as you meditate. These thoughts are yours to accept or reject. They are constantly available to you. It is only necessary that you desire them, if you wish them. This is our service to the people of the planet

Chapter 1: The UFOs

Earth at this time. This is not our only service, but it is our most important service.

Why are your people at this time not very interested in these thoughts? We have said, time and time again, that thoughts of this nature are what the people of this planet need. And yet they show very little interest. This puzzled us at first, until we became more familiar with the reasons for the thinking of the population in general of this planet. We are now aware of some of the problems involved in bringing truth and understanding to a people so very long in the darkness that has been generated by those that have gone before them in the history of this planet.

It is a very difficult thing to change thousands of years of erroneous thinking in a very short time. It is something that we will not be totally successful in doing. However, we will be, and we have been, partially successful in bringing certain [information] to those who would desire it. This is the key, my friends: desire. If the individual does not desire what we have to bring to him, then he will not receive it. This is exactly how the creation is designed: so that each entity, no matter where he is or who he is or what he is, will got exactly what he desires.

Unfortunately, in some places certain actions of one entity with respect to another cause an infringement that was never designed by our Creator. This results in a discrepancy in the plan of the creation, and creates unfortunate situations, as it has upon your planet. It is necessary for man on planet Earth to realize this, and to individually correct his understanding of himself, in order to bring himself back into alignment with the plan and design of our Creator.

Each individual must make up his mind, and he must do it now. He must decide whether he is going to attempt to understand and to serve in the light of the infinite, or whether he is going to seek for himself, and follow a pathway that has been laid down for him by man on Earth, rather than that provided by the Creator of us all.

February 25, 1974
We of the Confederation of Planets in the Service of the Infinite Creator are here at this time for a particular purpose. This purpose is to serve you. This is our only purpose, to serve the people of this planet. We are serving them at this time to the very best of our ability, and we will continue to serve to the very best of our ability. What we can do is limited by what you can do, and by what the people of this planet can do. The more that you can do, the more that the people of this planet can do, then the more that we can do.

February 9, 1974
We of the Confederation of Planets in the Service of the Infinite Creator are here for one purpose. That purpose is to communicate with the people of your planet. This communication takes many forms. However, the most important of these forms is that communication which you receive in your daily meditation.

We are able to use channels such as this one to communicate concepts for your intellectual evaluation. However, these concepts are always of a limited nature. We find, however, that it is helpful for many of those of your people who have not yet learned the necessity for daily meditation.

We will continue making contacts such as this one, and developing new channels for communication, and we will hope to reach more and more of the people of your planet as time progresses.

March 3, 1974
I am of those who inhabit what is known to the people of your planet as flying saucers.

Chapter 1: The UFOs

I and my brothers have been in the vicinity of your planet for many years. We are at this time educated in the ways of your peoples. We have observed the people of your planet for many of your years, and we are familiar with the thoughts of the people of this planet. And we are familiar with the thoughts of this group.

We have been contacting groups such as this one for several years. We have been doing this through individuals such as this one, and others in this room, who have learned to receive our thoughts and pass them on to others of your planet who desire them. We do not wish to impress our thoughts upon any of the people of this planet who do not desire them. For this reason, we have found it convenient to speak to them in this manner, and we will continue to speak to them in this manner, using the people who dwell here who wish to, like us, serve in the name of our Creator in aiding us to give what we understand of His thoughts to the people of Planet Earth who desire it.

We are here to bring to the people of this planet what we consider to be of utmost importance to them at this time. We consider that there is one thing of importance to the people of the Planet Earth at this time. This thing is an understanding of the truth of the [creation] in which they live. Our study of the people [who] inhabit this planet indicates that almost none of [them] understand the reality of the creation.

We have determined that almost all of the peoples of this planet are living within an illusion created by man on Earth through a number of centuries. We have determined that at this time it is very necessary that the people of this planet that desire truth be given it. It will be up to those who desire truth to seek it out. We will provide for them our understanding. Their acceptance or rejection of our understanding will be up to them. That is our understanding of the Creator's plan. Our understanding of the Creator's plan is that He provides for man in this creation to possess a total freedom of choice.

For this reason, we provide a total freedom of choice. We do not impress in any way upon the people of this planet a necessity for accepting what we bring to them as our understanding of truth. This is our reason for contacting the people of this planet through instruments such as this one, who receives our thoughts in what you consider a telepathic manner.

Our craft have been seen many times in your skies. Some of the people of this planet believe that these craft are what they really are: our craft, craft from elsewhere in this Creation. Some of the people on this planet do not believe this. This is their choice, and this is the choice that we provide for them. This is our understanding of one of the principles of this creation. It is necessary for us, if we are to operate within the limits of our understanding of truth, to act in such a manner as to not force upon anyone that which he does not desire.

March 3, 1974
If you perceive separation, then this is illusion. We do not perceive separation. For this reason, we serve ourselves by serving those of the planet Earth who desire our service. This is our mission, and this is our objective: to serve ourselves by serving those of the planet Earth who desire our service.

But it is necessary that this desire be present. We will direct aid to all who desire our service. This service is to give to those who desire it the creation. This is the only gift that we have. It is the only gift that exists. There is an infinite creation all about you. It is yours for the asking. We will give it to you, for it is yours to begin with. If you wish to accept, then do so. All that is necessary is that you avail yourself to this gift through daily meditation. Nothing else is necessary.

Chapter 2: Channels And Channeling

The Function of Channels

> "'We suspect that a psychic naturally ... attunes his brain waves to the rhythm of another person's brain,' one of the younger physicists told us.
> 'This rapport helps him get the other man's thought ... We think that many people can learn to tune to each other in about three months.' He didn't say how."
> —Sheila Ostrander and Lynn Schroeder

Comment

The Confederation suggests that anyone can learn to receive the messages telepathically. It is only necessary to want to, and then to follow their simple instructions. That's one way the UFOnauts' information has some points over information on telepathy from other sources: the Confederation does tell you how people can learn to become telepathic receivers.

Channeling Selections

January 4, 1974
Many of your peoples at this time would wish to know exactly what has happened, but they are not provided with the correct information. The information they are given should be correct. And it can be given them only by those who understand what is correct, or those which are channels and can speak directly, using our thoughts. Many people are crying out for this knowledge, but they are confused. They are confused by so many erroneous thoughts and erroneous sayings and erroneous deeds.

In the past, our space brothers contacted some of your people and attempted to pass on through them certain information. In each case, this resulted in failure. These contactees were not understood or believed. It led to their ridicule, and a considerable waste of effort for those who were contacted and on the part of the Confederation. In some cases, it did them harm. It seems that each time your people are contacted, it does them harm, to some degree.

So it will take strength to serve at this time. It will take strength to be a link between our brothers in space and our brothers upon the surface of your planet. But this is very necessary. More necessary, my friends, than anything else that you could do at this time. It will not be an easy task, but it is not an impossible task to alert those of your people who would wish to know what is actually occurring. It will be necessary that enough of your people believe in what we say for the Confederation to land upon your surface. It is not necessary for the people of this planet to believe in the Confederation; it is necessary that they believe in the Creator, and that they believe what the Confederation says.

There are many people here that already believe this, that already know this, for it is truth. However, this knowledge is lying dormant, below their level of consciousness. It is necessary that this knowledge be brought to their surface [consciousness]. A reawakening, a self-examination of their inmost thoughts, is necessary for them to release themselves from the hypnosis created by their present social conditions.

It is therefore necessary that channels such as yourselves act at this time, to give to the people of this planet a reminder; a reminder of truth. Those that are ready will awaken. Those who are not ready will ignore.

Chapter 2: Channels And Channeling

January 7, 1974
It is only necessary that our words be made available to your people. Those who will recognize them as truth will do so. Those who cannot recognize them as truth will not. It is as simple as that. There is no need to impress this information any further upon your people than simply exposing them to it. This, however, has not been carried on in sufficient quantity. It is for this reason that we are now attempting to impress upon channels such as this one the need for greater dissemination of that information that we have to present to your people.

We of the Confederation of Planets are here, and have a job to do. We have been working diligently at this job for many of your years. We are aware of the problems that you face in attempting to make more of the people of your planet aware of our communications, but we will assure you that we will aid you in doing this. As time progresses, more and more aid can be given. You will have noticed that in the past twenty years attitudes have changed considerably. Things that were very difficult to talk about with the general population are now relatively easy to talk about. Their acceptance of our presence is much greater than it was in the past. Your own expeditions into space, however slight, have aided greatly in the acceptance of your general public's attitudes toward possibilities of extraterrestrial contact.

We of the Confederation of Planets in the Service of Our Infinite Creator are here to contact you now. We must emphasize this: we are here to do this. This is our purpose. We must, however, make this contact very, very carefully, in a predetermined way. That is what is happening in this room at this instant. There can be no variation from this technique at this time. We have had many experiences in contacting peoples. It has always been found that it must be done with extreme caution. There are grave consequences when an alien society is impressed directly upon another society, especially when technological separation is as vast as is ours.

Your people would not understand at all. They would not accept us for what we are. We could not walk among them and be accepted, and this is what we wish to do: be accepted. For, my friends, we are all exactly the same. We could not speak directly to your people and have them gain benefit from our teachings, for they would feel that they must accept, without question, what we say. This is of no benefit, my friends. You are here, at this time, as we are where we are, primarily to seek. To seek in our own way that which is the path back toward the Creator of us all. An interruption that is too great in this personal seeking is not a very good thing. For this reason, we are unable to contact your people directly. We must provide them, however, with that which they need. And this we are doing to the best of our ability.

January 8, 1974
It is important for you to prepare yourselves now, so that you do not confuse them. If it is necessary, then we will work directly with them but you must be very careful in your attempt to serve, for the service that you perform must be correct, or it will only confuse them.

There is, unfortunately, considerable false information as to our purpose, our reality, our motives and our being. It will be a great help to our effort to have additional vocal channels such as this one. These channels will be able to talk directly to the people who initiate seeking as a result of seeing our craft. If we are able to do this in sufficient quantity, then we will be able to circumvent discrepancies and wrong information with respect to our presence.

We of the Confederation of Planets in the Service of the Infinite Creator are engaged in a definite program of action. This action, for the past twenty or so years, has been limited.

Chapter 2: Channels And Channeling

It has recently become less limited. Certain aspects of your civilization and its intellectual growth have made greater stimulation through a greater showing of ourselves a distinct possibility. In other words, many, many more of the people of this planet are [now] open to suggestions of a nature that would have seemed all too radical just a few years in your past.

Many of your people are now ready to open their minds to things that were beyond belief for them just a few years ago. There has been a great increase in the dissemination to the general public of information with respect both to travel in space and to what you call metaphysical phenomena. This attitude makes it possible for us to initiate what I will call a second phase in our program in awakening the people of this planet to the truth that they so badly desire.

We of the Confederation of the Planets in the Service of the Infinite Creator are about to embark upon a most interesting phase of our mission. It will be interesting for us, and it will also be interesting for you. If you are to be of service in the program we are now instituting, it will be necessary that you very, very carefully control what you say to those who seek from you, and it will also be necessary that you are very careful about the way that you act. In this way, you can be of maximum service.

It has been said, in your language, "Physician, heal thyself." If you do not demonstrate in your daily living an understanding of the teachings of those of the Confederation who profess the understanding of the way of the Creator, then you will not be of as much service in your attempts to help enlighten your people as you would be if you would so demonstrate this knowledge.

January 10, 1974
In a very short period of time, there will be considerable activity with respect to our presence, and considerable

awareness of this form of contact. At this time, those of you who can serve us will have a great duty to perform, for you will, like us at that time, be actively and directly in the service of our infinite Creator.

Join with us, members of the Confederation of Planets in His service, to act as a steppingstone from the darkness that now abounds upon your planet to the light that is so ever-present in this infinite creation.

February 22, 1974
We are here to help those of this planet who would help themselves and, by doing this, would help others. Each of you will be a channel of communication for the understanding of the truth of the creation that we bring to the people of this planet.

It is, I am afraid, a difficult thing to give to all of the people of this planet that which they desire. However, at this time, there are many who are on the brink of understanding. It is only necessary that they be given that which they desire and this is our duty to those of whom we speak. And this will be your service, to aid us in bringing to them that which they desire: An understanding of the true workings and principles of the Creation.

It will, however, require some effort. For it is not easy to communicate all the levels of understanding that exist at present on this planet. And, for this reason, it is necessary to have many channels such as yourself, so that each individual who is seeking will be able to receive exactly what he seeks. There are many questions that will be asked you in the future. And in order to answer these questions, it is necessary that each of you be prepared. And this will require effort.

It is not a simple task to raise the understanding of a large number of those who will shortly be seeking understanding. But, with effort and diligence, it will be accomplished.

We realize that it is difficult to find time for sufficient meditation in order to avail yourself to the understanding that is necessary for the task that you are to perform. But it is possible to avail yourself in meditation at various times during the day when meditation of what you might call a formal nature, such as you now indulge in, is not possible. This instrument has learned to utilize many portions of his day to clear his mind of the thoughts generated by the illusion that surrounds him and to become at one with the creative consciousness that is in all of us. This we suggest doing in addition to the type of meditation in which you now engage, for if you are to understand, it is important to spend time each day in the process of meditation.

We of the Confederation of Planets in the Service of the Infinite Creator are here for one purpose and one purpose alone. We are here to bring truth to those that seek it. But, my friends, it is necessary that an individual seek truth, if he is to find it. This is a natural principle of this Creation, for it was within the original Thought that created us that we should have exactly what we desire. For this reason, it is necessary to desire to return to the original Thought of love and unity in order to return.

Concern yourselves, therefore, with those who seek. For they are the ones we are here to serve. It would be a direct violation of the principles of creation to attempt to serve those of your planet who do not seek our service. We can advertise our services to some limited extent. But it is not possible for us to impress upon any individual at any time a service that is not sought. For this reason, our mission is wrought with several problems. [One is] the problem of communicating with those of your people who seek our service, while not disturbing to an overt extent those who do not seek.

For this reason, we act as we do now, using those of you who seek this understanding and also seek to serve others who would seek the understanding. The degree of your service will depend upon the degree of your seeking. This is always the way.

We are very privileged to be able to work with you. And your service in many ways is much greater than ours. For you must work within conditions that are much more difficult than those within which we now work, However, each of you will be successful in your efforts to serve your fellow man. For this is what you seek. And, as I have stated earlier, it has been provided for by our Creator that if an individual seeks anything, this is what he shall find. And if he seeks to be of service to his fellow man, this he shall surely accomplish.

February 23, 1974
There are problems that will confront the people of this planet very shortly. We have said this before, but the time now grows very short. We have ways of telling this. There will be a need for channels of communication, whether they be of the type of this instrument, who can directly channel our thoughts, or whether they simply be of the type able to relay this information from groups such as this one to groups who seek it and direct them to a group. We have far too few groups of this type to accomplish that which we seek to accomplish: to bring to the people who desire our aid, the aid that they desire.

We are striving and doing our utmost to help your people and to make them aware of the situation they are in, but they are not paying attention. We can only do so much. The more attention your people pay, the more that we can do. It is a simple matter of direct free will. If the population of a planet seeks for our services then we may give them freely. If only a portion of that population asks then we must limit our services. If none of the population asks for our services, we are unable to give any of our services.

Chapter 2: Channels And Channeling

For this reason, you find us in a state of hiding, you might say, at this time. For far too few of the people of this planet have asked for our services. Consequently, we must act through instruments such as this one to speak to you and tell you of the problems that now exist for us and for you and for the rest of the population of your planet. We suggest that you, as individuals, attempt to evolve as best you can on an individual basis and at the same time attempt, in your own way, to act as examples of this evolution. By doing this, you will draw attention by maintaining a knowledge of truth.

Through meditation you will be examples. You can be nothing else. Those of your people who are in great need of truth and of understanding will notice that you are different. They will notice that you will have an inner peace and tranquility. They will notice many things about you. Then they will seek you out for information. At this time, you will be able to serve them as we are able to serve you.

It is a difficult thing, my friends, to serve all of the people of your planet that wish service. Many of them do not know that service is available and they do not know how to recognize the service once it is offered. Each one of them is a different problem and there is not too much time left, my friends. Shortly, many of your people will be seeking much information. More and more of them, at this time, are seeking information. But they are difficult to communicate with because of their mixing with those who do not wish to be served. We must, therefore, increase the number of channels such as this one and we must increase the amount of information that is given to your people by other means.

I am sorry that I have taken a little more time than I expected on this particular aspect. But at this time, we consider the dissemination of our information to the people of your planet of utmost importance. It must be remembered though, that caution must be used. And, as a general rule, the information should be presented so that it may be rejected. It is necessary to create within the individual an intense seeking that is his own, rather than to force upon him information that he does not request. Therefore, act as you are directed through your daily meditations. And, we will, with you, succeed in bringing the truth that your people require at this time to them.

There has been much strife and much confusion upon your planet, and there continues to be much strife and much confusion. And even those who attempt to follow the examples of the teachers who have demonstrated the Creator's light do not understand, and there [also] is confusion. All of this confusion, all of this misunderstanding, all of the strife that is occurring upon your planet, is primarily due to a lack of meditation.

We realize that we will be successful with only a relatively small percentage of those whom we contact. However, this will be sufficient, for the time being. For from these seeds will grow a wider understanding of the truth for those who desire it.

April 25, 1974

We of the Confederation are pleased that so many of the peoples of your planet have begun to avail themselves to our thoughts. We have been attempting for many of your years to contact your peoples. Recently, our efforts have been very fruitful. And through the extension of our contact to your peoples we can shortly contact many more.

It will be your privilege in the future to offer your services to your peoples. There is much work to be done. And you should look forward to this time as being a great opportunity to advance yourself in His service.

Many of your peoples do not comprehend that which you have come to accept. You need to grow in confidence in order that you may be of beneficial service to these people. Many will approach you and will begin searching because of the new vibration in the Creation. Your vibration shall rise and shall be felt by those who you come into contact.

Use the time that remains to develop your confidence in His will. The Father wishes all to join in this seeking and all shall have the opportunity to seek. But only those who desire shall do so. It cannot be accomplished by any other individual. it is controlled by your desire.

Channeling

> "So Samuel went and laid down at his place.
> And the Lord came, and stood, and called as at other times, Samuel, Samuel. Then Samuel answered, Speak; for thy servant heareth."
> —*Bible*, I Samuel 4: 9-10.

Comment

The Confederation seems to be remarkably unorganized in nature, and does not manifest any desire to promote organizations of any kind, including religious ones. They recommend only personal meditation and group meditation where questions can be freely asked through channels. The following information was given in answer to a mother's questions about how best to raise her child so that it might have the best spiritual start in life.

Channeling Selections

April 14, 1974

The question of how to instill the type of training of the spirit to which we refer is a question that is very difficult for us to answer for you. It would be necessary to have communities centered around the great truths of the spirit. It would be necessary to have in each person and in each group of people who have banded together a spirit of understanding and seeking. It would simply be necessary to have a completely different type of environment than you have.

There is much that can be done within the sanctity of your own life. Those people of like mind may provide for you and those dependent upon you an atmosphere conducive to spiritual growth. In your own household, much may be done to encourage the constant awareness of the love of the Infinite Creator, where growing entities are aware, as their bodies and their minds mature, that their infinite and eternal spirits are real and are capable of maturing also.

If there were a place they might choose to go and, with no pressure or suggestion, seek their own peace and find their own truth, then the training for the spirit might be a much more possible thing for those upon your planet's surface. Needless to say, my friends, we have not found rich earth for planting this idea in many places.

April 24, 1974

Children are born with a type of personality or manifestation of awareness which is their heritage of previous experiences and knowledge. This varies extensively from entity to entity. For the most part, those who are now incarnating on Planet Earth have a considerable background of latent understanding because they have been called to the Earth at this time for experience involved within the ending of this cycle. Therefore, for the most part, the entities who are called children upon your planet at this time are somewhat advanced, before they are taught any lessons within the physical illusion.

However, the physical illusion is designed for further teaching. The teaching, my friends, is of two kinds. The first is the most important, especially upon your planet. That is, as you say upon your planet, "the school of hard knocks." This phrase indicates the school which will teach children the lessons, for the most part, that they will learn. Within this

Chapter 2: Channels And Channeling

school, the most informative stance that those who wish to aid a child may take is that taken by the Master known as Jesus. When asked for understanding, Jesus spoke to the best of His ability. But more importantly, in this aspect of His service, he exemplified by his life that which he wished to make known.

The experience of children, as regards those around them, is to a great extent built upon not what they are intellectually manifesting, but what they are manifesting by their existence. This again is your greatest area of teaching of any child. And that is the area of example.

Upon the planets in which the atmosphere is spiritually more centered upon seeking, the use of the intellect in aiding spiritual seeking in children would be greatly enhanced. However, the influences which are upon your planet at this time are, for the most part, quite baffling to spiritual impulses. Therefore, the most earnest and sincere attempts at teaching of spiritual concepts will be frustrating to the teacher and to the child.

It is therefore, recommended that when the opportunity for this type of intellectual teaching arises, that the truth be spoken and that the frustrations connected with attempting to live the spiritual life within the confines of an unfriendly environment be accepted without undue disturbance or strain.

It is to be expected that there will be difficulty and confusion. Therefore we say to you, there are three simple ways to attempt to aid. One is to be aware that children are, for the most part, already somewhat mature and that, therefore, they only need direction.

The second is that the best direction comes from the daily abiding of yourself with the light of your own spiritual awareness. This is your best contribution to anyone that you meet. It is your life itself. By example, more have been aided than by any other more elaborate means.

The moment-to-moment existence within the physical provides you with your third form of aid to another entity. The attempt to speak the truth as you know it, when asked, is always a good thing.

We remind you that to forgive and to encourage amidst difficulties and setbacks and even failures is also a service. It is to be remembered as a principle that you are part of the infinite Father and just as you, yourself, as a child, spiritually are taught, but also welcomed upon whatever terms, so in expressing yourself, you may remember that you may teach but, always above all, accept and love on any terms.

We wish that we could tell you that there is a way to ensure that a human entity will surely be aided and given the right concepts. We cannot tell you any such joyful news, my friends. We have been attempting to aid each entity upon your planet for many, many years. Some may be aided, some may not. They may be aided only when they desire it. It is within each entity to choose what he will learn and what he will not learn. All that can be done by example is to have the awareness ready to be shown to those about you.

We are sorry that we cannot give you any surer method than those about which we have told you. But the Father gave us all free will. The least and the greatest are equal spiritually. Be stayed in the knowledge that all things are fulfilling the purposes for which they were intended. And you have only to respond to each day's request for help to the very best of your ability and to the very furthest of your knowledge and you will have been of service to those who you wish to serve.

Graded Groups

> "My soul, sit thou a patient looker-on;
> Judge not the play before the play is done:
> Her plot hath many changes; every day
> Speaks a new scene; the last act crowns the play."
> —Francis Quarles

Comment

Of course, it's never easy to divide beginners from intermediate groups, or advanced from intermediate. But in general beginners are those unfamiliar with this type of contact. Intermediate groups are familiar with the contact and are coming to terms with whether or not they wish to become channels, and whether or not they wish to stick with daily meditation. Advanced group members are usually either channels or self-aware people who do not feel this as their service but are committed to daily meditation. The small intermediate groups will predictably be the ones which develop the great majority of channels.

Channeling Selection

February 25, 1974
The limits of what we wish to give you are always limited by those receiving. We can only transmit that which is acceptable to those who are receiving it. We cannot, shall I say, go over the heads of the receivers. For this reason, we are hopeful that the grades of people who receive our communication are not too mixed. We would request that groups of relative advancement be made. Putting a new person, who is unfamiliar with what we have to give to you, with a group that is somewhat advanced in its study of philosophy, limits us to a communication that would be acceptable to a new person. It is, therefore, requested that you keep this in mind

when forming groups of people who listen to our communications.

Being a Channel

> "In that day that now approaches, the day of the great telling, it is necessary that ye are all channels, in one way or another."
> —Brother Philip

Comment

You can learn to receive telepathically. It's actually very simple. But, like most other things, you have to want to do it enough to work at it. As you will see from the following messages, the instructions are simple: meditate and avail your consciousness to their impressions. The difficulties and obstacles are those of the busy intellect, with its questions and analyses.

Channeling Selections

January 6, 1974

I will return to this instrument another time, for he is becoming fatigued. It is difficult to use control for a long period. It is difficult to translate all that I have to say to an understandable framework for you, because of limitations of concepts. But we will continue, and we will attempt to bridge this gap.

January 8, 1974

I am Laitos. I am with this instrument. I greet you, my friends, in the love and the light of the infinite Creator. As you know, it is my privilege to condition those who are to become channels. I am here this evening to condition each of you. Each of you will feel my presence and the effect of my conditioning. All that is necessary is that you avail yourself to me. If you desire my contact, you will receive it. This is my duty and my privilege.

January 10, 1974

We are called to instruments such as this one by a so-called direct telepathic thought. This is the way that you explain it in your language. We do not think of it this way. We do not think of it as a possibility of separation. Since the creation, my friends, is one thing, it is very difficult for us to suppose that you could separate minds.

January 17, 1974

There are many ways of achieving a contact such as this one. There are several ways we can impress an intellectual thought upon an instrument. The form of contact that we are using most of the time with this instrument is a form that presents to him a concept, or a portion of a concept. He is able to use his own fabrications of language to describe the concept. At other times we use muscular control to aid the instrument in forming words to fit the concepts impressed upon him. If the concept is of a totally new or different nature from his thinking or his realization in meditation, we use a great deal of muscular control. If the concept is familiar to him, we allow him great leeway in his intellectual analysis of the concept, and therefore his verbalization of it.

You can experiment by saying a word to yourself without speaking. You will hear it in your mind. One part of your mind has said the word, and another part has heard it, although you have made no sound. It is possible for two, or more, or all minds to work in this manner. It is necessary that they don't, for this would result in an unimaginable confusion and constant noise in the mind. However, it is possible, by willing it, just as you hear the unspoken word that you have thought in your mind, to direct the same word to another mind. It is also possible to direct a muscular action, a response, to another mind. It is also possible to impress an intellectual concept upon another mind. It is also possible to impress a non-intellectual concept upon another mind.

These are just a few of the simple principles of communication, mind-to-mind. We have some difficulty at times, and there is confusion. This instrument is aware of the possibility of generating thoughts and repeating them as if they were from a source external to him.

My friends, I have stated earlier that there is only one source. It is the Creator.

January 15, 1974

I am sorry that I could not use the instrument known as R this evening, although he received some of my thoughts. With practice, he will be able to speak using my thoughts as easily and freely as this instrument. All of you here tonight are capable of doing this in the very near future.

It is not a difficult thing to do. It only requires that you have confidence in your ability to do this, and that you avail yourself to these thoughts in meditation.

This instrument has had quite a bit of experience at receiving my thoughts. I realize that when you are new to this process, it is easy to get confused and to suspect that you are speaking your own thoughts. This sometimes happens. But when this happens, you are corrected. If your thought, however, is a thought that is ours as well as yours, then there is no need for correction.

If there is an obvious error on the part of the channel, then he is immediately corrected. Do not disturb yourself that you might give false information by this process, for if information is to be available at all, there must be some process by which it is generated. It is unfortunate that we are limited to this process, the process of telepathy, as you call it. But for the

Chapter 2: Channels And Channeling

time being, there is very good reason why we limit ourselves to this form of communication.

We of the Confederation of Planets in the Service of the Infinite Creator are experienced in contacting planets such as this one, and we find that this form of communication is highly desirable over other forms.

This instrument is practiced enough at receiving our thoughts that it is not necessary for him to achieve a deep or extremely tranquil state of meditation in order to channel our thoughts to you. However, meditation is the process by which this ability is generated, and you will find it helpful to meditate as best you can each day, in order to gain the ability to translate what we have for you clearly.

January 16, 1974
This instrument receives my thoughts, and relays them to you. These thoughts are not my exclusive property. They are the thoughts of an entire creation of our infinite Creator. It is not necessary for the instrument to be used for you to know these thoughts. They are available to all people in all places at all times, for they are the thoughts of the Creator. And these thoughts were meant for all of mankind, in all places. These thoughts are the thoughts with which the Creator created us.

These thoughts are very simple. They are a simplicity that is unique, for they are the very foundation of the creation. This is what we are attempting to give man on Earth, this original Thought. This is what he needs at this time.

This Thought can only be approached using pure language. It is not a common concept among the people of your planet. This is the reason for their difficulties. The Creator never imagined difficulties in His creation. They are the product of man's erroneous thinking. We have said to you many times that meditation is necessary. Through this process of meditation, it is possible to know this Thought; we have called it love, but this can only be understood through meditation.

In an environment such as yours, meditation is of even greater importance than in an environment such as ours, for we have very, very little to overcome in our understanding of our fellow man. It is suggested, therefore, that through the process of daily meditation, you will develop an understanding of this Thought that created all of us.

February 4, 1974
There are thoughts that are available to all of the individuals who would receive them. These thoughts are available, but they are not necessarily received by all who may desire them.

The problem, then, is to produce a condition in which all who desire the concepts that are available receive them. In order to become able individually to receive and understand these concepts, it is necessary that an individual first initiate a spiritual seeking himself. In order that he initiate this seeking, it is sometimes necessary to provide a catalyst. In other words, if the individual is to generate the proper state of mind so that he may achieve an awareness of the concepts that are given to him in his meditation, then it is necessary that he first be given some ideas and thoughts to generate an attitude of seeking an awareness of truth.

Therefore, in order for the individual to break away from the concepts which are primarily of an erroneous nature to which he has been exposed in his present environment, it is first necessary that he verbally be given concepts of a more spiritual nature.

This then, is the reason for communicating through channels such as this one. This process then builds upon itself. As an individual becomes aware, intellectually, of certain spiritual truths, and since these truths are, in actuality, within him, but to some degree forgotten, he will then begin to seek on his own.

When his seeking reaches a state where he will be useful in generating intellectual communications of a channeled nature, he then experiences what is known as conditioning. This conditioning occurs after the seeking which he performs as a result of his new awareness reaches a level of intensity high enough to create reception of what I will call a blanket conditioning wave. This is automatic. It is quite similar to tuning a radio receiver, assuming that the reception of this wave is in some ways unique, since the tuning necessary is somewhat unique upon your planet.

An individual, having reached this level of seeking, undergoes a transition in his mental awareness. As he moves to this more rarified awareness, he becomes aware of this conditioning wave. It is of such a nature to act upon him in a physical way at his desire.

Questioner: Is it a machine?

No.

Questioner: Does this keep you from meditating?

No.

Questioner: It seems like sometimes it interferes with your meditation.

The results achieved in meditation are not exactly apparent in a way you might expect. If this conditioning is not desired, then the instrument will not receive it. This instrument receives very little conditioning. This instrument receives conditioning only slightly prior to channeling our communications telepathically. You will experience the same transition.

There is a good reason for the conditioning you experience at present. There are many thoughts generated. The thoughts are generated by yourself, by those around you, by those not in a physical form around you, and from many other sources. You become aware of these thoughts as you meditate. In the case of a new channel, it is difficult to identify thoughts which are of a direct and beneficial nature and thoughts which are of no particular value.

This conditioning wave is operating at a sufficiently high spiritual level so that if a thought of this level is brought within the consciousness of the channel, then it is possible for the conditioning to unify or match with this concept. At this point the muscular reaction that results from the conditioning wave produces an attempt to speak the first portion of communication that is matched in spiritual quality with the conditioning waves. If the thought is of little value, or if it is not desired as part of a transmission, then it should be noticed that there will be no attempt to initiate this portion of the communication.

It is necessary for a new channel to experience a large amount of conditioning in order to separate thoughts that are intended for communication from thoughts that are not so intended. The reason for the long period of conditioning is so that the individual channel may experience the muscular reactions when he has achieved a sufficient spiritual quality of attunement for reception.

February 11, 1974
This instrument is still skeptical in regards to this communication. He has always been skeptical of communications of this nature. I can assure him that I am Hatonn, and am communicating through him from a craft, and that the thoughts that I have given him and the words which he has spoken are correct. And if he will kindly maintain a clear and open mind, I will use him as an instrument. He should not think of anything. He should not try to analyze these communications. He should not be

skeptical of what he is saying. He should simply relax and allow me to use him as an instrument.

February 18, 1974
We are serving you at this time by conditioning you, if you desire it, so that you can receive our thoughts. We find this service to be effective, for these thoughts generate in you your own thoughts, and augment, to some extent, that which you are able to seek within yourself. It will also be important in the future that we have channels of communication instantly available, and this technique is highly effective, especially when the channel is as trained as is this channel.

It is a simple process, and if you desire this form of communication and this form of service, it will be given unto you. We can only do as much in this area as you desire. For this is the limitation of all of our service: to do only as much as is desired.

February 18, 1974
It is a great privilege to work with you in conditioning new channels. It requires some experience in receiving our thoughts to communicate as easily and accurately as does this instrument. However, even this instrument at times questions as to whether the thoughts are from those of us who identify ourselves as the Confederation of Planets in the Service of the Infinite Creator, or are thoughts generated within his own thinking. We can assure this instrument and those who are present here this afternoon that if there are errors made by him due to misinterpretation of what we relay to him, we will correct this by using control. He has experienced total control several times during communications in past weeks, and is quite familiar with this technique. We use more control with new instruments than with instruments who are as experienced in receiving our thoughts as this instrument is.

Chapter 2: Channels And Channeling

Each of you can arrive at this ability very easily. It only requires that you spend some time in availing yourself of our contact to receive as clearly and as rapidly as does this instrument. He, too, went through a long period of training and conditioning, but through the years of his practice in availing himself to us, he has developed the ability to receive our communications at his convenience. It is only necessary that he think that he wishes our contact, and he has it. For this, as we have said, is our service to you. We are available to you at all times, and we only require that you desire our contact for the contact to be made.

It is helpful to be able to channel our thoughts as does this instrument, for there will be many of the peoples of this planet seeking truth who have not become aware of it through meditation, simply because they have not been aware of the necessity for or the technique of meditation.

This will be the service of the channels such as yourselves, to initiate the concepts of meditation and the concepts of which we of the Confederation of Planets in the Service of the Infinite Creator have become aware.

There will be many of the peoples of your planet who do not desire this information, and who do not desire that it be proved to them, as they express it, that such information is correct. This we do not wish that our concept of truth, that which we know to be true, be forced upon individuals who do not accept these concepts and would rather bury within them the realization of this truth. This is the Creator's plan, my friends: that each of the Creator's children has what he desires regardless of the consequences.

February 21, 1974
There is a common difficulty when using new instruments. That difficulty arises due to their inability to accept that they are receiving thoughts and then speaking the thoughts that

Chapter 2: Channels And Channeling

they receive. In many cases they believe that these thoughts originate within themselves, and for this reason do not wish to speak these things. It is a simple task to act as does this instrument, as simply a receptacle, with no thoughts of his own.

This is something that each of you can learn by practice. It requires meditation and practice in speaking without thinking. This instrument is doing that now. In fact, he has but little knowledge of what is to follow each of the words that he speaks, and by long practice is able to clear his mind of the transient thoughts that disrupt a communication such as this one.

Therefore I suggest that each of you who is new to this method of communication simply relax and allow the mind to think of nothing. It is better that you make errors in communication, which we later correct, than it is for you to fight, as it were, the concepts which we impress upon you.

February 23, 1974
The process of giving information to you through a vocal channel such as this one is at times quite varied, and is only a small aid in creating a condition by which you can avail yourself of the total knowledge of the creation. We do find, however, that in using channels such as this one, that there is a service performed in helping those who desire it to seek the knowledge that is within them.

There are some misunderstandings about the uses of instruments. For this reason, a new instrument sometimes has difficulty in channeling our thoughts, for he confuses his thoughts with our thoughts. But in all of these processes, we are simply awakening in you the part of you that is us, and the part of us that is you. It is what you might consider a reduction of your isolation, so that instead of being isolated, you are in unity with the creation. For this reason, it is

Chapter 2: Channels And Channeling

sometimes difficult for those of you who are so much conditioned by the illusion that is created on this planet to understand within the boundaries of the language that we are forced to use when speaking through an instrument the concepts which we are attempting to give you. It is necessary that an instrument such as this one spend much time in meditation, so that these concepts may be developed within him.

February 25, 1974
It is only when you clog your mind with your own thoughts that it is very difficult for us to get through to you. This is why we request that you spend time in meditation. This is the only way that you will become practiced enough to transmit our thoughts as easily as this instrument does. He has been practicing now for many years. It was difficult for him at first because the people of your planet are not used to this form of communication and, therefore, are not aware of the simplicity with which it may be accomplished. It is not at all complex, my friends, and thinking about nothing is not at all complex. It is, as has been stated by to this instrument, something like learning to ride a bicycle. Once you learn it, you do not forget it, but you must practice it to maintain a high degree of efficiency.

Sometimes this instrument has difficulties and at those times, it is necessary for us to condition him further. This conditioning, my friends, is simply a means of causing the individual to be helped to think of nothing. We hope that each of you here in this room will learn to do the same, because then you will be able to receive and speak our thoughts as readily as this instrument. He sometimes begins to wander in his thoughts as we transmit to him. When he begins to think of something *[else]* or begins to think of the transmission, rather than simply relaying it to you, it sometimes becomes garbled, shall I say, or somewhat difficult.

Chapter 2: Channels And Channeling

For this reason it is necessary at times to stop and condition him once more and then resume the communication. Errors are possible due to this same phenomenon, but we correct these, if these are out of limits of what we wish to give you.

This instrument has learned to go ahead and speak the thoughts that we give him. He has also learned to clear his mind to almost a 100% extent. This varies somewhat, depending on the conditions that are surrounding him. At this time, the conditions are quite good, and he is receiving my words almost in a word-for-word fashion, since I am familiar with your language, and am also able to transmit the words that I wish the instrument to speak.

This type of communication is good for communicating information of a specific nature. It does, however, require a greater degree of control of the environment. In other words, the conditions for reception of my thoughts are at this time quite good, and this instrument is able to repeat word for word what I am giving to him. Each of you may learn to do this, with practice. It is necessary to clear the mind of thoughts. You practice this through daily meditation, and also through use of the channeling technique. You will not arrive at the fluidity of speaking which this instrument has without practice in doing so.

For this reason, we recommend that you simply relax and allow us of the Confederation of Planets in the Service of the Infinite Creator to impress upon your thinking our thoughts. And then, as these thoughts enter your mind, instead of analyzing them, simply repeat them. The analysis that you make of what you are doing is detrimental to the type of communication that we are making.

This instrument is doing very little analysis of what we are giving him at this time. He too, at the beginning of his channeling, had some difficulty, because he analyzed, at that time, what he was saying. For this reason, it took a great deal

Chapter 2: Channels And Channeling

of time to transmit a thought through him, and there was very little success in using this form of communication.

At this time I am going to tell a little story to you in order to allow you to focus your thinking on that upon which is necessary for you to focus your thinking in order to receive our thoughts very simply. This story has to do with a small child.

This small child listened to its parents, and its parents spoke to it. The child, before listening to its parents, could not speak, but after listening to its parents, it could speak quite fluently.

However, the child was totally unaware of the process by which it learned to speak. It simply was there, and it simply learned to speak. This is the process that we are using. This is not to say that you are a little child. That is the problem! If you were as a little child, we could speak through you with no difficulty.

The problem is that you are not as a little child. We recommend that you think of yourself as you would of a little child, and relax and know nothing. In this way you will learn very rapidly. This is what is necessary if you are very rapidly to learn to channel our thoughts. The child, you see, has no knowledge of what it is supposed to do. It simply speaks. This is how it is possible for you to learn to do this rapidly.

We have found that some people of your planet learn much more easily than others. We find people in a technological society such as yours sometimes requires great effort, because they have learned to question quite carefully everything that is presented to them. If you do not question what we are attempting to do, but simply relax and let it happen, it will happen.

Chapter 2: Channels And Channeling

March 2, 1974
We are grateful for those such as yourselves who would join with us and bring this truth to man on Earth at this time. However, we caution you that we have discovered that man upon this planet is difficult to teach. Therefore, it is necessary that the individual seeking to aid us in our endeavor to increase the awareness of those of this planet do it only after he has availed himself to the understanding that is necessary through his daily meditation. When he is ready to join with us in a direct effort to help those of his fellow man who seek his aid, at that time he will be aware of his readiness, for it will be apparent to him in his meditations.

Proceed then, with this in mind: that it is necessary for an individual to seek out understanding in order to achieve understanding; and it is also necessary that he be given that which he desires, if he is to achieve what he desires. It is available for all of mankind at all times. If you wish to act as an instrument in delivering what man on this planet desires, do so by preparing yourself. Do this through daily meditation.

My friends, there is much to be done sometimes when one begins the process of conditioning to become a channel. This does not have to do, my friends, with your basic vibration. This does not have to do with the level of awareness, except in a very general way. What it has to do with is the amount of intellectual activity which the individual who desires conditioning is allowing his brain to function with.

It must be understood, my friends, that to become a channel is temporarily to trust another entity with the use of one's vocal mechanism. This involves letting the control go completely and not retaining any amount of judgment over it. This is very difficult or impossible to achieve, if there is any thinking going on at all on the part of the channel.

The conditioning is sent out and is deliberately intended to be effective only to thought. This, my friends, is a challenge, indeed, and one which we are aware is very specialized and can be very difficult. However, my friends, there is no doubt that each of you may be instruments if you desire to become instruments. You need only complete relaxation and a complete ability to refrain from analyzing any thoughts that you receive. It may take some time, as you know time. However, it is not only possible but inevitable if you continue to desire this service. We will, my friends, attempt to help you in every way that we can, as always, and we are extremely privileged to be allowed to be conditioning you.

April 25, 1974
When the conditioning wave is given, the thoughts that are of a creative or spiritual nature will vibrate within your mind. And you will feel the impulse to speak. The question of whether these creative thoughts are yours or ours is somewhat unspiritual in that those thoughts which are of a spiritual nature are the thoughts of the Creator. As they are in me, they are in you. And as they are in you, they are in everyone, every entity in whatever planet and in every station in all of the realms of the creation.

April 26, 1974
It is difficult at times for a channel, even an experienced channel such as this one, to clear his mind totally and to refrain from analyzing the concepts that are given unto him. However, this may be done with practice. It is easier if the new instrument has had a period of time of meditation prior to attempting to receive our contact. It is difficult to come directly from one's daily activities and involvement in intellectual exercises and to reach a state of meditation and freedom from intellectual thought that is required for a good contact. With practice, however, this may be done. It will be

Chapter 2: Channels And Channeling

possible if one will practice through meditation to go directly into a state of non-intellectual analysis.

This instrument is able at times to channel our thoughts very accurately. At other times, he finds it somewhat difficult to receive our contact. The problem is always the same. The problem is one of analysis and use of the intellectual mind. At this time, this instrument is not using his intellect or analyzing what we are giving unto him. He is simply repeating what is given unto him. This is what is necessary if a channel is to become a good, functioning channel.

As I have stated earlier, the way to accomplish this is through meditation, a divorce of the intellect from analysis, a total freeing of one's mind of intellectual thoughts. This may be done through practice. This practice is simply meditation, a meditation in which the mind is allowed to relax and to discontinue its thoughts of that which affects you in your daily activities.

Chapter 3: The Channeling Experience

> "Now the hand of the Lord was upon me in the evening ... and had opened my mouth: ... and my mouth was opened, and I was no longer dumb."
> —*Bible*, Ezekiel 33:22

Comment

As you have read in the messages, all that is needed to begin a meditation group, and to initiate contact with these sources of information, is the desire to do these things. If you can make contact with an already existing group in your area, that is recommended, for the guidance of their more experienced people is helpful.

However, a group of people can simply begin a group by holding group meditations at least twice weekly, and practicing meditation in some form daily. It is to those who will attempt to contact the Confederation that this chapter is given. Perhaps some of the experiences which you may encounter will be described in these interviews with developing channels.

Our only word of caution is a request that as you seek contact with the Confederation, you seek specifically that cosmic level of information which is beyond all the planes of this density, including the astral plane. Astral entities are often very interesting entities with whom to communicate, but their expression will have some degree of the subjective illusion under which those of this density labor. Therefore, their information is not dependable. Consider your consciousness as a radio tuner, and as you desire contact, simply desire the tuned contact.

Chapter 3: The Channeling Experience

(Editor's Note: Carla refined her procedure for making contact with any kind of discarnate entities and put her instructions in her 1988 book, A Channeling Handbook, *and it is recommended reading before one attempts to do any kind of channeling.)*

After the Confederation and you have established a dependable contact, then these other avenues may be explored.

A word about the variety of time spans for the development of these channels: Two of the new instruments, J and M, were professional men in settled professions, which tended to make the development a longer process, due to the high involvement of the intellect in daily activities. D1 and D2 also experienced this difficulty due to the intellectual needs of their jobs. H, S1 and R work with their hands, and seemed to progress more quickly. And S2 was extremely rapidly developed, probably because she had been highly trained, previously, in Eastern forms of meditation and realization. Once aware that contact with this source of information was possible, she developed the beginnings of contact immediately.

The longest it ever took, in my personal experience, for a person who desired it to achieve contact with the Confederation, was twelve years. On the other hand, S1 and S2 experienced the conditioning within the first week of their meditations. I have witnessed great "control," with much conditioning, movement of tongue and mouth; and I have seen people achieve contact with little or no conditioning. The youngest channel I ever heard was 18. The oldest: 68. It makes no difference as to your sex or your previous experiences. The key to the meditations is simply your desire.

I can picture you asking, "What happens if I get this contact, and then one day I decide I don't want it?"

Chapter 3: The Channeling Experience

The Confederation abides totally by the law of free will. If you desire their presence, they are there. If you will not accept it, they are gone. One of these new instruments has already stopped coming to meditation meetings. He tells me that he still meditates, but the meetings and the channeling were not the path for him. This is very acceptable to the Confederation. What it is attempting to do is to get its information across to people of Earth. They have no "strings" on those people to whom they have been able to speak. They simply rejoice that they were able to speak.

I stress this because much has been written recently about the difficulties of getting out of contact with "occult" powers, once contact has been made. The Confederation is not such an "occult" contact, but a cosmic contact with no strings attached!

Interviews with Developing Channels

Interview with R on February 4, 1974

R: I sat down and tried to quiet myself, and I guess after about 20 minutes I just realized that I was making all these weird movements with my mouth. And you, know, it's stuff I'd done as a kid. I just came to the realization that I'm doing it, I'm doing this. And I didn't know what it was. I guess maybe a few days later it hit me that it was probably conditioning.

Carla: And what do you experience now in the way of conditioning?

R: Well, sometimes it'll start as half a yawn. And sometimes it'll be that as I kind of quiet or relax, my mouth will just start opening, and then I'll just start making all these weird things.

Carla: Does your tongue move?

Chapter 3: The Channeling Experience

R: Yeah, everything [moves]. It's almost like I'm trying to get out of my body. In fact, I think that might even have been what I thought that first time, as I think about it. It was almost like a yawn you just couldn't grab a-hold of or something. You know, like my jaw was pulled out.?

Carla: Dislocated?

R: Yes, dislocated. I think it can happen. And then, a lot of times it gets really, really tiring, and a lot of times I cop out. I'll say, "Well, not now, and the next time we'll do it longer." Because it is kind of a hassle. I don't mean like pressure. I mean like energy would be if someone shone a bright light at you behind your back. You could feel it.

Interview with J on February 10, 1974

J: Vocal channeling is an interesting kind of a personal phenomenon. It's kind of hard to describe, however. When I became interested in the possibility of extraterrestrial communication—or for that matter from even a cockroach that was able to do it—it took a period of about three months of conditioning for me, between three and six hours a day, and at the end of this time I was an awkward channel in that I required a lot of control, because I would fight the message.

The fact that intrigued me was that even though the information that was being channelled would change from instrument to instrument, the format and subject matter was also the same, and I'm talking about at a single session. This would be following the same thread. In fact, there was an episode where I came in late, and I was the last channel used. And when the speaker signed off, as it is, he used his name, and I was afraid at first to sign off for him, but I proceeded, and it was the same channel who had identified himself earlier, before I had arrived at the meeting.

I have a slight stutter in my speech, but when I channel I seem to be completely free from it.

As to the content of the messages, that's a great big argument I always had. Are these my thoughts or other thoughts? When you channel you get a physical control but also a thought wave, and the more proficient channels are able to function on the thought wave without a whole lot of physical control. And I was always in an argument with myself over whether the thoughts were mine or someone else's.

Carla: Tell me, what physical reactions did you have to conditioning? What it felt like?

J: Well, it's kind of a weird feeling, as if it isn't you, but then again it has to be you, because that's what's causing that popping noise that you hear. There's a lot of tongue wiggling, flying open of the jaw, and kind of a grunting sound, and when you receive conditioning, you think that something has turned loose in your brain, and you're having some kind of fit. It actually seems to be quite controlled, and the speakers that I would channel would have their favorite methods of control. For example, Hatonn would always want to begin the sentence with "I" or "I am," whereas Laitos would begin with "we," or occasionally "I,". What you have is the word formed in your mind and your jaw seems to move to form it but it isn't really a conscious effort. I can't seem to put it any better because I haven't analyzed it completely.

Interview with S2 on February 17, 1974

Carla: Just describe what you have felt after two meetings with a group of this type.

S2: Well, I started my first experience with conditioning when I was meditating and keeping myself open as a channel of love and light for the Creator. And suddenly my tongue started moving around in my mouth. It was being moved by others than myself. I received some messages, such as "Have no fear, sister," and the word or name "Ezekiel" came into my head very strongly twice. I wasn't familiar with him, although that evening I read all about him in the Bible. George Hunt Williamson also has a chapter that explains [who Ezekiel is].

And after that, since I was eager to be a channel, throughout the day and evening I would leave myself open, and they would start conditioning me, continue conditioning with my tongue, sort of exercising.

And then yesterday, I was meditating for about three hours, and my whole mouth and face started being moved like R's. I got a mirror, and was watching my face change with all the contortions, exercising the muscles to stimulate the telepathy. I didn't get very far as far as words, but my mouth was going through the motions of the words.

The strongest feeling was when I could feel something creaking, in the bones of my face, like something was coming in me, it was very much similar to the whole feeling and sound of having a baby. I can't explain it. Anyway, it continues whenever I open myself to it. When the being is coming in you to channel it's not a grinding sound, but sort of like a forcing of another entity in yourself, sort of a stretching of your whole frame and structure. It actually makes a noise.

Carla: Did you feel anything on your head?

S2: I felt all through my head. I was watching my face in the mirror, and the whole face was moving. The top of my head was feeling very open too.

Carla: Were you getting any words?

S2: "I am Hatonn." That was it.

Carla: And how long has it been since you first experienced this?

(The two figured together; it was five days. She had heard about the space meetings a week before that.)

S2: I was getting a lot of thoughts which I didn't mention because it was without control and I didn't know where it was coming from, whether it was coming from me or where it was coming from, but certain phrases kept being repeated, such as, "You are an angel," and "Avatar." I don't know if that was for me, because I guess I don't understand the nature of that. It would never occur to me that it would be possible to look on my past life, you know?"

Interview with Michael on February 17, 1974

Carla: Describe what you experienced during the process of conditioning.

M: Well, it started last summer. What you experience in the beginning is really strange. You don't know quite what's happening. But it started with an uncontrolled opening of the mouth, which is in the form of a yawning sensation, and there's a stretching of the muscles of the jaw, which opens and closes the mouth in sort of an uncontrolled manner. You really don't have any control over it once you relax and let your body be free. It just happens, you know? A muscular exercise seems to be taking place in the jawbones and in the throat.

The second stage seemed to be when the inner throat and the tongue started to roll up, and to me that seemed like an exercise for forming words, that's the feeling I was getting. A lot of the times I felt, later on this winter, that just prior to actually speaking, that words were actually being formed in my mouth, but I didn't know what they were. But there was the feeling that something was happening there.

One other thing, for me anyway, there was a lot of crying of the eyes, like a lot of tears flow from the eyes during the stretching of the mouth, and also there is some movement of the neck and the head, a kind of back–and-forth movement that kind of relates to the stretching of the jawbone. I think

Chapter 3: The Channeling Experience

it's a natural movement. And as the jaw is opened up the head is thrust backwards. It's kind of hard to describe. It just happens.

Carla: Have you felt anything on your head?

M: Yes. My scalp has gotten really tight-feeling, and I've also felt a whole lot of warmth. The whole top of my head starts almost sweating. It gets really hot, almost like an energy field is there, you know?

I feel like there has always been a certain amount of doubt, just because we kind of grow up with all kinds of conditioning and blocks which make us think that anything having to do with outer space communications is Buck Rogers, unreal, almost. But in the last year I feel like I've been trying to clear out a lot of that kind of thinking, and really open my consciousness up to a more universal consciousness. And in doing that, I felt a lot freer and a lot better about it.

When you try to look at the kind of content of the messages that we are receiving, I don't think there's any question about the truth that lies in the spirits, the way it's being talked about. I've never really ever experienced any negative thought in any of the channeled messages that I've experienced here or with anybody else that's been associated with it.

Carla: Did you ever wonder whether anything that you ever channeled was your own thought?"

M: Yeah, I feel like there is some part that goes on there. That's the hard part to separate, and that's like a big hurdle and a big transition that you have to make with your own conscious being and any kind of message that you're possibly picking up telepathically. When you first get a few words, you naturally wonder whether they're yours or someone else's, out there. But again, it just comes from being able to relax your own consciousness and let it flow. It's been a problem for me,

I feel. It's a problem for everybody, probably, in different degrees. But I do feel like it's real.

Interview with D on February 19, 1974

D1: I was talking about the feeling in the back of my head. Well, yesterday was when I had the feeling a little bit stronger. And it felt a little bit like you were wearing a yarmulke. It felt like someone was touching you just enough that they were touching the hair, not the head but the hair. And I'd been meditating long enough that I had that floaty feeling—I'd been sitting still long enough—and I got this feeling at the back of my head, and then I got this tendency to move my head backward, and at the same time almost uncontrollably wanting to open my mouth wide.

It's very hard to fight personal anxiety, where you feel, well, maybe I'm getting something, maybe I'm not, and then you get just a rush of frustration and tense up a little bit. And then you say, "Well, this isn't any good, I'm going to have to relax if I'm going to get anything." And then when you relax you find that there's a little pressure this way or that way, so you totally let yourself go. And you feel your mouth very slowly moving either one way or another. And it seems as though it's coming mentally. I feel like moving my jaw sideways. And then don't know whether I'm moving it or whether it's being moved. I'm sort of floating into the path of least resistance.

And you have to be very, very quiet and very relaxed in order to find out which way the path of least resistance is. And you just float into it. When I was feeling it stronger, because I wasn't relaxed, I was sitting on the floor and about the time I started getting the feeling on the back of my head, it was a little like leaving my body. And that was when I had the feeling of being separated from my jaws.

And I don't know whether it was like my consciousness was very, very tiny, and I was conscious of a large mouth, or whether it was just an illusion, but that was it. Suddenly I had left a connection with all of my senses, and I was just kind of floating there, and I was feeling this flowing, the path of least resistance, with my mouth. And my consciousness was at the top of my head where the skullcap was, and I was mentally looking down and aware of the mouth.

Interview with D2 on February 19, 1974

D2: Probably the most vivid experience for me was the first time, and that was really bizarre. I was meditating, and I'd been trying to get into a lot of 3-D eye things.

Carla: You mean, feeling the third eye?

D2: Actually, inner vision, I guess. I don't know what you'd call that.

Carla: What had you been doing? Thinking about it?

D2: Yeah. When I meditate, I try to focus on it. And I was very much aware of two parallel lines set out about at arms' length. It was almost like rickrack. There was a green [zig-zag line] and a blue one. And they were vibrating intensely. And although I was staring straight ahead, I was able to see both of them perfectly, which was really bizarre. And if I could maintain my attention on those two things, I was going berserk. And my heart was—I'm surprised that everyone in the room didn't hear it. And my breathing was erratic. It wasn't nearly as slow, I think as yours.

Carla: People have different types of conditioning, but it all involves moving the mouth and jaw.

D2: I don't get anything. My tongue doesn't seem to be getting any motion at all. My jaws are killing me! Why do they make the jaws go way over here, or way over there, or …

Carla: All I can think is that they're trying to get us all set up to say "we."

D2: Yeah, I do "eee" a lot.

Carla: Or "I" or "you."

Debbie: Yeah, I get those two a lot. Yup. I get that "I" when yawn. "I."

Carla: Yeah, and then you get all the way into the yawn and you find that there's nothing to yawn?

Debbie: Right!

Carla: Thank God we do this mostly at night, that's all I have to say!

D2: I'll get my mouth all the way into a yawn, and I can't get it closed. It'll lock there. They're just killing me, my jaws are.

Carla: Well, the only thing we can hold to is that eventually we'll be channels, because eventually it'll happen only a little bit, when we channel. Like R, who doesn't get conditioning any more. He only gets conditioning just before he channels. And I know that's true of Don.

Debbie: But I'll be driving the car—Oh! And it's about to take off my head.

Carla: That's happened to me, too.

Interview with H on March 6, 1974

H: It first happened here, a week ago today, at the meeting we had. And we were told in the contact coming through Don that everyone in the room was receiving conditioning. And I had never, ever even thought I was or felt anything until then, and then I did start conditioning lightly, not a great deal.

And then that evening after I went home I was meditating I started receiving it quite a bit. It impressed me as not being anything that I myself could not do. But I also realized that I was attempting not to do it, and it was still happening.

Chapter 3: The Channeling Experience

Well, as far as to the first time it happened that's it. And like you say, it doesn't impress me to be anything I couldn't do. And that is what's so hard to decide - to let go of that feeling of whether you're doing or they're doing it. It's really a hard decision to make.

Carla: What kind of effects did it cause?

H: The first couple of times it was mostly to the side. And then after a couple times of meditating my mouth started to open wider. And the supposed-to-be yawn started coming. The first half of the yawn would come.

Carla: And then you found out there was nothing after.

H: Yes, and then there was nothing left once my mouth was open. But at first, it was like a really vigorous side-to-side and then about the third or fourth time my mouth started opening. But it's still mostly side to side. Uh, except Sunday night. We were out at the meeting at Hal's. And it was really strong that night, just every which way. Really, really strong. Strong as it's ever been. Probably due to the energy out there, for sure.

Carla: Have you felt anything besides the primary conditioning of the jaw and mouth? Have you felt anything on any other part of the body?

H: There are things I felt prior to the conditioning. I felt a small amount of other energy during my conditioning. Prior to my conditioning I have felt some very strong energies in my spine, in my forehead …

Carla: Third eye.

H: … on top of my forehead, on top of my head. One night, I wouldn't sign an affidavit, but I could swear my hair was standing up. And this was the same night that I meditated about three hours and got this really, really sincere feeling that if I went out I would see a ship. And it was snowing and it was really cold out and sat there after done meditating and tried to talk myself out of going out. "You know, this is really strange." But I went out anyway and drove around in the snow.

Nothing happened. But the next night, I very vividly saw a ship. So from then, I realized, well, that was definitely was some type of telepathic impression that I got during my meditation, because it was so strong and I really tried to talk myself out of even thinking that way, thinking I was psyching myself up for something, you know. I really felt that I had psyched myself up for something when I went out and nothing happened. I wasn't even thinking about it the next night it happened. That was really strange. But that night, like I said, about three hours sitting and meditating, I had energies just rushing all over my body. I've not had them that strong since.

Carla: You think it was just the length of time you had concentrated on meditation?

H: I really don't know. I've gone several times for an hour, an hour and a half, nothing unusual.

Interview with S1 on March 6, 1974

S1: Well, I just noticed my urge to move my mouth in this direction. I got those urges, those jerks of my arms, and we talked about it for awhile before we meditated. And D1 mentioned the fact that he is conditioned to form the letter "I." I don't know if I was myself making myself do it or what, but I got like that *(demonstrates motion)*.

And the other night I was meditating by myself and I think I channeled, "I am Hatonn. It is a pleasure to be with you this evening." Then I decided that I was probably doing it myself. Didn't do anything after that. The night we meditated over at D2's house. I was getting some really, really heavy conditioning. It was just static everywhere. I really had a strong urge to start out talking. I just held it back and then a few minutes later D1 started talking. I should have gone ahead and said, " I am Hatonn." I don't know. I know now that the words were trying [to come].

Chapter 4: About Specific Information

> "Write it down," he said patronizingly. "Why not? You seem to be more comfortable writing."
> Don Juan, a Yaqui Indian, to Carlos Castaneda

Comment

The Confederation is not particularly interested in the type of specific information included in this short chapter, and in light of the philosophy which they have to teach us, I can certainly understand their preference for working with us at every opportunity on the basic spiritually oriented thoughts which they have to offer.

However, occasionally a specific question will occur to a group member, following some event read or heard about. The following are answers which the Louisville group got to two such recent questions.

Channeling Selections

May 14, 1974

Questioner: Who were the UFO's that picked up Betty and Barney Hill, as told in *The Interrupted Journey*? Were they invaders? Were they evil, or to be feared? Do evil planets attempt to invade Earth?

Hatonn: We wish only to help all of the Creator's children, as we wish only to help you. We are, unfortunately, unable to help some who do not wish our service at this time. Therefore, we are content to wait until such time as they require our aid.

Chapter 4: About Specific Information

Meanwhile we regard them with the love of the Creator for all of his created beings. To be afraid of such entities as you have called invaders is to be afraid of yourself, my friends. And it is not needed to be afraid of anything or anyone.

I am aware that this does not satisfy your questions very well, and I will attempt to use this instrument for a more specific answer, although she will find it somewhat difficult, because there must be more control used, to which she is not used at this time.

The entities of which you have spoken were friendly. They were a scientific expedition which had good intentions, but their knowledge of life forms on this planet was lacking. They had no intentions to commit any sort of infringement. They had been cautioned by the Confederation that it was best to refrain from investigating in areas populated by people. They wished only to collect specimens of the fauna of some parts of the planet and to gain data about the predominant life forms.

They did not attack them. They will not attack you. Their intentions are positive. They are aware of our presence. Their presence is not an harbinger of any sort of enemy.

May 18, 1974
Hatonn: I am aware that you wish to know something about the confrontation between a combatant from another planet than your own and two of your people.

The Pascagoula landing, my friends, was, as far as we are aware, not a completely isolated instance. However, it is the only instance which has been delivered into the hands of public knowledge.

On the other hand, although it is not the only landing of that particular group of alien individuals, it is one of the very few.

These peoples are members of a type of combatant group. There is not the idea of the soldiering or war as you know it.

However, it is the closest interpretation which your language and the use of this instrument will permit. These people were interested, simply as passersby, in the phenomena which they saw; and, not having strong enough leadership, they decided to take a closer look. There was no intention of any harm intended at all.

It is doubtful that this type of craft and this particular group of beings will cease passing this particular area of space, for several reasons, none of which are in any way connected with the planet on whose surface you now reside.

Therefore you may again discover some evidence of such a contact. But we assure you that it is merely a rare, scattered, and unharmful confrontation.

Do you have a further question?

Questioner: Were the people who came from the spacecraft people or robots?

Hatonn: These were beings with consciousness and individuality. They were, however, not precisely of the nature which you would call human. You are not at this time aware of the possibilities that exist in the creation. However, these people are not robots.

Questioner: Can you give me some idea of what you meant by combatant?

Hatonn: There is a great deal of difficulty in working out of the language of your culture in explaining another culture, especially an alien culture. I am attempting to give to this instrument an idea of the structure of thinking upon the planet from which these people come. I am giving her the name but she does not seem able to understand it. However, the structure is somewhat more totally conscious of illusion than your own world structure. Each of the projects and difficulties of learning within a density somewhat comparable to yours results in an externally expressed series of movements

Chapter 4: About Specific Information

which eliminates for these people the need for inner fears and doubts. By the structuring of the illusion, they so recognize it and deal with it in a highly stylized fashion.

They have a good record of advancement along the spiritual path, using this technique. The closest that this instrument can come to explaining the concept she has been given is probably the concept of a few people, accepting the responsibility for many peoples' ambitions. They go, therefore, a far distance to take part in a game which has much of the characteristics of war, but which is entirely mental.

Due to the type of structure which these people have obtained throughout many generations of this discipline, the outcome of this combat will be final, just and completely acceptable to each who has depended upon the combatants of each different opinion.

These people are progressing along a different path that yours, and this is true throughout the infinite creation. But they are progressing towards the same goal that we all share.

Have you a further question?

Questioner: With respect to progress, what would be their relative progress and understanding with respect to this planet's general progress?

Hatonn: I am afraid that it is difficult in the extreme to state where a relatively stable, progressive culture lies, in comparison to the somewhat uneven picture which is represented on Planet Earth. The potential which is within very many of those upon the planet Earth is somewhat, shall we say, more advanced than the basic vibratory level of the planet.

However, the average vibration upon that alien planet is far more advanced than the lower average of those upon Planet Earth who stubbornly sleep. We are afraid that as those of

Earth have much potential, so they also have little time to translate their potential into the actuality that they in truth can deserve and have.

Both planets are within the same basic vibration. And the planet upon which you enjoy physical existence is far more advanced through its cycle within this particular vibration.

Is there another question?

Questioner: what type of sensory equipment do these individuals have? Do they see, hear and communicate like we do?

Hatonn: No. They are aware. The material which covers them is aware of more than all of the physical senses upon this planet are aware of, in unison.

Chapter 5: Cycles

The Concept of Cycles

> "And I examined the records of the stars of heaven, and of the Earth, and the accounts of Jehovih's harvests, and I perceived the bondage and labor of the Red Star were of the seventh magnitude in the advance of habitable worlds."
> —Oahspe
>
> "The sky is falling,
> The sky is falling."
> —Chicken Little

Comment

Many different groups, with widely divergent beliefs and solutions, are predicting some sort of final crisis, whether they call it Armageddon, depression, the polar shift, a final economic catastrophe, world starvation, political disaster, or what. These following messages present the Confederation's slant on the concept of this ending of a cycle.

Channeling Selections

January 6, 1974
You will see many changes in the coming years. These changes will be both of a natural type and a man-made type. There are certain things that will take place. But do not be alarmed. For you will be with the Creator.

January 7, 1974
We are here for a special purpose. We are here to serve. Think of this. We are here to serve. This is important. As you now near the end of a master cycle, there will be changes in your physical world. These changes should not be feared. They

should be welcomed. For they are signals to you that a new age is dawning. If you understand it, and walk among your people unafraid, then you, too, will serve. For they will see in you an inner knowledge, which we will provide you. We will also serve you through the absolute limits of our ability.

There are cycles in time, and cycles in space, and all things operate in cycles. Your planet now approaches the end of a great, great cycle of time. This has been a learning time, an evolving time, a time of growing. And many of the people of your planet are now ready for a transition to a much more glorious existence.

But they will not understand this transition unless they are told. There have been many contacts speaking of this transition, but too few of your people are presently aware of what is shortly to take place. It will be necessary to provide them with the reasons for what they experience. It is only necessary that you avail yourself in meditation to be able to understand and therefore serve. This is your call. This is why you are here, where you are.

We of the Confederation of Planets are aware of all of the problems which confront you, for we are in contact with you at all times. It is not an easy place to exist, your world. But pay it no attention, for it is not a lasting world. Everything that is happening and will happen is not really of any importance. It will shortly be gone. We speak of a lasting creation, an unchanging but infinite creation.

January 25, 1974
Due to the situation that now is evolving on your planet, that of transition from one vibration to another, it is necessary that we come to you at this time. It is also necessary that you avail yourself to us at this time, for there will be many, many things to be given to the ones who will accept the Creator's plan and way. These limitations of travel, and many, many other things

Chapter 5: Cycles

will be lifted, for these are of a sufficient vibration to accept them.

February 4, 1974
Hatonn: There are many vibrations within this creation. It has been written in your holy works that "in my Father's house, there are many mansions." This was a statement of these conditions. The mansion, or vibration, in which an entity finds himself is a result of his desire. If there is a separation, or choice, to be made, then it is up to each entity to select, according to his desire.

For that reason we visit your planet at this time, to attempt to help those who would wish to make their choice. There are many who have chosen already, even though they are not aware of it.

There will be an experience in this illusion, in the not too distant future, which will be alarming to some of the people of this planet. We are attempting to provide an understanding of the truth of this experience prior to its occurrence. Our service is to aid those who wish to choose a different mansion.

If an entity has chosen a particular mansion, then he will receive it. It is not a good place or a bad place. It is simply a different place.

Questioner: Is it a place without suffering?

Hatonn: There is no suffering except in the mind of the individual experiencing it. And if he experiences it, it is because he desires it. This may seem strange, but this is how the creation is designed.

February 17, 1974
Be aware, my friends, that a great opportunity is presented to all of your peoples at this time. Those among your peoples who can raise their consciousness rapidly enough can take part in what you might call a great graduation. Your planet moves

to a higher vibratory area and is even now at the entrance to this higher vibratory area. Only those individuals whose vibration can be raised along with that of the planet will continue into the golden age which will soon dawn upon your surface.

It is a spiritual age of beauty, grandeur, and true love of which I speak.

As an individual, each of you has everything to gain by following our simple suggestions, which will raise you in consciousness, and which will raise your individual frequency of vibration. You have nothing to lose but a small particle of what you call your time.

Ask yourselves, my friends, in all honesty, do you not find the time for those things which are important to you? It may simply be a matter of readjusting in your own thinking that which is important to you.

February 18, 1974
It is not too often that the condition that you are soon to experience in its total sense occurs. This experience is the reason for our visitations, and it is the reason for your present meeting. Each of you will become channels of communication between we of the Confederation of Planets in the Service of the Infinite Creator, and the multitudes of the population who dwell upon the surface of the planet you now enjoy.

February 23, 1974
There will be conditions manifesting shortly upon your planet, conditions that will be obvious to many of the people of your planet. They will be conditions of physical change. These conditions will bring about much seeking among the peoples upon your surface for one reason or another. In this time there will be many channels such as yourselves there to

speak, using our thoughts, for we have an understanding of these conditions and of their consequence.

February 23, 1974
Shortly upon your planet there will be conditions which will alert all of the people to something. Many will not understand what has happened, but they will know that something has happened. It is a situation where the people of the planet will have their attention focused upon something of which they will all be able to speak in common. It will be a natural phenomenon of a great magnitude, from your point of view. This will be something that many of the people who dwell upon your surface will fear. However, groups such as this one will be able to aid them by not fearing this phenomenon. There is no fear necessary.

I will continue now, since this instrument is able to receive my thoughts without using control.

My friends, many of the people of this planet will know, for the first time in their present life, that there is a creation, because, my friends, the illusion that man has created upon this surface will suddenly become totally insignificant. They will be awakened from their slumber and look about them in amazement, and see about them the creation of the Father for this first time in its reality.

Unfortunately, this awakening for most of them will include the reaction of fear. And this was never intended by the Creator. And this reaction, my friends, will be because of their ignorance. Those of you who wish to serve with us of the Confederation of Planets in His Service will have the task of educating those of the people of this planet who would seek an education. And, my friends, many, many will do this. For, as I say, many will have been awakened.

It will not be an easy task, and there will be many at your door. And there will be much misunderstanding. My friends, there is one thing that is always understood and that is love. Your demonstration of this principle will be the greatest benefit that you can offer to those that seek to learn.

It will be necessary that you prepare yourselves, so that you demonstrate your knowledge of truth and the creation of the Creator. It is written in your holy works, "Yea, though I walk through the valley of the shadow of death, I will fear no evil, for Thou art with me." These words are not false words, my friends. These words are meant for you.

You have heard it spoken through a channel, that, "He does not leave their shepherds without their staffs." These are not false words, my friends. All that is necessary is that you desire to seek, and then desire to serve, and then you shall do both of these things.

You shall seek understanding, and you shall gain understanding. And you shall serve, and give to those who seek it, understanding, for this is the Creator's way. There will be many, many of the peoples of this planet who cannot be served, for they will not seek. They will not seek the understanding that you offer. They will not be able to comprehend these concepts. For the illusion which they have created will be much too strong.

This is unfortunate. And these are the ones that you will not be able to serve. And this will sadden you. But there will be a great, great number who will seek. And these are the ones whom you will be able to serve. And this will give you great joy. For this, my friends, is the source of true joy: to serve, to serve in a way that provides that which is actually desired.

Within each of us—within each individual in the entire creation—there is this desire to seek. But many, many have buried this so very deeply within them that it will take even more than you shall shortly experience to uncover it. Concern yourselves, therefore, with those who seek.

Chapter 5: Cycles

February 23, 1974
Hatton: There are several events that will occur. There will be events of a physical nature. These events will be, from the point of view of those who are living within the illusion, of a very destructive nature. However, there is no such thing as destruction. There is only change. This you must understand. If you understand this, then you will understand the truth of what is to occur.

There will be change, a physical change. This change will be very beneficial. However, the people of this planet who view these changes from their present state of ignorance will consider them to be quite destructive.

This is unfortunate. However, the people of this planet have had a sufficient length of time to become educated. They have, however, sought to educate themselves in the ways of their illusion, rather than the ways of the Creator. This illusion is so strong in their understanding that most of them have no awareness in a waking sense of reality. These people will be very difficult to communicate with. They will view the changes in their immediate creation as destructive and irreversible.

R: Well, is it going to be an earthquake, like, or a depression, or what?

Hatonn: The changes will be of a physical nature. The depression of which you speak is of no consequence. It would be viewed as nothing compared to the physical changes that will occur. It will be necessary for members of groups such as this one who wish to serve to understand fully the reality of these changes, and to understand fully the accuracy of the statement made in your holy book which states that "Although you walk through the valley of the shadow of death, you will fear no evil." This must be kept uppermost in your consciousness. For you will walk through this valley.

Chapter 5: Cycles

And you will demonstrate to those who seek your knowledge of truth. And only your ability to demonstrate this knowledge will alert those who seek the knowledge that you are a true and knowing channel. For many false channels will at this time be lost. For they will not be able to demonstrate their knowledge of truth. For they will cling to the illusion that has surrounded them, and will display the fear that this illusion brings upon them.

This change is looked upon by those of us who understand it as an extremely beneficial change. It is also looked upon, by those members of groups such as this one who have realized the truth of this information, as extremely beneficial to all the peoples of this planet. It will be difficult for some of the members of groups such as this one to demonstrate an understanding of these truths, since they have been strongly affected by the illusion that has been created by the people of this planet.

However, this understanding is a necessity to be demonstrated.

R: What's going to be happening, exactly?

Physical change, of all types. There will be massive destruction wrought upon your surface. It will be of such a nature as to change the surface of your planet totally, This destruction is within your planet at this time. It has been put there by thought. It has been put there by the thought of the population of this planet through thousands of years of thinking this thought. This thought is of a vibratory nature.

You are at this time passing through the last portion of what you know as the third-density vibration. Shortly, your planet will be sufficiently within what you know as the fourth-density vibration. At this time there will be a disharmony between the thought that creates the vibration that is your

Chapter 5: Cycles

planet, and the thought that dwells within the density that is the fourth.

Much energy will be released of a physical nature. This energy will create physical changes within your planet. There will be changes within your land masses and changes in your atmosphere, changes in all of the physical manifestations of your planet. This will be of a nature that will be considered to be cataclysmic. This is a very good thing. However, it will not be considered good by those that are within the illusion.

Labeling this change good or bad is something that is dependent upon the individual observing the change and his orientation. My friends, the reason for this change being of a cataclysmic nature is that the thought that has been generated upon and in your planet for the past several thousands of years is a thought that is out of harmony with the new vibration into which your planet now goes. The Creator never conceived of the condition that is shortly to manifest upon your planet. This condition is manifested as a result of the desire of all the individuals that dwell on this planet. They are not aware of this desire, but their desire has created this.

They have created a condition by their desire that is shortly to be severely out of harmony with where they will physically be. Due to this, there will be a large energy release, which will manifest itself upon your planet in the form of earthquakes, storms, volcanic eruptions, and in fact a shift of the poles of your planet with respect to their orientation in space.

This change that will shortly manifest itself upon your planet is, as I have said, a result of the mismatching of vibrations of your planet and its new position in space. This change will alert many of the people of your planet who are very lightly slumbering, and many of the ones who are slumbering relatively deeply. Many of these people will at this time be what is known in many of your religions as "saved." It will save them, because they will get the violent awakening that is necessary to cause them to raise their vibrations that last amount that is necessary to get them off the fence, so to speak.

There will be those who are more deeply slumbering, so to speak, who will not make the transition. It is up to you to provide those who will be awakened with the information that they desire. We have stated that this transition is both good and bad.

Ultimately, in its most broad sense, it is a good transition.

However, it is an unnecessary transition. In a normal transition there would be no energy release, since in a normal transition, the vibration of the planet would match closely enough and be in harmony with the new and higher vibration. This would result in no energy release, and the planet would continue in a relatively normal sense from a lower vibration to the higher. Your planet is an aberration in the evolution of the spirit of the people of the planet and of the planet. The change that will take place will be a beneficial change. However, the mechanics of the change will seem anything but beneficial.

Those of the people who dwell upon this surface at this time, who are totally aware of the results of this change, and the reason for it, will not in any way be affected by this change. Those who are not aware of this, but who are aware of this in a spiritual sense, will be affected only emotionally, because they will not understand. These are the people with whom we wish to communicate.

March 3, 1974
Your planet, along with its neighbors, is moving, as your galaxy is, into a new area of space, a new vibration. In this creation, there is nothing but order. It is only necessary to look about you to see the order and perfection of this universe.

Chapter 5: Cycles

You are about to experience a gift. This gift will be a new understanding of love. Some of you have already begun to experience this, and as the progression takes place, it will become more and more apparent to many of those of Earth.

We are here to help with this experience. This is the reason that so many of your brothers from space, as you call it, are now here with Planet Earth. We are here to serve and to help the Creator's plan bring to you the love that you desire.

March 23, 1974
Our understanding, my friends, of this illusion, which is taken for the physical life upon your planet, is that it consists of a path, of a road to be followed, and of lessons to be learned. There are as many paths as there are people, my friends, and there are no set lessons. But after a great many lessons have been met, my friends, there comes a time when all of the lessons change to a different set. And those who are ready for the change go on to a new set of lessons.

It is our understanding, my friends, that the planet known as Earth approaches the end of one set of these lessons and that graduation is at hand for some and not at hand for others. There are many people balanced very delicately between going on and repeating these lessons for another cycle of time. It is our desire, my friends, to aid those who are almost ready to graduate. We have had some success in the past in giving this service to other peoples in other places and times. We are hopeful of doing this same thing here. This is our fervent desire, for in our service to you lies our service to ourselves.

April 26, 1974
Everything within your present physical world shall be changed. And when this is mentioned, it is usually considered that we mean only the planet which you now occupy. But it shall also include planets in your system and all of the heavens surrounding.

You pass into a new vibration where all shall vibrate with a new and great intensity. This intensity, or shall we say, the vibration, shall be attuned directly to receive the love and awareness of the Creator. It shall not be affected by any negative vibrations, for the vibration shall not be able to be penetrated by negatives. As these changes occur, so shall your awareness. Enjoy your present situation with the awareness that, through your meditation, you shall be within this new level of vibration.

The Concept of Vibration

> "If this is a universe of motion in which matter is a complex of motions, then motion is logically prior to matter."
> —Dewey B. Larson

Comment

The concept of "good vibrations" has been before the public since the Beach Boys' song of that title a few years ago. According to the Confederation, the Beach Boys had a handle on some good information!

Channeling Selections

February 4, 1974

You speak of the concept of vibration, and in your mind you think of various grades. We do not think in this manner. There are simply different experiences for an entity to choose - different experiences, but the same creation, an infinite creation, experiencing an infinite number of experiences, separate but the same, graded but ungraded, separated by vast distances, but all in the same place, expressing many thoughts and desires, but being only one: the thought and desire of the Creator.

Chapter 5: Cycles

March 11, 1974
Life is composed of two materials. One of them is what you might call consciousness. The other is light. But my friends, consciousness is love, and light is its physical manifestation. All that you are able to experience in the way of a physical universe is composed of one ingredient. This ingredient we will call light, since this word is closest to what we wish to express, and it is the only word that we have available in your language to express the basic building block of our Creator.

Originally, the Creator expressed a desire. This desire was expressed in a state of consciousness that is best described in your language using the word, love. The Creator, then, expressing desire through love, caused the creation of all matter. He caused the creation of light. This light was then formed in its infinite configuration in the infinite universe to produce all of the forms that are experienced. All of these forms, then, are molded or generated through the expression of consciousness that is love. They are composed of a fabric that is light. For this reason we greet you each evening, with the statement, "in his love and his light." For this, then, encompasses all that there is: the consciousness that creates and the fabric that is love and light.

The love that produces the configuration of light occurs in what we term various vibrations, or, using a word in your language that is not sufficient but somewhat descriptive, "frequencies." Love occurs, then, in various vibrations or frequencies. These vibrations or frequencies are the result of free will. When the Creator produced this original concept, the concept included the gift of freedom of choice to all of the parts that He created. These parts are then totally free to change the original Thought. In doing so, they change what you understand to be the vibration of some portion of the original Thought.

Chapter 5: Cycles

Each of you here this evening has a vibration. This vibration is yours, and you have control over it. Your freedom of choice has created the love that manifests the light that is the fabric molded into your physical form.

This is the simplest analysis of all created forms of all of the creation. Each part of it is able to utilize its own consciousness, through the principle of freedom of choice, to vary or change the original vibration. The creation, therefore, continues to be self-generating, in an infinite variety. This was provided for in the original Thought of the Creator. It was provided that He might generate, in an infinite way, an infinite number of forms.

Through this use of freedom of choice, man upon planet Earth has generated many forms. Some of these forms were never envisioned by the Creator with the original Thought. However, they were allowed for, due to the principle of freedom of choice.

This is perhaps the most important principle in this creation: that each of the Creator's parts be able, throughout eternity, to select for themselves what they desire. In experimenting with this desire, there have in some instances become a slight problem in straying away from thoughts and desires that would be most beneficial. In experimenting with these desires, some of the created parts have lost contact with the original desire.

This has occurred in many places in this creation. We are here at present to communicate, to those who desire to find their way back to the original Thought, information leading those who desire the path back along the path to the original Thought. It is necessary that we act in such a way so as to lead only those who desire this pathway along it, therefore not violating the important principle of total freedom of choice.

As I was saying previously, each of you and all parts of this creation have particular vibrations or frequencies. This vibration or frequency is the only important part of your being, since it is an index of your consciousness with respect to the original Thought. When an individual is aware of life in its infinite sense, he is also aware of the benefits of matching this vibration with the vibration of the original Thought.

It is our effort to match our vibration with that of the original Thought. This is the reason that we of the Confederation of Planets in the service of the Infinite Creator are here now. For this service that we perform is a service that would be in harmony with the original Thought. This, then, produces within us a vibration more harmonious to the original Thought. We are attempting to give instructions to those of the planet Earth who would seek the instructions of how to produce within themselves the vibration that is more harmonious with the original Thought.

This, as I have stated before, was demonstrated upon your planet many times before by teachers. The last one of whom you are familiar was the one known to you as Jesus. He attempted to demonstrate his thinking by his activities. His thinking was in harmony, much more than those about him, with the original Thought. His vibration was, therefore, much more in harmony with the original vibration. For this reason he was able to work what were called miracles.

However, the original Thought was that all of the parts of the consciousness that were of the original Thought should be able to generate by thought and consciousness what would be desired. The man known as Jesus desired, and therefore created, since the vibration which he generated was in harmony with the vibration which the Creator used to form the creation.

It is only necessary, then, that an individual come into harmony with the vibration that formed the creation in order for him to act within the creation as did the Creator, and as

Chapter 5: Cycles

does the Creator. This was demonstrated to you by the one known to you as Jesus. Not only did he demonstrate what could be done, in a very small way, but also how to think in order to do this.

Unfortunately, man upon Planet Earth has misinterpreted the meaning of this man's life. At this time we wish to point out the true meaning of this man's life. It was desired that those who were aware of his thinking and his activities then follow the example and, as he did, become more in unison and in a harmonious vibration with the Thought of their Creator.

We are here to bring you information and to impress upon you in a nonintellectual way during meditation the idea that is necessary for you to increase the vibratory rate of your real being so that it is harmonious with the original Thought of our Creator. Our teachings will be simple, as were the teachings of the one known to you as Jesus. It is only necessary that you attempt to understand these teachings. Understand them in depth. Understanding in depth can be done only through meditation.

And then, once these teachings are understood, it will be necessary that they be applied, and that the individual so desiring to apply them demonstrate in his daily activities and in his daily thinking the concept that was the original Thought, the concept that we have spoken to you as being love. We have used this word, as I have said, because it is as close as we can come, using language, to the original Thought. However, this word is miniature compared to the original Thought. The original Thought can be obtained in your intellect only to a very small degree. It must be obtained in your total being, through the process of meditation.

Once this is done, and once your activities and thinking reflect this Thought, your vibration will increase. At this time you will find the kingdom that has been promised to you. It is truly all about you. It is only necessary for you to grow in order for you to receive it. This growth is simple: spend time in meditation and learn of its simplicity.

Chapter 6: Entering the Silence

Meditation

> "I am only an egg ... Waiting is."
> —Valentine Michael Smith in Robert Heinlein's *Stranger in a Strange Land*

Comment

Since there are several distinct types of meditation which are currently practiced in this country, we perhaps should explain that this recommended meditation is of a passive nature, as opposed to a concentrative nature. The goal is to arrange for the body's comfort, and then allow the mind to cease its everyday functioning or "computing." Within this achieved stillness of mind and body, an attitude of inner listening is practiced, as the spirit within awaits the "still small voice."

Meditation upon subjects or objects, and that type of meditation closely allied to prayer, are quite valid procedures to follow. However in them both the meditator is speaking, rather than listening. The goal of the meditation recommended by the Confederation, as we have said, is a receptive and listening attitude on the part of the ones meditating. In this attitude, the very silence is full of cosmic information.

Channeling Selections

December 18, 1973

Do not concern yourself if an individual rejects an attempt you might make to awaken him. This simply means he is not yet ready for this truth to be given unto him. Concern

Chapter 6: Entering the Silence

yourselves with those who would seek the truth, and make it available to them in any way that you can.

There are many people upon your planet at this time who are attempting to cloud the memory of this truth. They are not aware of what they are doing. This is not their fault, but it is unfortunately the condition. It is not a simple task that we have outlined, and I am afraid it will require a great deal of effort. We have not been as successful as we had hoped to be when we initiated this project some years ago. The people of your planet do not actually wish to be awakened for the most part. Those who are sleeping very, very lightly are all too few. However, you will know them as you find them, and you will recognize their lightness of slumber by their activities, for they will not be as enmeshed in the insanity, if we can call it that, that is so prevalent on your world today.

These people are already seeking. In this case, it will be but a simple matter for you to convey to them that which they need. It is, however, very important that you be able to give them what they need. For this reason, we suggest that you continue to meditate, for only in this way can you be prepared to serve them. I speak not only of the preparation to act as does this instrument, as a vocal channel, but also a preparation of your own thinking, so that you will know the truth with no doubt or hesitation in speaking it. It is within you, my friends, and we will reawaken it within you, for your slumber is but very, very light. It is only necessary that you avail yourself to us through meditation.

January 12, 1974
I am going to instruct the people of your planet on the use of love. This will be done in an unusual way, but please bear with me. We have found that it is necessary to do things in unusual ways, as far as you are concerned. It is necessary to teach to you a way of thinking that is not common to the people of your planet if you are rapidly to gain understanding

of the concepts that are of utmost importance in your present progression. There are three ways to achieve a knowledge of love.

The first way is to relax and let your mind become at rest. This is the method of meditation. If this is done on a daily basis, then it is not possible to shut out the love that is ever present. You will become aware of the true creation and its meaning.

The second way is to go forth among the people of your planet and serve them. They will return to you love, and you will absorb this love and store it within your being. I must at this time caution that this service to your people must be done in such a way that it is service that they wish. Do not make a mistake, as so many of your people have done, in trying to impress an unwanted or unsolicited service upon your neighbor. To go forth and to serve your fellow man at this time upon your planet requires much care and planning, for it is at this time rather difficult to accomplish, for interpretations of service vary greatly, and it is necessary that you understand what service is, in order for yours to be effective. This can only be done by following the first step or plan, which is meditation.

The third technique is to give all that you have to your fellow man. If this is done, then you will not be encumbered by material possessions. You will no longer give part of your love to material possessions. Giving love to material possessions is an extreme waste of your abilities. This is a mistake that is made by most of the people of this planet. It is necessary, if one is to attempt this method of gaining love, to divorce oneself from the desire for material things.

January 13, 1974
We in the service of the infinite Creator are here in great numbers. What we ask of you is very simple. We ask that you

meditate. This is important, for if we are to contact you, this will be the way.

January 14, 1974
Meditation, my friends, is a very, very effective tool if you are to accomplish anything. But first you must understand what we mean by meditation.

We have stated that it is necessary that you clear your mind of thoughts. This is not always too easy to do, but it can be accomplished. There are many techniques that may aid you in doing this. Various sounds are sometimes used, and things to concentrate on are sometimes used, so that a single thought is allowed to remain. And then, from this single thought, no thoughts occur. It is necessary, if you are to be totally successful in meditation, that you totally relax. It is, however, necessary that you do not go from this relaxed state to a state of sleep, for this defeats the purpose.

It is therefore recommended that you remain in an erect, sitting position. This, for the most part, eliminates a great deal of tendency to sleep.

January 26, 1974
I am Laitos. I would speak to you at this time regarding your personal daily meditations. This is becoming increasingly necessary as we near the coming events upon your planet.

Your daily meditation is necessary in order that the veil might be lifted, and all things which you have been promised will be shown.

There is much about this creation that the people of your planet are not aware. I have stated that the principles are extremely simple. Everything is provided for the individual. All knowledge is yours. It is only necessary that you seek it out within you. Everything that we do is within the abilities of everyone else. All of the people of your planet are also able to do all of these things. It is only necessary that they return to an awareness of these abilities. This awareness is an awareness of the love and understanding with which they were originally created.

This is the only thing that blocks them from their abilities and their knowledge. It is recommended, therefore, that through meditation it is possible to regain this knowledge and these abilities. For this reason, we continually impress upon you the need for meditation, and the need for understanding your fellow men. For only through this process can you return to your rightful position.

The people of your planet are not aware of the simplicity of this process. If they could learn how very simple it is, and not forget this, then they would not any longer have the difficulties that they experience. I must be very emphatic about this, that the entire process is of an extremely simple nature. It is only necessary that the individual realize that he is a part of the creation, and that the creation is one single thing, and that in so being, he and all of his brothers and sisters throughout all space are one being. This realization will result in an ability to demonstrate only one reaction to anything: that reaction will be love.

February 11, 1974
We have suggested that meditation is the best avenue for acquiring the non-intellectual understanding of the use of the creative force. This is possible for anyone at any time. It is only necessary that they avail themselves of the knowledge that they already possess. It is a difficult thing to do sometimes, when surrounded by vibrations created by desire that is of a nature never intended by the Creator. We understand the difficulty arising in realizing this simple truth when impressed with the thought of those who would desire other than this truth.

Chapter 6: Entering the Silence

However, it is quite possible to insulate one's consciousness from these influences of thought, and realize the truth of one's origin. The one known to you as Jesus was able to do this. Do not believe that this man was unique in his ability. He was demonstrating to you that this was possible. He was demonstrating that each of the Father's children could do the same thing that he did. It is only necessary that you meditate to realize this, and then it is only necessary that you demonstrate your knowledge of it through your thoughts and your actions.

You, then, as did he, will be able to use that force that is yours to use: love.

This is the word, my friends: love. But it is not understood. Love: it means all that you think it means. But it means much more. Learn what it means, and you shall truly be free.

February 13, 1974
We have stated many times that meditation is very necessary. If you are to understand what and how to serve at this time, it is necessary that you find this through meditation, for this is the only process that will allow you to understand this information in its totality. So it is necessary that you spend time each day in meditation, and become aware of the technique of fulfilling your desire to serve.

When you have done this, you will find that you are experiencing something that is phenomenal. It will be an event that is beyond your wildest dreams. It will be of a nature that you might consider impossible at this time, but it will take place.

February 18, 1974
We of the Confederation of Planets in the Service of the Infinite Creator suggest that there are certain things that are important if you are to meditate effectively.

Chapter 6: Entering the Silence

The first and most important is that you allow the conscious mind to relax. It is necessary to relieve it of thoughts that are of a transient nature, and we find that thoughts concerning most of your daily activities are of a transient nature.

In order to allow the mind to become receptive to things of other than a transient nature, it is suggested that you sit in a quiet place with the spine erect. This is the most important of the techniques of meditation.

A silent place is very beneficial. However, it is not necessary. It is more beneficial to an individual who is starting to meditate than it is to an experienced individual.

In order to remove the concepts of an intellectual nature that involve the mind in transitory thoughts, it is suggested that something to fascinate the intellect can be at times of use, such as music, or what you have called a mantra. This, however, is not necessary.

What is necessary is that thoughts that are of an intellectual nature be allowed to leave the consciousness.

We have said many times in the past that it is necessary for you to meditate. We have said this as an instruction to allow you to erase the illusion that has grasped so many of the people of this planet within its clutches. This meditation that you perform brings you to an understanding of reality. Reality is all about you. But it is not the illusion that continually occupies the thinking of the larger number of your planet.

We have said this to you many times. It is up to you to understand what we are saying. And there is only one way to understand it. This way is to understand it in meditation.

February 21, 1974
Desire is a thing that dwells within each of the Creator's children. The desire of each of them, however, is different. What this desire is, is dependent upon the vibratory level of

Chapter 6: Entering the Silence

the individual. The lower the vibration, the more basic the desire. The higher the vibration, the higher the desire. You will find, as you increase your vibration through meditation and seeking and service, that your desire will change. The things that are desired by those that are tightly locked within the physical illusion are not those desired by those on the verge of freedom. And the reason for this verge of freedom is the desire, which goes hand in hand with the increased awareness or higher vibration.

However, it is possible to achieve what you actually desire, by removing from your thinking desires of any nature except those of unity with the creation and those of service for your fellow man. The technique for doing this, my friends, is a simple one. We have stated it many times. It is to avail yourself to the reality and truth of the creation through meditation, and then act upon the desires generated by the availing. These desires will be somewhat different from the ones you experienced before you spent time in meditation and seeking. The desire to seek will be generated from seeking. It is a self-perpetuating phenomenon. We have belabored this point many times, and we will continue to do this.

Why do we do this, my friends? Why do we continue to tell you to meditate? So [that you can] understand your desires, understand yourself, and become aware of seeking and what it is you actually do.

Why do we spend so much time on these subjects that so many on your planet would consider to be trivial? The reason for this, my friends, is that these are the only subjects that are not trivial. It is of no value at all to seek within the illusion that you now know as your physical world. What you seek there, and what you find, is not lasting. It is stated in your world that you cannot take [it] with you. This is fact. What you take with you past the boundaries of the physical illusion is one thing. That is your mind. This mind that you take with you is, in reality, all that there is.

February 23, 1974
There are several ways of becoming aware of your desires but there is only one that we recommend. This is meditation. Each of you had all of the information that this instrument has given you, before he gave it to you. You have all of the information that he is going to give to you. We of the Confederation of Planets in the Service of the Infinite Creator are unable to give you any new information, for you are already in possession of all the information that exists. Each individual in the creation possesses all of the information in the creation, for each individual is a portion of the creation. The only reason for a lack of availability of this information is that this individual has desired to limit himself for the sake of his own experience.

For this reason, we have stated many times that it is necessary to meditate. Through this process, you regain the communication with yourself that is necessary to be aware of all the information of the creation. There is one single, simple Thought behind all of it. This Thought is the original Thought of the creation. In your language, this thought is expressed as love. This word most closely approaches the concept, although it is totally inadequate for an expression of the love that is the creation.

March 2, 1974
Upon your planet at this time, there are many, many individuals performing many, many services. Very few of these services, however, are services of a nature that we would consider to be in the service of our infinite Creator. We find that upon this planet, man is primarily concerned with serving himself.

Chapter 6: Entering the Silence

There are many ways to serve, and there are many attempts at service. However, much of the service performed upon this planet which is an attempt to serve, as we do, our Creator, is not service of this nature.

The reason for this is always the same. It is because of a lack of meditation. We have said to you many, many times that it is necessary to meditate. This is the most important truth that we bring to you, for if one practices meditation, then one has no questions about service.

Each of you here this evening desires to serve, and each of you is serving and will serve to an even greater extent in the near future. However, in order to be of the most efficient service, it is necessary to prepare for that service with daily meditation.

March 8, 1974

Consider, my friends, that each man has a handprint uniquely his own. No one else's handprint in the whole world can match it. Consider each leaf or snowflake, and realize that there has never been a duplicated entity.

The way from this illusion, which is a tiny part of reality, to reality cannot be measured, and is as individual as your handprint. There is however, a quality whereby the circumstances for understanding may occur. This quality is more possible to obtain in meditation, for by it the intellect, which is responsive only to the illusion about you, is stilled.

April 24, 1974

We are shepherds of your flock. And we see the needs of the flock. Our only desire is to aid those of the flock who seek our aid. The aid you seek, my friends, has become very much more focused upon true seeking than that of most of the sheep of the flock. Therefore, what we can say to you intellectually is more and more lacking in complete satisfaction. It is for this reason, my friends, that we stress to you, even as you are gaining advancement, the continued need for more and more meditation.

For, my friends, what we can give you through use of the intellect and language is a very small percentage only of what we are able to give you by direct contact, mind to mind.

Desire

> "The soul selects her own society,
> Then shuts the door;
> On her divine majority
> Obtrude no more
> Unmoved, she notes the chariot's pausing
> At her low gate;
> Unmoved, an emperor is kneeling.
> Upon her mat.
> I've known her from an ample nation
> Choose one;
> Then close the valves of her attention
> Like stone."
> —Emily Dickinson

Comment

In 1975 I omitted a comment here. If the tone seems to shift, it is because some 34 years have passed since I wrote these comments.

Desire is that from which we all move. We might desire to have a meal or to change the world. The faculty is the same. The Confederation philosophy finds desire to be vitally important because it is only our own free will that moves us, and we move according to our desires. Through meditation, the Confederation hopes that our desires shall become more educated, so that our choices can become more polarized towards service to others.

Chapter 6: Entering the Silence

Channeling Selections

January 21, 1974
My friends, of what substance is the universe made? We have told you that this substance is light. You may also call this substance energy, vibration [or] consciousness. And yet, my friends, by itself, this substance, this fundamental unitary substance, would remain in an incorporate state. The shaping force, my friends, is love.

And so we greet you in love and light. For there is nothing but these two substances which are, in fact, two aspects of the single building block of the physical and the spiritual universe. You, my friends, in your spiritual reality are articulated light shaped by love in such a way that you possess freedom and desire. Your light is shaped by the love of freedom and the love of desire.

January 26, 1974
The illusion that is now impressed upon you because of your limitations in a physical condition, as you call it, are limitations that are not at all ordinary. They are limitations that are impressed upon those who desire them for certain experiences. Each individual in this creation is able to select precisely what he desires. This is exactly the plan of the Creator. He not only gave man free will, but he also gave man the ability to select exactly what he desired. There are many, many paths to take through this creation—in actuality, an infinite number—and the choice is always left up to the individual.

Some of those who have explored, have explored in a direction that led them away from the all-knowing One, the all-loving One, the Creator. In wandering away, there were conditions encountered that were at that time desired by the individual who was wandering. But as he wandered farther and farther, he became more and more immersed in an illusion that he created. This illusion is at present so very strong that many of the children of the Creator find themselves confused and unable easily to find the pathway back to the infinite light.

It is necessary that they realize for themselves how to do this, for the principle given to them by their Creator is still totally in effect. It allows them to do precisely what they desire. It is therefore necessary that they realize for themselves what they desire, and then it is necessary that they seek this realization. In order to do this, it is necessary that they become aware of the techniques of bringing about this understanding. This is our purpose at the present time: to help those who are presently seeking the pathway that will return them to the love and the light that they now desire. It is necessary for us to help those who desire this, in order to act within the plan of the creation. It is necessary also that we do not overly disturb those who do not overly desire at this time such activity.

February 1, 1974
The creation was initially conceived by our Creator to be of a property so as to reflect the impressions given to it by man. It was so designed to express his desires in any way that he chose. There are various levels or densities in this creation, levels and densities that are not yet suspected by your physical scientists. Each of these levels is expressing the desires of those of the Creator's children who are acting within it.

Each level or density is moldable or may be acted upon by the thoughts of the individuals within it to greater, or in some cases a lesser, extent than that appreciated by those who dwell upon the surface of your planet at this time. It is only necessary to desire an effect to create it. This is what the Creator of us all provided for us. This is not understood at present by the population of the surface of your planet. However, it is in actuality the truth of the Creation that they are experiencing at this time. The conditions that you

Chapter 6: Entering the Silence

experience in your daily activities are a result of your thinking and the thinking of those about you and others on your surface.

February 9, 1974
Your desire is extremely important, for the Creator planned that all of his children throughout all of the universe would get exactly what they desire. That is how the universe works. That is how the Creator planned it.

The people of your planet at this time do not understand this, though it is evident to us that this is the cause of all of the conditions that you enjoy on your planet. These conditions range from those that you would call enjoyable to those that you despise. However, my friends, all of these conditions are a result of desire. Man on Earth does not realize that he creates everything that he experiences through the mechanism of desire.

This, my friends, is why meditation is so very important at this time. It is because man on Earth does not understand his desires, and, since he does not understand his desires, he does not understand the gifts of the Creator. He interprets them quite erroneously. And, my friends, the Creator never planned for his children to be the recipients of that which they did not desire.

However, man on Earth is desiring things that he does not want. But he does not realize this. He can realize this, very simply, through the process of meditation. He may know himself and his true objective. That objective, my friends, is the same for all people throughout all of the creation. Even though, as on your planet, they do not realize the objective. The objective, my friends, is a return to the Creator and a return to the true creation.

Many of his children have wandered far from truth. They have forgotten that condition in which they were originally

Chapter 6: Entering the Silence

created. They have wandered from this condition due to a desire to experience other things. And these experiences have led them to other desires which have led them even farther from the original truth.

Man on Earth at this time is in a state of ignorance with respect to the principle of desire. This principle has been stated many times. You know of it as, "Ask, and you shall receive." We say, "Knock, and the door shall be opened." Open to what, my friends? Open to truth, a truth that will make you aware of what you actually desire. "Seek and ye shall find," it has been said. Seek this truth, and know your desire.

But first, my friends, it is necessary that you desire to seek. All of you here tonight desire to seek, and you are seeking. But many of your fellow beings upon the surface of this planet are not even aware of the possibility of seeking or of the fruits of seeking. They continue living in a state of desire that is erroneous to that which their true being would achieve.

It is necessary that we make available to as many of the people of this planet as would receive our thoughts the principles upon which the creation actually functions. It is necessary for the people of this planet to understand the principle of desire.

February 13, 1974
Your people on this planet seek many things. However, they seek these things in what we would consider to be a very strange way. They seek the result of their desires almost exclusively within what they know as the physical illusion that they now enjoy. Since they are unable to experience in their waking state anything but this physical illusion, they then think that this is all that exists, and they attempt to find expression of their desires strictly within this illusion.

This results in the fulfillment of false desires. The people who fulfill these false desires wonder why, having fulfilled them,

Chapter 6: Entering the Silence

they do not find happiness. This has been demonstrated upon your planet many times, but little heed has been taken of it. The desires still remain very strong, and the people about you strive with much energy to fulfill them.

Having fulfilled them they then, as I have said, wonder. They wonder why they still have desires, for as soon as they have fulfilled one, they have generated another.

We are going to attempt to give you instruction at this time on the proper use of desires so that you may work within the truth of the creation and become once more knowledgeable about its function. There are certain desires that every individual has within him. These desires are a natural state, and they should be fulfilled. The reason the individual has these natural desires is that he is a part of the creation, and the Creator had an original desire, which continues throughout all of time and all of space.

This desire of the Creator was to provide an experience for all of His parts that would fulfill in totality the desire of all of His parts. But since all of His parts have this same desire, then it should be evident that this desire is to serve the other parts. This is how we have interpreted the functioning of creation. This is why within each individual throughout all of the creation there dwells a desire to serve the creation in any way that he can.

This dwells within each of the people, all of the entities of this planet, for all of them are a portion of the Creator.

It is possible to fulfill this desire. As we have said, the Creator has attempted to provide only good for all of His children. But since all of His children are a part of the Creator, and since all of us, and everything, is in actuality one thing, then we have this necessity occurring within each individual in all of the parts of the creation, an attempt to serve. This is natural. The planet upon which you now stand serves you. The growth that comes from the planet serves you. Its atmosphere serves you. Its water serves you. The entire creation serves you. You feel the energy from your sun. It serves you.

This principle is simply the original concept of the Creator being expressed through all of its parts, for this concept remains undiminished. For this reason, you will find that you will achieve what you actually desire only if you are to serve the rest of the creation. This is a law that is natural. This law is the creation.

February 23, 1974
We desire to serve our fellow man, as the teacher known to you as Jesus desired to serve. We desire to serve you. We must serve you to the best of our ability. This will include meeting with you when this will result in what you desire. What you desire is that you grow in a spiritual sense, so that you may better serve your fellow man, fulfilling your desire, [your fellow man's] desire and the desire of the Creator. When our meeting with you will increase your spiritual growth and therefore meet your desire, we will desire to meet with you. I hope that I have made this point more clear.

You are desiring at this time that of which you are aware that is desirable. The reason that you are not aware of what you actually desire is that you are conditioned to understand that which has been given to you as the illusion. If you will avail yourself to truth through meditation, then you will understand what you desire. What you desire is that you grow in a spiritual sense in order to serve your fellow man and in order to fulfill your desire, his desire, and the desire of the creator.

Seeking

> "Ask, and it shall be given you; seek and ye shall find; knock, and it shall be opened unto you. For every one that asketh, receiveth; and he that seeketh, findeth; and to him that knocketh it shall be opened."
> —*Bible*, Luke 11: 9-10.

Comment

(This comment was written in 2009.)

The Confederation's view is that Planet Earth's people are, for the most part, asleep in terms of being aware that there is more than this apparent world, its goals of comfort and security and the ambitions of the world for love, money and power. They hope to awaken those who are sleeping lightly and to offer them thoughts which will wake them up.

And so they talk about meditation. They feel that with meditation, a person's thoughts will begin to come more and more into conformation with the one original Thought of the Creator, and the seeker of the truth of love will be born.

Channeling Selections

February 9, 1974
Seek truth, and you must surely find. Ask, and it will surely be given. These truths are in your sacred books. This is a law of the universe, for your desire sparks cause and effect.

February 9, 1974
We are always available to aid in guiding your seeking. But, my friends, we cannot do this, if you do not seek. This message is not meant so much for this group as it is for those who will read it at a later time. For this group is seeking. Seek, my friends! Seek! This is the word that opens the door to

Chapter 6: Entering the Silence

everything that exists throughout all of space and all of time. Seek! Seek!

And what will you find? You will find love, for that is all that there is to find. For that is all that there is.

February 25, 1974
Be patient for all things come to these who seek. Seeking, my friends, is the most important thing that you do. All of us in this creation seek. What we seek is the important thing. Many of your people seek, but they do not seek things that are of any value. Every day you are given suggestions of things that you should seek, but if you will examine them, you will find that most of them are of very little value. When you seek that truth that is permanent, and everlasting, then you seek that which is of significance. We of the Confederation of Planets in the Service of the Infinite Creator are here to help your people with their seeking. As I have said before, there are all too few of them who are even aware that such seeking is important. Actually, they have chosen their physical incarnations at this time for the purpose of seeking the truth of which I speak. They are, however, for the most part, unaware of this. This is unfortunate.

We are attempting to remedy it in many ways and we are enlisting as much aid as we possibly can. For at this time your people are in very great need of knowledge of how and what to seek. They have been seeking for so long within the material realms that most of them are totally unaware that seeking is possible within the spiritual realms.

The religions of your world have, for the most part, eliminated the responsibility for individual seeking. This, however, is an extremely erroneous point of view. It is very necessary for the individual to seek truth, knowledge and the ultimate and supreme love, of the Creator if he is to grow in strength and spirit and understanding and at some future time take his rightful position in the Father's creation. This, my friends, is why seeking is so important. It is the only way for your people to get from where they are to where they should be.

March 8, 1974

It is a great privilege once more to be able to speak to those who seek. There are not too many on this planet who seek. We of the Confederation of Planets in the Service of the Infinite Creator are here to help those who seek. It has been written in your holy works that if you seek, you shall find. We are here to help those who seek. We are here to help them find.

And what, my friends, shall we help you find? We will help you find life: life as it was intended; life as you desire it. There is what man on Earth presumes to be life abundant upon this planet. However, this life is not acting in a manner ever intended by our Creator.

There are many problems upon the surface of your planet. All the life that is so abundant about you is reacting to the conditions that are not in harmony with the Creator's plans.

Yes, my friends, these conditions affect not only the people who dwell upon this planet, but all life forms. We of the Confederation in the Service of our Infinite Creator are here to attempt to teach to those who would wish to learn how to live.

We have stated many times that there is a great advantage in living as the Creator intended. However, there is no way for us to show you what such a life is like. It is only possible for us to show you how to live such a life. When you do this, you will then understand what the Creator planned for all of us.

I am aware that many of you are anxious to succeed with your seeking. I am aware that some of you think that your progress is all too slow. This is nothing about which to be concerned.

Chapter 6: Entering the Silence

It is only necessary that the individual first desire to seek that which our Creator intended, and then, if he continues in his seeking, all of those things which he desires in his meditations will be added.

The seeking, my friends, is very important. This is of utmost importance. There are many people upon this planet who are seeking something. However, very few are seeking what was meant for them to seek by their Creator. They are seeking things that are within the illusion that they have created. They are seeking these things because they don't know of anything else worth seeking.

There is only one thing worth seeking. There are many ways of defining it. There are many pathways to it, and there are many names for it. But, my friends, no matter how you name it, no matter how you reach it, no matter what it is that you achieve, there is only one objective. That objective is the same for each of us. It is only necessary that man realize that he has this common objective with his fellow man. Once this is realized, and once he begins to seek for this objective, he will be guided, for this is the way the creation functions.

And to what will he be guided? What, my friends, is this objective that we all seek? It is very simple. As I have said, it can be called by many names. And it can be reached by many pathways. However, it is simply a return to the awareness, to the thinking of our Creator. This thinking has been demonstrated in the past. Guidelines have been set down for the people of this planet to follow. For they were not able to reason these pathways themselves. They were not ready to seek and actively find that common goal. But in laying down these guidelines and in showing these pathways there was a generation of misunderstanding.

For this reason, we say that it is necessary to meditate. For then and only then can you understand the true meaning of

Chapter 6: Entering the Silence

these guidelines and of these pathways that lead to our common objective.

March 9, 1974
I am going to speak on the subject of seeking. This is a very important subject. It is perhaps the most important of all subjects that could be spoken about.

I would like to explain why seeking is important. Seeking is a way of growing. In truth, for the people of this planet at this time it is their only way of truly rapidly growing; growing, my friends, in a sense that is spiritual.

The people of this planet at this time are almost all children, in a spiritual sense. Most of them are not at this time seeking spiritual growth. This is very important, if an individual is to rapidly grow, spiritually. All of us throughout all of space are growing, in a spiritual sense. However, some of us are growing much more rapidly than others. The reason for this growth is simply that these are the ones that are seeking.

It is written in your holy works that it is necessary to seek if you are to find. This is with reference to finding spiritual enlightenment. This is in reference to developing the awareness that is necessary for man on Earth to develop if he is to take his rightful place in the creation.

We of the Confederation of Planets in the Service of the Infinite Creator are aware that seeking is necessary if one is to get where he wishes to be, and one wishes to be at a higher state of awareness. Look about you, upon your planet. There are many conscious beings, in many forms of life. There are the animals, and birds, and the fish, and man on Earth. And each has a state of higher awareness. But it seems that man has the higher state of awareness. And yet we tell you that this awareness is very minimal. And the awareness of man on Earth can be raised to an awareness that he would consider godlike.

Chapter 6: Entering the Silence

But, my friends, this is what was meant for man to have. This was the original concept of the Creator: that this awareness would be possessed by all of His children. This is what it is necessary to seek, if you are to find this awareness.

The reason that it is necessary to seek this awareness is that it cannot be given to you. It is something that each individual must find for himself. It is not a difficult thing to find. It is a very simple thing to find. It is only necessary that the individual go about seeking in a proper way. We are here to attempt to aid those who desire our aid in seeking our awareness, to find it. We will not attempt to confuse those whom we wish to aid with complex lectures on various problems and concepts. We will simply give to them the simplest of the Creator's ideas. For, my friends, His ideas are not complex. It is man, especially man on Earth, who has made a complex set of rules and conditions for spirituality. The Creator's concept, my friends, is extremely simple.

This we are here to bring to you. It is only necessary then that you seek an understanding of this simplicity. Then, upon understanding it, demonstrate it in your daily lives, and in your activities and associations with your fellow man. Then, my friends, the awareness that was meant for you will be yours. It is an extremely simple process. It is only necessary that, first, man on Earth seek.

Seek, my friends! This is what is necessary. This is the first step. Seek awareness. Seek the spirituality that was meant to be yours, and surely you will find it. For this is the Creator's plan, that all of his children should have this.

Seeking, my friends, is extremely simple. And yet, through the powers of your intellect, with the best of intentions, it is possible to make it seem complicated.

There is the complication in your vision of the concept of time; and there is the complication in your vision of the concept of space. And you say "Where, and when, may I seek?

Chapter 6: Entering the Silence

In what place may I find holy ground? And at what time may I seek the Creator?"

My friends, you are the Creator. For the Creator is you. And, my friends, as it is written in your holy works, the place where on you stand is holy ground.

There is no complication in time, for all time is here and now.

There is no complication in space, for all space is here and now.

My friends, there is naught but seeking; there is naught but the Creator. It is only necessary for you to turn inwardly, into the light, and enter the light.

These words are poor, but they lead the way to a new understanding. It is not necessary to have the most perfect meditation or the most proficient spiritual moments in order to be seeking. It is necessary only to turn your will.

March 23, 1974

Seek understanding, my friends. Seek through meditation and seek to know the reason that the master teacher known as Jesus retreated from time to time to a place where there was [silence.] There was something he was seeking. Seek for the silence, where there is much understanding awaiting you.

April 26, 1974

Our only concern is to help you with your spiritual seeking. A great deal of activity has already taken place upon the surface of your planet and within its atmosphere by way of interaction between those of us in the Confederation of Planets in the Service of the Infinite Creator and those who dwell upon the surface of your planet. Each confrontation of whatever nature was intended in some aspect or another to turn those people involved toward an attitude of seeking. In many cases, my friends, we would say the majority of cases, this attempt worked, in that whatever anomalistic phenomenon—out of the ordinary, at this instrument would put it—occurred created the alerting mechanism in that entity's mind which it was intended to create.

Our problem, my friends, is not in gaining the ability to catch the attention of the people of your planet. Our difficulty is to aid them in a way that is truly consistent with all of their desires. We cannot transgress the principle of free will. This holds us in check so that we can come only as close as thought or, in some isolated instances, isolated contact. More definite contact must wait until we are more definitely welcome.

Therefore, what we have to offer in the way of confrontation is largely a thought value. This is as it should be, my friends, and yet we put it to you: there is a continuing difficulty, not in alerting the consciousness of man of Earth alone, but in keeping those who are alerted within the active attempt that they are making. We have seen many, many people who have gone through some sort of confrontation and have gained a sense of seeking, only to place it far back in the closet of their mind, to be taken out at some future time.

You cannot lose awareness, my friends. Yet, there is little time. And it is our desire that we may help each of you who truly desires it to seek not only when there is a reason for seeking that very day, but to seek each day in a self-perpetuating way, so that your thinking is completely independent of such things as physical or thought appearances of a controversial nature which turn you toward seeking.

Seek ye first, my friends, is written in your holy works. Seek ye first the Kingdom of Heaven. If we can lead you to this level of seeking, then we will have been able to have produced in you the capacity, which you have always enjoyed, for continual, lifelong and productive seeking. Furthermore, once this seeking has taken its place within your life as knowledge which needs no impulse to give it the central place in your consciousness, then you are within the boundaries for a true

Chapter 6: Entering the Silence

discipleship in which you join the service of the infinite Creator.

May 17, 1974
There are many ways, my friends, of gaining what you seek. However, what you seek now will change. It will change as you seek it, for this is the nature of seeking. For as you seek, you find, and as you find, you understand. And as you understand, you continue in seeking, but at a different level.

So do not attempt to understand that which at present seems to be beyond you. Simply go within, and you will be led to an understanding that will place you upon a new plateau, from which you will be able to view much, much more of reality.

Seeking, my friends, is not a direct attempt to understand each intellectual question which crosses your mind. Seeking is the attempt to know one's Creator. There will be in your seeking an unfoldment of understanding. Each step will show itself to you. When it does, raise yourself upon it, so that you may find the next one.

We bring to man of Earth understanding, and yet we cannot speak to him and cause him to understand. We cannot communicate this understanding through channels. We can only point out directions for his seeking. For it will be necessary for him to change his point of view. And to change it, he must understand. And to understand, he must seek.

There will be many paradoxes in your seeking, for this is the nature of seeking. But as you continue, these will dissolve, for you will reach a new plateau and a new understanding. And the seeming paradox that you have bypassed will appear in its true light.

Meditation, my friends, is the only method of which we know to allow an individual rapidly to form this new basis for his understanding. For this is not dependent upon preconceptions. It is not dependent upon the definitions of a language that was never intended for spiritual seeking.

Redefine that which you experience. Redefine it through your seeking and through your growing awareness of the creation and our Creator. And then, my friends, you will not question, for you will know. For you will have grown in your understanding.

It is sometimes frustrating to be unable to find answers to those questions that seem paramount, and directly in the path of your seeking. But these, too, will fade as you pass them by and become more and more aware of the single truth that permeates all things and answers all questions.

We will continue to aid you in any way that we can, but primarily we will point out to you the wonders and the joy of the creation that you experience. And we will attempt to bring to you an understanding that will grow with each day, an understanding that will be a result of your meditation.

Service to others

> "We are all one, beloved ones; and to serve others is only to serve yourself."
> Brother Philip

Comment

This concept of service to others is perhaps the most basic concept given by the Confederation, after the concept of meditation. The drive which leads us to this material is a desire for knowledge. Once we begin to attain a degree of this new knowledge, the drive progresses within us to a desire to be of some service. The following messages are attempts to elucidate these concepts.

Chapter 6: Entering the Silence

Channeling Selections

January 4, 1974

I am in the Service of our Infinite Creator. I am here, as are my brothers, to serve your people. This has been told you this evening. But there are some other things that should be told unto you at this time. We are here for another purpose. This purpose is to serve ourselves. For, my friends, in serving you, we serve ourselves. This is the way that the creation is built. It is made so that if you serve anyone or anything in this creation you are serving yourself. This is a truth that cannot be varied. The creation, my friends, is one thing, and it is impossible in this creation to act without affecting yourself. This is not realized by most of the people of your planet, and for this reason they have affected themselves in a miserable way. We are very sorry for this because in doing this they have not only affected themselves, they have affected us. They have made us very sad.

We are sad because we are very sorry to see people as miserable as are yours. It is not necessary, my friends, to be miserable. It is necessary only to be extremely ecstatic at all times, for this is the way that our Creator intended it. When it is understood that all things are one, and it is impossible to serve anything without serving yourself, then the state of ecstasy that I spoke of becomes reality.

January 8, 1974

Service, my friends, is very natural. It is the way of the Creator. It is the plan of the creation. Everything in the creation is performing a service. The vegetation that is abundant on your planet performs a service. But your people ignore this. The animals upon your planet perform a service but this is largely ignored. The flowers, the very air, the water, perform a service, but this is ignored. If it were taken fully into consideration, it would become obvious that everything in the creation is here to perform a service.

This includes all the Creator's children. Each of you is here to perform a service. This is the plan of this infinite creation. This is how it works. It is only necessary to understand this and then all things are possible.

Unfortunately, upon the planet that you now enjoy, this principle is not understood. Very, very few of those who inhabit the surface of this planet understand the simplicity and totality of this plan. It is the way the creation functions. It is only necessary that you understand this, and then perform with the best of your ability these services to your fellow man, and then you too will be functioning the way that the Creator of us all planned.

January 12, 1974

We, the Confederation of Planets in the Service of the Infinite Creator, are waiting to meet as many of the people of your planet as would wish to meet us. The reaction of the people of your planet is quite varied [as] to their realization of our presence. Some of them seem convinced that we are here now. Some of them do not believe in us at all. That is exactly the condition for which we have strived. It is a condition which will produce a maximum effort on the part of the individual to seek: to seek the truth of our existence or of our nonexistence. This seeking will lead him upon other ideas. These ideas have been presented in many forms in your literature in the past many hundreds of years.

In his seeking he will, if things are correctly progressing, discover certain truths that have been available throughout all time. He will also, if he is fortunate, come in contact with some of the material that we make available through channels such as this one to the peoples of your planet.

Chapter 6: Entering the Silence

This condition of questioning, seeking and thinking about things is precisely the condition that we have attempted to generate by our rather nebulous contact. It is always much more satisfactory if the individual finds something out by his own efforts than it is if he is taught a principle. The mental activity required for the individual to seek out and find the basic truths of the creation allows him time to reflect and examine with his own point of view each one of the propositions offered to him. This results in an understanding of the propositions that surpasses any understanding that he could achieve if these propositions were made to him in a relatively short period of time.

January 14, 1974
It is necessary, my friends, to serve if you understand, for this is the only route open to us. I am aware that you have certain questions as to how one is to serve. There are certain problems in performing this service. We are very limited in our ability to contact your people, because we must be careful. We know what the limitations are and why they should be as they are. It is necessary that each individual serve in his own way. If you can understand how to serve, then your service will be effective. It is necessary to avail yourself to meditation to know these things.

Many of the people of your planet attempt to serve, in many, many ways, but they are not effective. They have not availed themselves to the Creator through meditation. Service, my friends, must be performed with care. However, it must always be performed.

We of the Confederation of Planets in His Service do not have the difficulty in serving our fellow man elsewhere in this Creation that we are having at this time. There are so many limitations upon your planet at this present time that service is extremely difficult. However, it is possible for ones such as yourselves to serve the people of the planet in a much more direct way.

It is, however, necessary that you be qualified, if you are to serve. These qualifications include many, many things, each of which may be obtained through meditation. When the individual is fully ready to serve, then it is time to go forth and perform the service. It is not wise, however, to act beyond your limitations.

You will know your ability to serve by availing yourself to this knowledge through meditation. Many of your leaders attempt to serve the people of your planet but they are unaware of the necessity for meditation. If this is not done, then it is very difficult to serve with intelligence. It is necessary for all who are in His service to spend time in meditation. We cannot overemphasize this necessity. It eliminates the possibility of making errors that will result in nullifying the effect of the service.

February 2, 1974
Service, my friends, is an extremely difficult task to perform effectively. It is necessary first to define the objectives of true service in order to understand how one may serve. There are two classifications under which all services may be divided. The first classification includes those services that are of a transient or un-lasting nature. These are the services that you perform in your daily activities for your fellow man, and they are truly services.

But there is a test that may be administered in order to determine whether the service performed is of a transient or not of a lasting nature, or whether it should fall into the second classification, which includes all services of a permanent and non-transient nature. The test is to determine whether or not the service is of such a nature to cause spiritual growth for the one served.

Chapter 6: Entering the Silence

This, my friends, whether it is known to the individual or whether he has forgotten, is in truth his only real objective.

The people of your planet are, for the most part, in a state of ignorance with respect to their real objective, which is the evolution of their spiritual awareness. This, then, is what must be served if the second classification for service is to be met.

Each of those two classifications is desirable, and we would like to perform for the people of your planet acts which would be classified under both classifications. However, since we are aware that the second classification is by far the more important of the types of services that may be performed, it is necessary at this time to postpone performances of services of a direct way, to aid in a physical or more transient nature. We are quite fortunate that we are able to act as we are doing now, to provide the people of this planet with information that they may use in order to augment their seeking in a spiritual sense.

February 3, 1974
We endeavor to use instruments such as this one to help in guiding you so that you may, using the information that we present, find similar truths within your own consciousness, for these truths are the ones that are of great value. We only hope to remind you that you have these within you. We only hope to help guide you to a remembrance of what you seek.

February 9, 1974
It is a great privilege to be of service, for that is our purpose. That is our <u>desire</u>: to serve. This, my friends, is also a principle of the creation, for in serving you we serve ourselves. For it is not possible to serve anything within the creation without serving yourself. The creation, my friends, is one thing. You are simply a part of that one thing. It is impossible to separate yourself from it, because you are it.

Chapter 6: Entering the Silence

The people of your planet are living an illusion. This illusion includes the concept of the possibility of separation; the concept of the individual.

There is difficulty in using your language, for it was evolved with concepts that are erroneous. It is necessary in using it to use terms such as "the individual." However, this term should be simply, "the Creator." As you look at your fellow man, see him for what he is: the Creator. For there is no part of this creation that is any more, or less, than any other part.

February 10, 1974
We of the Confederation of Planets in the Service of the Infinite Creator are here for this express purpose: to serve those who seek. Our service is, unfortunately, very limited, but these limitations are limitations impressed upon us by those who are dwelling upon your planet. We are limited to use of a channel such as this one in order to serve those of the people of this planet who are seeking our service: who are seeking truth.

February 13, 1974
Your people on this planet seek many things. However, they seek these things in what we would consider to be a very strange way. They seek the result of their desires almost exclusively within what they know as the physical illusion that they now enjoy. Since they are unable to experience in their waking state anything but this physical illusion, they then think that this is all that exists, and they attempt to find expression of their desires strictly within this illusion.

This results in the fulfillment of false desires. The people who fulfill these false desires wonder why, having fulfilled them, they do not find happiness. This has been demonstrated upon your planet many times, but little heed has been taken of it. The desires still remain very strong, and the people about you strive with much energy to fulfill them.

Chapter 6: Entering the Silence

Having fulfilled them they then, as I have said, wonder. They wonder why they still have desires, for as soon as they have fulfilled one, they have generated another.

February 18, 1974
The reason for life in the physical sense is to experience service. For this is very effective in creating a deep and complete understanding of the Creator's plan for the creation. In this plan was the concept of service. Through His love, He instilled in each of the parts of this creation the desire to serve.

This desire to serve is within everything that exists. It is within the planet upon which you walk. It is within the vegetation, the atmosphere itself. Everything about you exists to serve. And unless an entity becomes involved too deeply in thoughts generated as an action of his freedom of choice, he will maintain this awareness of his desire to serve, as does the vegetation upon your planet, as does the atmosphere that you breathe, as do we of the Confederation of Planets in the Service of the Infinite Creator.

This, then, this experience, is what is needed for many of the peoples of this planet at this time: an opportunity to act and to demonstrate this desire to serve. Many people who now live upon the surface of this planet act in such a manner so as to serve their fellow man.

Some of these desires for service are unfortunately misdirected. This is not a bad thing for the individual, for all that is necessary is that this desire be realized. However, it is sometimes unfortunate that the service is misunderstood and misdirected, for it is not as effective in this case as it would have been with more intelligent direction.

For this reason we have suggested that everyone who will attempt to serve first avail themselves to a knowledge of how to serve. This they can do through daily meditation, and only in this way can they serve intelligently.

Chapter 6: Entering the Silence

February 18, 1974
We suggest, in order to create an atmosphere desirable for service, that each of you avail yourself of the knowledge of how to go about this, which is within you. Do this through meditation, and then your service will be effective.

There are many ways to serve. However, a knowledge of the real objective of service is of great importance. There are many illusions of service that result in little or no service. Before attempting your service, spend time in meditation. You will realize what is necessary if you are to serve in an effective manner.

There are two possibilities. One is to be in the service of the infinite Creator. One is to be otherwise. The definition of "in the service of the infinite Creator" is very simple. It is applied to those who go forth, in this infinite universe, with a purpose that they understand to be a purpose desired by their Creator. This purpose they have determined through an understanding of the principles which govern this creation.

There are many ways to be in the service of the infinite Creator. We are demonstrating only one of these ways. It is possible for an individual to demonstrate a knowledge of this service at any time.

In order to do this, you must understand what you are doing. In order to understand what you are doing, it is necessary for you to meditate, to avail yourself to the knowledge provided by the Creator of us all.

Upon your planet at this time, there are many, many individuals performing many, many services. Very few of these services, however, are services of a nature that we would consider to be in the service of our infinite Creator. We find that upon this planet, man is primarily concerned with serving himself.

Chapter 6: Entering the Silence

There are many ways to serve, and there are many attempts at service. However, much of the service performed upon this planet, which is an attempt to serve, as we do, our Creator, is not service of this nature.

The reason for this is always the same. It is because of a lack of meditation. We have said to you many, many times that it is necessary to meditate. This is the most important truth that we bring to you, for if one practices meditation, then one has no questions about service.

Each of you here this evening desires to serve, and each of you is serving and will serve to an even greater extent in the near future. However, in order to be of the most efficient service, it is necessary to prepare for that service with daily meditation.

Upon a planet such as yours, which is not at all used to service, there is considerable difficulty in serving your fellow man. And he is in dire need of that service. There is considerable difficulty for us of the Confederation of Planets in serving man on Earth. Man on this planet is extremely confused. For the most part, he has lost sight, almost entirely, of reality. He has built a myriad of illusions, and these illusions are so very strong that he is locked within them and cannot be served.

For this reason, it will be necessary for him to experience the strong catalytic action of his physical environment in order for him to break his self-made illusion. Many of those who are locked within an illusion of their own are, nonetheless, of a nature willing and eager for service in the light of our Creator. These will be the ones who must be contacted. These will be the ones who must be educated. And this will be quite a large problem.

Groups such as this one will have information given to them by us of the Confederation of Planets. This information should be of a form that is available to the many who will seek and understand this information when their illusion is destroyed.

March 10, 1974
You have desired our presence, and we are with you. We are of the Confederation of Planets in the Service of the Infinite Creator. We are always with those of the people of this planet who desire our presence. This is our service to the people of this planet at this time. This is our technique of seeking. It may seem strange that we would seek through service, but this is our understanding of seeking.

It is stated in your holy works that it is necessary to seek in order to find. We have found many ways of seeking. One of these is to serve your fellow man. And this is our form of seeking at this time.

We are seeking understanding: understanding of the Creator. For this is our desire. We are seeking this understanding through service, through serving our fellow man on Earth, and aiding him in his desire to understand the Creator.

And through aiding him and fulfilling his desire, we aid ourselves in fulfilling our desire. For in doing this, not only does man on Earth perhaps learn more of this creation and the Creator, but also we. For it is a law of this creation that only through service may one be served. In serving others, we serve ourselves, as even does man on Earth. For this was the original idea that generated the entire infinite creation: the idea of mutual service, the idea of mutual understanding and the idea of mutual love.

This we are bringing to man on Earth: an understanding of that which is within him; an understanding of that which created him; an understanding of our service and the need for his. It is unfortunate that there are so many that do not understand the true principles of this creation. We are attempting to help them realize this truth. It is within them.

Chapter 6: Entering the Silence

And this is our service: to help them find what they desire to find: the realization of the Thought that generated not only them, but also all that there is. And the thought that provided that all that there is acts in such a way as to serve all that there is.

May 19, 1974
The many attempts which each of you makes to give service to others are more successful than you know. The simple turning of the self from the seeking for sensation in self to the seeking towards service gives the seeker the ability that he seeks.

However, my friends, if you wish to improve and expand your service, we can only suggest to you that you turn within, away from all sensation, and towards meditation. There is no power without you. There is nothing that you can smell or taste or experience in the physical that can cause harm or give aid. The power that you seek is the power of the reality of the love and the light of our infinite Creator, and it lies within. Go within, my friends. Meditate. Seek that which you desire, and it will come to you.

We are aware that those present desire to serve. This is a true and worthy desire, and we find there can be no greater desire. For, as we have often said, a service performed by any entity towards another is also service towards that entity. For as we comprehend, this creation is but one thing; that is, this creation is love, and is the manifestation of the Creator. And within it exists no separation. Therefore, any service rendered unto the creation, in any portion of it, is also service to oneself.

Language

> "Polonius: What do you read, my Lord?
> Hamlet: Words, words, words."

Chapter 6: Entering the Silence

—William Shakespeare

Comment

(This comment was written in 2009.)

After practicing channeling for 35 years and counting, I am highly sensitive to the place of language in offering potentially helpful information to seekers of truth. Language can be used to persuade or to control people. That is never the Confederation entities' intention. Indeed, these entities look for emotionally neutral ways to talk about spiritual matters.

When I enter into the channeling process, I do not receive language for the most part. I receive concepts. My job is to translate these concepts into words; to clothe them with language. And I attempt to do this without infusing these concepts with my emotions or biases.

I believe that there is permanent and inevitable frustration on the part of the Confederation entities at the fact that they must submit their concepts to the narrowing and flattening influence of language so that their concepts may be offered to humankind. Sometimes, faced with infinitely intricate and profound concepts, I join them in their frustration, for I know that I shall never be able to do these concepts the justice they deserve.

But words are all we have, here in third density Earth. And so I am grateful for them, as is the Confederation, I am sure.

Channeling Selection

We will not be able communicate with you unless you are able to avail yourself to our thoughts in meditation. We cannot contact you in the manner you are accustomed to using upon the surface of your planet. This would be of no avail. We do not have concepts in your language that we wish

Chapter 6: Entering the Silence

to convey; we have concepts that are not within your language.

(2009 Editor's Note: The 1975 Editor's Note here suggested that the reader see the channeling of February 10, 1974, which is included in the last chapter of this volume in its entirety. However I did not find that channeling useful. It is possible that the channeling to which the note refers is a second channeling done on the same date, and that this channeling session has been lost to us.)

Chapter 7: The Original Creation

The Original Creation

> "Just open your eyes
> And realize the way it's always been.
> Just open your mind
> And you will find the way it's always been.
> Just open your heart And that's a start."
> —The Moody Blues

Comment

The messages up until now have concentrated on giving us information on how to achieve a contact with cosmic sources of information, by means of meditation. These next chapters on the original creation, the physical illusion, and the intellect, contain information on the fruits of meditation. The messages that follow describe a view of the universe which is quite different from the popular wisdom's concept. Try this view out. It may grow on you.

Channeling Selections

January 14, 1974

In addition to practicing this form of meditation, it is necessary for you to become aware of the original creation, and not creation of man. Pay attention to that which is natural. Become aware of it. People of your planet are not aware of the original creation. They have created a very false illusion. Therefore, they are not in awareness of reality. If you think that you are totally aware of the original creation at this

Chapter 7: The Original Creation

time, then you are mistaken. For, if you were, you would see us, for we are part of the original creation.

There is a technique for increasing your awareness. This technique will be given to you a little at a time, so that you may employ each step. The first step will be to seek to understand each thing that you see that is a portion of the original creation. Take these things one at a time, consider them in detail, and try to establish in your mind a totally detached understanding of them.

If this part of the creation happens to be a leaf, then study it with care. Become aware of it. Do not rely on old impressions. Develop an awareness of each thing. This will be the first step.

January 16, 1974
This instrument receives my thoughts, and relays them to you. These thoughts are not my exclusive property. They are the thoughts of an entire creation of our infinite Creator. It is not necessary for this instrument to be used for you to know these thoughts. They are available to all people in all places at all times. For they are the thoughts of the Creator. And these thoughts were meant for all of mankind, in all places. These thoughts are the thoughts with which the Creator created us.

These thoughts are very simple. They have a simplicity that is unique, for they are the very foundation of the creation. This is what we are attempting to give man on Earth, this original Thought. This is what he needs at this time. This Thought can only be approached using pure language. It is not a common concept among the people of your planet. This is the reason for their difficulties. The Creator never imagined difficulties in His creation. They are the product of man's erroneous thinking.

Chapter 7: The Original Creation

February 1, 1974

It is evident that all creations throughout this infinite creation are the works, in either a direct or indirect sense, of the Creator of us all. It is unfortunate that the people of this planet are unaware of the principles that were provided for the extension of the principle of creation. Our Creator provided each of his children with abilities quite similar to His own. Each of you has within you these abilities. They are not possible to be removed. They are within all of the children of the Creator, and will always remain with them. It was so designed by our Creator.

He wished for all of his children to have and to use the abilities to govern and mold their environments at will. Unfortunately, the people of this planet have forgotten the principle that was within each of them It is only necessary that this principle be remembered for each of the children of our Creator to fully manifest them.

The teacher that was known to you as Jesus was able to use many more of the abilities than the people of this planet. He was no different from any of you. He simply was able to remember certain principles. These principles are not at all complex. They are very simple. And an understanding of these principles is what we of the Confederation of Planets in the Service of our Infinite Creator are attempting to give to the people of this planet who would desire them at this time.

These principles are not necessarily of an intellectual nature. They are of extreme simplicity, and may be realized by anyone at any time. It is only necessary that you avail yourself to our contact through meditation in order to begin to re-realize that which is rightfully yours: the truth of the creation and the truth of your position in it.

Unfortunately, on this planet there is what we might term as interference. This interference occurs because of erroneous thoughts that are manifested in most of the areas of your planet. These erroneous thoughts are of a nature so as to cause a problem in the realization of truth.

These erroneous thoughts must be totally obliterated from the thinking of an individual if he is to be successful in returning to the original thinking with which he was created.

We have attempted many times to suggest to you that this original thinking is one of total love and brotherhood. This is not enough. It is very difficult for the people of this planet to understand these concepts in an intellectual way. They have for a very long period of time been mentally conditioned by erroneous thinking so that they cannot easily become intellectually aware of the principles that are simplicity and truth themselves.

It is therefore suggested that the intellectual mind be circumnavigated, and the principles be directly communicated to the soul or spiritual mind through the mechanism of telepathic impression in a non-intellectual or a conceptual sense. This we have found to be highly effective with respect to any attempt to get from an intellectual thought to a deeper understanding and awareness of the truth of the principles of our infinite Creator. It is for this reason that we have asked that the individuals who wish to understand these truths avail themselves to daily meditation, so that these impressions may be analyzed by them at a deeper level and therefore a true and complete understanding be achieved.

If this process of daily meditation is continued, then each of those who avail themselves of this will find that they begin to become aware of things about then in a new sense, and that they find that they begin to appreciate the true creation in a greater and more beautiful way.

March 10, 1974
It is very difficult for man on this planet to look about him and realize the truth for what it actually is. He has been

Chapter 7: The Original Creation

conditioned, through his thinking and through the thoughts of others, for a very long period of time, to see things as they are given to him, rather than as they really are. The way that they really are, my friends, is extremely simple.

This simplicity is within each of the children of the Creator. Each of them possesses all of the knowledge that was the original creation. It is only necessary that they avail themselves of that knowledge. And this is very simple. It is done through the process of meditation.

When this is done, all the truth and beauty of the original creation becomes apparent. And then it will not be possible for the individual to be fooled by the illusion. He will not see his fellow man in any form but perfection, even though within the illusion he has been taught to disdain. This was not planned by the Creator. The Creator only planned that each of his creations should express itself in any way that he chose. This, my friends, is perfection. If man on Earth could only realize this, he would once more think in total harmony with the original creation. This may be done on an individual basis. It is not necessary that this be understood in an intellectual sense, or by anyone else than the individual endeavoring to reach this understanding.

This has been demonstrated upon your planet before. The man most familiar to you who demonstrated his understanding is known to you as Jesus. He made the simple realization, and then demonstrated it by his activities this understanding. It was not necessary that he be understood by his fellow man, for it is impossible to force, externally, this understanding upon another individual. It is only possible that this understanding be attained from within.

But yet this man demonstrated this understanding, pointed out a pathway, a guidepost for others, so that they too could find the original creation, and once more lead themselves from darkness to light. For light, my friends, is eternal and infinite and real. The rest is illusion. Go within. Become aware of reality. It is within each of you.

The Concept of All-Consciousness

> "Let the sea make a noise, and all that therein is;
> the round world, and they that dwell within.
> Let the floods clap their hands, and let the hills
> be joyful together before the Lord ..."
> —*Bible*, Psalm 98:8-9

Comment

The idea that all things, including so-called inanimate objects, are possessed of consciousness is a very old one. The scientific community, with such experiments as the series of tests of emotional response from plants, is beginning to explore this concept seriously.

Channeling Selections

December 18, 1973
There are many wondrous things that we would freely give you, if you would simply avail yourself to us. Those gifts are freely given. It is not only our pleasure and our privilege to do this but our duty, as it is your duty to pass them on to others, for this is the plan of the creation. The creation is a single entity. Each part of it is designed to aid and help all the other parts. This is the original plan. It is a very simple thing for you to understand if you will relax and look at the original, true creation. Forget that which was created by your fellow man upon the surface of your planet that you now enjoy, and think of the plan and the working of the Father's original creation. It is quite obvious that each part was designed to aid and benefit each other part.

Unfortunately, due to the action [of] the free will that He gave to its parts, there have been some errors, shall I say, made by some of the parts, and they have strayed from the original plan, confusing themselves and confounding the workings of this plan. It is only necessary to realize the truth of this plan to know its workings. It is only necessary that you meditate to have all of these things given to you, or reawakened within you, for all of this knowledge was originally given to all of the parts of this creation. It dwells within every living thing—and every thing in this creation lives.

February 4, 1974
All planets, all of the creation, is consciousness. It is possible to communicate with all parts of the creation, regardless of form.

Healing

> "And who comes here to wish me well?
> A sweetly-scented angel fell.
> She laid her head upon my disbelief and bathed me with her ever-smile."
> —Jethro Tull

Comment

This subject is important enough to have a place in the Table of Contents, and yet in the messages received, the subject of healing is closely interrelated with the subject of love. Therefore, for information on healing, please refer to the message dated February 11, 1974 in the section on Love later in this chapter.

Jesus

> "I can of mine own self do nothing: as I hear, I judge: and my judgment is just; because I seek not mine own will, but the will of the Father which hath sent me."
> —*Bible*. John 5:30.

Chapter 7: The Original Creation

Comment

(This comment was written in 2009.)

The Confederation entities have always used Jesus the Christ as an example of a man who had awakened to the truth of the Creator and who lived according to the ways of love. I believe this is because Jesus is one spiritual leader whose whole message is love, who said, "Thou shalt love the Lord thy God with all thy heart, and with all thy soul, and with all thy mind. This is the first and great commandment. And the second is like unto it, Thou shalt love thy neighbour as thyself."

While Jesus held wisdom, in His way, this is not His most valuable at trait in the eyes of the Confederation. It was His all-embracing love that caused them to mention Him often in their messages to humankind.

Channeling Selections

February 18, 1974

This man known to you as Jesus was born into the physical upon your planet. He was able to realize the truth of the creation, and then he was able to demonstrate this truth to those about him. This man came into the physical on your planet as have many teachers in the past. Each of these teachers came into the physical for the purpose of serving the people of this planet. However, it was up to them to carry out this service. Each of them did it in his own way. This is within the limits of our understanding of the intent of our Creator.

These teachers were limited: limited by the same conditions that each of you and that each of all the people on the planet experience. The people of this planet have misinterpreted the meaning of these men. The people of this planet are at this time misinterpreting the meaning of the man known to you as Jesus. His purpose in his life was to demonstrate that it is possible through an awareness of the Creator's truth to experience what the Creator planned for each of us. This man worked what was called miracles. These were truly miracles to those who thought of them as miracles, but this was given to each of the Creator's children. He was simply demonstrating the result of thinking in the original way as planned by our Creator. He was also demonstrating that it is possible for anyone, at any time, to demonstrate this type of thinking, and therefore, the abilities that accompany it.

Unfortunately, the people have very much misinterpreted this man's life and teachings. He was attempting to provide an example of understanding so that each of the children of the Creator could seek the same understanding. This is the task of any teacher upon this planet or any other place in the creation. This is our task at this time.

February 23, 1974
There was a teacher once known to you as Jesus. This man had desire. His desire was to serve his fellow man by demonstrating a knowledge of the Creator's love. Through this desire he accomplished things that you know as miracles. His thinking and the Creator's were the same. And [through studying Him,] you will know the meaning of love.

I hope that I have been of assistance in giving to you my concept of truth. We of the Confederation of Planets in the Service of the Infinite Creator are expressing our concept of truth, a concept that is the result of our seeking.

When we look at you, we see our Creator. This is our understanding. When we look at this infinite creation, in all of its wonders, all of its vastness and all of its splendor, we are seeing the Creator. This is our understanding. And when we look at the smallest form of life, or even an insect, we are looking at our Creator. This is our understanding. For our understanding is that the Creator is expressing himself throughout all of the infinite manifestations that we experience. And his Thought in all of these manifestations is a Thought of love.

For this was the Thought that created all that there is. Seek this Thought, my friends. Seek this understanding, my friends. And then you will know. You will know love. For this is the Creator.

Love

> "All you need is love." "Love is all you need."
> The Beatles

Comment

(This comment, and indeed this entire section on Love, was written in 2009.)

In my long and error-strewn life, I occasionally make a big error, and leaving the section on love out of this manuscript, back in 1975, ranks with the biggest goofs ever. Love is central to the Confederation philosophy. So it has a place in this Table of Contents. But the section from 1975 has gone permanently missing. The channeling selections below, therefore, are chosen by me in 2009. However, I am using only those channeling sessions generated within the time period of this book's creation – basically, 1974.

Later in our channeling's development here at L/L Research, we received information which clarified love's place in the Confederation philosophy. Free will is the first distortion of the Law of One, said Ra, and love, or the Logos, or the one great original Thought of love, is the second distortion. This love, then, generated light, which manifested all that there is, from the greatest star to the tiniest sub-atomic particle, and everything in between. Love is all there is, and all that there is, is love. Sometimes that love is very distorted. Untangling the distortions, however, one inevitably finds love, love, love.

Channeling Selections

January 10, 1974
We have spent considerable time studying the people of this planet, and we have found that there are a reasonably large number of them that can join us in the peace and the love of our Creator's infinite creation.

For this reason, we are here now. If there were none of your people ready for this, we would have no task. We would be incapable of arousing people that do not wish to join us in this love and light to do so. It is not possible for us to do this, my friends. It is only possible that the individual do this. Each of you must arouse himself to a state of seeking that which we hold out to you as the only worthwhile objective in the creation: that is, the love and the light of the creation itself.

January 12, 1974
This planet, my friends, is a ball in space. It is a ball of light. But it does not appear to you as what it really is. The reason, my friends, that it is a ball of light is that all things in the entire creation are comprised of nothing but light. This is the basic building block of all of the material creation. When we greet you in His love and His light, we greet you in the only existing ingredients of the creation: love, the formative force, and light, the building block.

I am aware that it is difficult for you to conceive of light as matter, but this, my friends, is the actual situation. Light is one of the two things that we always mention at the beginning of a contact. There is a good reason for this. There is a good reason for us to greet you in His love and His light. The reason is that this encompasses everything. And that is what we wish to do: include within this greeting everything

Chapter 7: The Original Creation

and everyone in the creation. For, as we have told you, it is true that all of these parts are one single thing.

Imagine, if you can, an infinitely large sphere of pure light. Impressed upon this is absolute love. Out of this, then, condenses the unimaginably vast number of created parts, each of those parts connected by this original force, the love of our infinite Creator. Each of us, my friends, and everything else, is made up of this single fabric—light. It is only necessary to learn the truth of what I say in its totality to be able to return to that place and stature that was designed for you by the Creator. Light, my friends, is the substance of which you are made. Light is the substance of which I am made. Light is the substance of which everything is made.

Love is the substance which forms light into the forms that you know as living beings, as planets, as trees, as stars, as air. It is all one substance. This substance, my friends, can be affected only by love.

Love, my friends, is not what you think it is. The word in your language has a meaning that has various interpretations. But it is none of these things. We use the word when we speak to you, because it is as close as we can come to the concept, using your language.

Love, my friends, is that force which does all of the things that are done in the entire creation; all of the things, my friends, even those that you would interpret as being without love. If it were not for that love, my friends, then the freedom of choice to do these things could not exist. It is only necessary that the individual realize the truth of what I am saying in order to be able to do those things that he was originally intended to be able to do by the Creator of us all.

The things that he was intended to be able to do are quite surprising. They extend so far beyond your present limitations that I could not possibly convey to you the scope and magnitude of these abilities. However, it is possible, let me assure you, through proper methods of advancing your understanding with respect to its present limitations, to regain what is rightfully yours, the knowledge that you have buried within you, the knowledge of the use of our Creator's light through love.

It is very, very important, my friends, that you seek an understanding of love. Do not be satisfied with your first interpretation of this concept, for it is much, much broader in scope than you might imagine. It covers everything that there is.

January 15, 1974

Analyses based on the false fabric of your material world are short-lived, and the intellectual process that is so prevalent among the peoples of your planet is invariably based upon this falsity. It has been stated, "Know the truth, and the truth shall make you free." Free from what? Free from many things, my friends. Free from many, many things. For cutting yourselves off from truth begins to put more and more limitations upon you. It is a difficult thing to relay to you, because you have been accustomed to another way of thinking. You have been accustomed to the proposition of cause and effect.

The cause, my friends, is the Creator. The effect is love. This is all that there is. This is the simplicity of the truth. Hear my words and understand them. Man was created with this truth within him. It is available to all men throughout all time. It is available through meditation.

January 16, 1974

This instrument receives my thoughts, and relays them to you. These thoughts are not my exclusive property. They are the thoughts of an entire creation of our infinite Creator. It is not necessary for the instrument to be used for you to know these thoughts. They are available to all people in all places at

Chapter 7: The Original Creation

all times, for they are the thoughts of the Creator. And these thoughts were meant for all of mankind, in all places. These thoughts are the thoughts with which the Creator created us.

These thoughts are very simple. They have a simplicity that is unique, for they are the very foundation of the creation. This is what we are attempting to give man on Earth, this original Thought. This is what he needs at this time. This Thought can only be approached using pure language. It is not a common concept among the people of your planet. This is the reason for their difficulties. The Creator never imagined difficulties in His creation. They are the product of man's erroneous thinking. We have said to you many times that meditation is necessary. Through this process of meditation, it is possible to know this Thought; we have called it love, but this can only be understood through meditation.

January 21, 1974

My friends, of what substance is the universe made? We have told you that this substance is light. You may also call this substance energy, vibration [or] consciousness. And yet, my friends, by itself, this substance, this fundamental, unitary substance, would remain in an incorporate state. The shaping force, my friends, is love.

And so we greet you in love and light. For there is nothing but these two substances which are, in fact, two aspects of the single building block of the physical and the spiritual universe. You, my friends, in your spiritual reality are articulated light shaped by love in such a way that you possess freedom and desire. Your light is shaped by the love of freedom and the love of desire.

January 26, 1974

It is only necessary that the individual realize that he is a part of the creation, and that the creation is one single thing, and that in this being so, he and all of his brothers and sisters throughout all space are one being. This realization will result in an ability to demonstrate only one reaction to anything: that reaction will be love.

It is extremely simple. First it is necessary to realize your relationship with everything that exists. It is then impossible to realize anything but love. This is the realization of the Creator. This is the principle upon which everything was created. It is that orientation of mind that is necessary to know all knowledge and to demonstrate all of the things that were intended for you to demonstrate through the expression of the Creator's love.

Do these simple things. Do not sway from this understanding and this love. Do this, and only this, and you will reach a state of ecstasy that is enjoyed by all of those of the Creator's children that are living in His light.

February 9, 1974
Seek, my friends. Seek. This is the word that opens the door to everything that exists throughout all of space and all of time. Seek. Seek.

And what will you find? You will find love, for that is all that there is to find. For that is all that there is.

February 13, 1974
Love is very misunderstood among your people. We express total love for all of your people. We cannot help doing this, for we express total love for all of the creation. It is impossible to do otherwise, when you are aware of the love expressed by the creation. In order to achieve this awareness it is only necessary to meditate, and then to serve, for with each service effectively performed, love will be reflected. This will generate within you more love, and the process will be repeated, or recycled.

This process will be self-generating and will continue to build. This is what occurred with the teacher you are most familiar with, the one known as Jesus. Why was this man much more effective in generating this love than others who have attempted this recently? The reason, my friends, is that he was able to fulfill his desire for service intelligently. He was able to do this in an intelligent manner because he sought answers to the questions of how to fulfill his desire for service through meditation.

Light

> "Now therefore whoso becometh a member of my kingdom shall practice light; but whoso practiceth darkness, will depart away from my kingdom of his own accord."
> —Oahspe

Comment

Michelson and Morley uncovered the paradox. Einstein and Lorentz showed that we were living a dream. The following messages suggest a possible reality behind the paradox and the dream.

Channeling Selections

February 11, 1974
This evening I would like to speak to you on the subject of light. We have spoken recently to you many times on the concept of love, and what this word really means. Tonight, however, I would like to speak to you on the subject of light.

We greet you each evening, as we speak through this instrument, in the love and in the light of our infinite Creator. These are the ingredients that comprise all of the creation. All of the creation, my friends, is composed of love and light.

Chapter 7: The Original Creation

We use these two words because they are the words that are closest in definition in your language to the concepts that we wish to communicate. However, they are, unfortunately, extremely lacking in depth of definition. I will attempt this evening to clarify to some extent the meanings of both of these words.

Love and light! As I have stated recently, love is the force that creates. Light is what it creates. My friends, the Creator is love. You are love. You are a part of the Creator. Therefore, you are love, But your love is expressed through the manifestation of light.

Light is the substance out of which the creation is formed. The Creator's love causes vibrations. This is what is meant when the term "vibration" is used. It is a condition of love. These vibrations are the building energies that compose all of the creation, in its entire infinite and boundless sense.

These vibrations produce a manifestation that you have come to know as the visible creation. The visible creation, and many, many invisible creations [are] invisible to you at this time. However, [they are] not inaccessible.

The vibrations produce the basic particle that you understand as a particle of light. This particle is associated with these vibrations. And therefore it manifests as a function of the rate of these vibrations, and produces the creation, the creation in which you and all of your fellow beings experience that which you desire.

March 8, 1974
I send to you my love and my light. And extend to you our warmest welcome. Join us, my friends. Join us in light. it is all about you. There is much light in this creation. We are here to lead you into this light. We know that it is what you desire, for this you have expressed.

Chapter 7: The Original Creation

The Creator's Law

> "Love is the Law, love under will."
> —Aleister Crowley

Comment

(This comment was written in 2009.)

Looking back at this, the harvest of my first year or so of learning to channel, I can see very clearly that the Confederation's message did not change at all when our research group contacted those of Ra in 1981, six years after these messages were sorted and compiled into this volume of our first fruits. The Law the entities were attempting to articulate was the Law of One. It simply states that all things are one.

The cosmology that this short sentence generates is eloquent in its internal consistency. This unitary creation was developed because the infinite Creator chose to know Itself, by activating the first distortion of the Law of One, free will. It generated a creation according to Its nature, which is unconditional love. Love, then, is the second distortion of the Law of One. This creation was manifested as light, light being the third distortion of the Law of One. And the manifestation that became the third-density planet that we know and love was and is full of polarity. To advance spiritually, then, is to polarize either in service to others or in service to self.

That's the Law of which the Confederation entities here speak in relatively fragmented form, in these early channelings.

Channeling Selections

December 18, 1973
Your people at present are totally unaware of [the Creator's] plan. Your scientists ignore it. They are extremely interested

Chapter 7: The Original Creation

in plans of their own. Unfortunately, their plans do not follow the plan of the Creator. Therefore, they waste much of their time and energy, and build devices that have no real valuable purpose. They are transient, I can assure you.

Your scientists should realize that there is a purpose to the creation that far surpasses what they suspect. They should avail themselves to the purpose in meditation. Then they would find that they would begin to understand the plan, and thereby they would be able to use their knowledge to build within the plan, not as they do now with no heed at all to the truth, and with plans of their own which have no relationship to truth.

Your governments make the same error. They do not work within the plan. They are not aware of the plan. They attempt to make law, but their laws do not work. They appear to have some value, but very shortly much strife is generated, and the result is war. They do not understand that the reason for this strife is that they have ignored the natural plan of creation, the natural order of things, and the law of the Creator that devised this. Your leaders should avail [themselves] in meditation to truth, as we do.

February 18, 1974
It is the gift of the Creator that each of his children should live as they desire. Unfortunately, there are certain natural laws. I say unfortunately—this is not correct, but it is unfortunate for these who choose to ignore them. These natural laws are as simple as the laws that your physical science experiences. The creation was generated by the pure love of the Creator. In generating this creation, He conceived of a creation in which all of the parts would serve all of the other parts. In order to create this creation, it was necessary to build it upon certain principles of love. These principles permeate all creation, and if properly understood, as is the

Chapter 7: The Original Creation

right of all of the Creator's children, it is possible to live in total harmony.

If these laws have been forgotten, as is the case with many of those who dwell upon the planet you now enjoy, then the consequences are somewhat unusual. These consequences are now being experienced by many of the peoples of this planet. These consequences, which they do not desire, are a result of their desire. A result of a desire that is not based upon understanding of the truth of the creation. There are, unfortunately, conflicting actions that result in creations and experiences that were never intended by the Creator. However, certain principles govern, and cannot be misinterpreted or misused.

This is our understanding of the manifestation, and reality of the creation.

Truth

> And ye shall know the truth, and the truth shall make you free.
> John 8:32

Comment

(This comment was written in 2009.)

The question of what is true is the meat of philosophical enquiry. As far as the Confederation is concerned, there is earthly truth, which is limited and relative, and then there is spiritual truth, which is infinite, mysterious and full of paradox and mystery, yet is as simple as: all is one, and that one thing is love.

Channeling Selections

December 18, 1973
We of the Confederation of Planets in the Service of the Infinite Father are with you, my friends, and you are with us,

Chapter 7: The Original Creation

in a single effort. Our effort, as I have said before, is to awaken the people of this planet to truth. This has been tried many, many times. They are sleeping very, very soundly. Yes, my friends, they are asleep, dreaming a dream that is fantastic. It is beyond the belief of those who know truth that such a dream could be a dream, but this is the case.

Many of your people have dormant within them the memory of truth. Many others have a less accurate memory. And a few have no memory at all. The truth, however, is within them, for it is within all men, in all places. For those of the first category, it is relatively easy to awaken them from their slumber. The second category is much, much more difficult, and the third, for the present, will be impossible for you to awaken.

Do not concern yourself if an individual rejects an attempt you might make to awaken him. This simply means he is not yet ready for this truth to be given unto him. Concern yourselves with those who would seek the truth, and make it available to them in any way that you can.

There are many people upon your planet at this time who are attempting to cloud the memory of this truth. They are not aware of what they are doing. This is not their fault, but it is unfortunately the condition. It is not a simple task that we have outlined, and I am afraid it will require a great deal of effort. We have not been as successful as we had hoped to be when we initiated this project some years ago. The people of your planet do not actually wish to be awakened for the most part. Those who are sleeping very, very lightly are all too few. However, you will know them as you find them, and you will recognize their lightness of slumber by their activities, for they will not be as enmeshed in the insanity, if we can call it that, that is so prevalent on your world today.

Chapter 7: The Original Creation

February 3, 1974
We of the Confederation of Planets in the Service of the Infinite Creator are always available to you for information and guidance. It is of great privilege to be of service in attempting to give you our viewpoints. We hope that these viewpoints will be of benefit in your understanding of the truth that is in you.

It is possible for you, like us, to find these answers directly, for they are within you as they are within everyone. However, we realize that conditions on your planet sometimes make it difficult to accomplish this understanding of truth that is abundant for all of us readily.

For this reason we endeavor to use instruments such as this one to help in guiding you so that you may, using the information that we present, find similar truths within your own consciousness, for these truths are the ones that are of great value. We only hope to remind you that you have these within you. We only hope to help guide you to a remembrance of what you seek.

February 9, 1974
Daily meditation, constant self-analysis, and love are the keys which open the doors to truth.

March 10, 1974
I and my brothers are here only to serve you, my friends. And it is a very great pleasure to be here. We offer conditioning to those of you who desire this. We serve you, and we seek. Serving is serving. The two words seem different: to seek and to serve. One suggests that you need something, and one suggests that you have something, for those who seek must need, and those who serve must have, to give away.

And so I would like to speak, my friends, about these two words. You are seeking and you are seeking to serve. It is a paradox, is it not, my friends? It is a paradox, as are all

Chapter 7: The Original Creation

intellectual things. And yet it is the simple truth, that they are one thing.

In this illusion of Earth, my friends, those of your planet are as though they were supplicants; poor, needful and ever lacking those things which they need to progress. And so they go on a pilgrimage, some to gain physical security, and some to seek the spiritual in life.

But there is the concept of seeking which will garner a type of treasure that can be held, and can be shown, and can be counted. Perhaps we could call this, my friends, dealing from a position of weakness. In this illusion, my friends, it would seem possible to be weak, to be limited, and to be in need. Yet this illusion is banished by reality. And this reality is what we seek. And when we seek reality, we turn either very far inward or very far outward—another paradox, my friends—into the light. And we find that we are not dealing from a position of poverty, but that we have all that we have been seeking.

But we are indeed dealing from a position of complete strength, because we are infinite. You, my friends, are infinite. You do not need help. You only need realization. All I can tell you, all you can learn, all that is possible in this infinite creation, is abiding eternally within you. For you are one with all that there is.

In the illusion, my friends, I am aware that I would be doing you a disservice if I did not realize that you have much with which to contend. For the illusion is very strong. But so much of the illusion suggests to you that the illusion itself lacks spirituality because various things are various and sundry ways, and they do not suit you. And it would seem perhaps that spirituality might consist in more manageable and more uniform things in your environment.

The illusion is as evanescent as a bubble. *Pop*, and it will be gone. It is as fleeting as a dream. Soon, you will awaken. It will change, as does day to night, and night to day. You need not do more than appreciate the infinity of the creation, even in the tiny part which is the illusion. And then, my friends, relax, and let the illusion float by you. Rest in the confidence of your seeking and of your seeking to serve. For you have much to give, my friends.

Unity

> "As a scientist, Frank, the best that I can ever do is to understand the will of God. But when I shimmy up a wild and lascivious hootchy-kootchy in my wig and sweatshirt, ah, then I *am* God."
> —Albert Einstein, to Franklin Roosevelt.

Comment

(This comment was written in 2009.)

The unity of all that there is, together with the concomitant declaration that this one thing is love, is at the foundation of the Confederation's teachings. In the Ra sessions, it was declared as the Law of One.

Channeling Selections

January 4, 1974
I am a member of the Confederation of Planets in the Service of Our Infinite Creator. I am here, as are my brothers, to serve your people. This has been told you this evening. But there are some other things that should be told unto you at this time. We of the Confederation of Planets in the Service of our infinite Creator are here for another purpose. This purpose is to serve ourselves. For, my friends, in serving you, we serve ourselves. This is the way that the creation is built. It is made so that if you serve anyone or anything in this creation you are serving yourself. This is a truth that cannot be varied. The creation, my friends, is one thing, and it is impossible in this creation to act without affecting yourself.

Chapter 7: The Original Creation

This is not realized by most of the people of your planet, and for this reason they have affected themselves in a miserable way. We are very sorry for this, because in doing this they have not only affected themselves, they have affected us. They have made us very sad.

January 6, 1974
All of us are one. If we are one, then we share all of the knowledge that there is. Avail yourself of this knowledge. It is yours to begin with. Do this through meditation. You all understand all there is to understand. It is a simple process.

January 27, 1974
I and my brothers in space, as you call it, are here with you. Yes, we are in space, and we are also here. This is a concept that is not too familiar with your peoples, that it is possible to be in more than one place at one time. However, we have told you that there is only one place. There is an ambiguity of concept when viewed from your limited state of awareness which you presently enjoy. However, it is possible to be, from your point of view, in two places, or many places, at one time. To us, they are all the same place.

This concept is not entirely new to the people of your planet, although it is not understood except by a very few of them. It is necessary that an individual reach an understanding of the reality of the unity of the creation in order to understand the reality of this concept.

There are many ways to state this idea in an intellectual way, but it is more revealing to experience it. This experience is available to all of the Creator's children. It was how they were originally created. Only through your own desires have you cut yourself off from the ability to experience the reality that is all about you. It is not necessary to be limited as you are. It was not intended that you be so limited. It is only your desire that you be so, It is a simple process to free yourself from the thinking that limits the people of this planet to their present locations. These locations are simply a consequence of their thinking, since in actuality, all places are one place.

This does not seem possible to most of the people of your planet. However, this condition is the true condition.

February 3, 1974
We of the Confederation of Planets in the Service of the Infinite Creator extend our hand to the people of this planet. It is not necessary that we appreciate ourselves in our attempts to serve. It is only necessary that we serve. This will be appreciated by the Creator, for, my friends, the Creator is all that there is. It is as impossible to separate the Creator from the creation as it is impossible to separate yourself from the creation.

Appreciate, then, this unity. Appreciate your oneness with the Creator and the creation. If this is done, then other objectives will be of very little value. For this is what the Creator meant for all of the parts of the creation to do: to act in such a way as to serve. He did not specify this service, and He did not demand it. He simply provided the opportunity.

February 4, 1974
I am love, and I am Hatonn, and I am light, and I am Hatonn. You are love and you are light. You and I are the same. You experience one thing. I experience one thing. But yet we are the same. For this is the creation. We are one. That is why I say that you and I are one and that you are with me.

February 4, 1974
Speaking with respect to the planet which you now enjoy, the higher degree of awareness is experienced by the people or individuals upon the planet. In this respect, they enjoy a dominion over the other forms of life. However, all the forms of life are one form: the Creator. They all express His love.

Chapter 7: The Original Creation

The concept of dominion, in the sense that there should be a separation by rank or privilege, was never a portion of the original Thought of our Creator. There are many experiences allowed the children of the Creator. There are many experiments which they may perform. However, there is only one truth, and it is the truth of unity and love.

February 4, 1974
To separate, classify and measure is not of the Creator's design. To unify, embrace, and love is all that is necessary.

February 18, 1974
There is no possibility of working against us. We are in the service of the Creation. We are attempting to serve those who desire our service. We extend our service to all of the Creation. We extend our love to all of the Creation. This is in no way limited. There is no possibility existing for a portion of this creation to work, as you say, against us, for it is part of us.

February 24, 1974
My friends, the Father is infinite and in everything you do and in everything you see and in everything you touch. There is nothing but the Father. For He is and you are. He and you are one and I and you are one and we are all one, beloved ones. There is nothing else but the Father and I.

When you go through your daily lives, know this truth. And demonstrate it in everything that you do. For this, my friends, is that which is truth. This is the truth that you seek. This is the truth that we all seek. For when we know this, my friends, there is nothing else to know.

Throughout your planet, my friends, there are many, many peoples of many, many races and each of them thinks many, many things. But you must see them and you must knew them as one. For each of them is a part of the Father as [each

Chapter 7: The Original Creation

is] a part of you. And all that is necessary for you to realize this is to open your eyes and see. For man on Earth has these eyes, but what he sees is, for the most part, something that he designed for himself to see.

The Father, my friends, made the creation. We are that creation. We are the Father. We are all one. It is impossible to be anything else. No matter where you are, what you think or what you do, this fact remains, that you and all of your brothers and sisters throughout all of this infinite creation are one, single, great, living being; not only [your] brothers and your sisters, but all of life, all of the trees and flowers and rocks. All of the foliage and all of the planets and stars are part of that one great being.

And yet, man on Earth attempts to separate and divide and subdivide. And this is not truth. And yet, he does not realize, for he is yet in a state of ignorance brought on by his own misdirected thinking. Truth is simplicity itself, and yet he has complicated this truth to such an extent that he has killed his fellow creatures in great profusion. And he has generated much hatred for his fellow creatures. And in doing so [he] has generated this hatred for himself. For to hate your fellow man, my friends, is to hate yourself.

And in doing so, he has brought upon himself terrible, terrible grief. For what could be worse than inflicting pain and destruction upon one's self? And this is what he does. There are millions and millions and millions of planets throughout the creation. And these are inhabited by millions and millions of people, people like yourself. And yet, they do not hate. They do not fear. They do not envy. They do not show greed. They do not judge. For how is it possible to do any of these things if there is only one being? For in doing any of these things there is nothing but a self-inflicted wound.

I and my Father are one. These are true, these spoken words. I and my Father are one. And each of you, as all people throughout all of the creation, [are] one. One! Know this and this alone and you will know enough. But know it, my friends. Do not think it. Do not speak it. Do not accept it. Know it. For when you know it, you will then know love.

February 25, 1974
Concentrate, my friends, on that which is all. Let your thoughts come. For all is one. Become aware of the one great all. Become aware that you are one and that one is all. Do not separate yourselves from anything. My friends, you are not separate from anything. There is only one thing. This one thing is truth. Truth is. It is all about you. It speaks to you. Listen to it and you will know it. Truth is in your sky. It is in your trees, in your fields, and in everything that is the Creator's. Do not be concerned with anything but this truth.

March 3, 1974
At this time I wish to speak to you upon our understanding of truth. We could give to you many things. We could tell you of many mysteries that would interest you. However, we consider that it is necessary first to provide for the peoples of this planet a simple truth that is in reality all that anyone in this creation needs to know. After this truth is understood, the rest of the mysteries vanish, for this truth is the key to a total understanding of creation. This truth is the pathway to all truth. I shall at this time speak upon this truth.

I and my brothers, who are with me in the name of the infinite Creator, understand a simple truth, that is the [most] important concept in this creation. This simple truth is that the creation is one thing. Everything that you can imagine, everything that you can see, everything that you cannot see, all that there is, is one thing.

This is not realized by most of the people of this planet at this time. Due to this, they are experiencing conditions that they do not desire. It will be necessary, if an individual is to find

Chapter 7: The Original Creation

the pathway that he desires, for him to realize the truth of this simple statement: there is no separation. Separation is an illusion. All things are one thing: the creation. To affect one part of the creation is to affect the creation.

We are here to aid the people of the planet Earth, but we are [also] here to aid ourselves. It is impossible to give service to others without serving yourself. For you and those whom you serve are the same: you are one.

March 8, 1974
I am Oxal. My friends, this is of no consequence, for I am the Creator. Yes, my friends, you are listening to the voice of the Creator. You hear the voice of the Creator each day, my friends, as you go about your daily activities. It is only necessary to recognize it.

As you meet your fellow man in your daily activities, as he speaks, then you hear the voice of your Creator. Birds singing in the trees, my friends, speak with the voice of the Creator. The very winds that blow through these trees speak to you, my friends. And this noise that you hear is the voice of the Creator. For His expressions are infinite. It is only necessary that you hear and see these expressions. And then when you hear and see them, it is then necessary that you understand them [and] understand that these are the Creator.

This is what is missing upon your planet, my friends: the simple understanding that all of these things are the same thing. They are the Creator. This knowledge is self-evident. It does not require a complex analysis. It does not require that I prove to you that what I am saying is true. Truth, my friends, speaks to you. It is all about you. It is the Creator.

It is only necessary for you to recognize this, totally, with no reservation, and then you will think as the Creator thinks. For the Creator recognizes Himself, and there is no part of

Himself that He does not accept. For it is He, and He is one thing: the creation.

It is impossible to separate yourself from the creation. It is impossible to isolate yourself from the creation. You are it, and it is you. And all of its parts speak to you, saying, "Be of the creation." It is only necessary that man on Earth listen to this voice, and then understand its words. Understand and then demonstrate this understanding. And then man on Earth will take his rightful place with those of us who roam through this infinite creation.

For this is our privilege. And this is your privilege. For we are all the same thing. We are love, and we are light.

March 10, 1974
All of the children of the Creator throughout all of the universe, all of this infinite creation, my friends, are truly seeking only one thing, whether they realize this or not. They are seeking understanding. For this is all that is necessary. For once this understanding is accomplished, then all things are possible, for this is the way that the Creator designed it. This is the way that He provided. It is only necessary that you realize this. It is only necessary that you demonstrate, in each thought, this realization. And then, my friends, you and the Creator are one; and you and the Creator have equal power. For this is truth. Each of us is the Creator.

April 25, 1974
This understanding, my friends, of which we are attempting to aid you in becoming aware is very, very simple. It is, in fact, unitary. There is only one. This unity within which the entire Creation resides is whole, complete, unbreakable and transcendent of all illusion.

Therefore, my friends, it is the most impossible thing to conceive of within the boundaries of your intellect and your consciousness with the physical. This consciousness of unity, which is your understanding described in one way, is available to you only through meditation. It is quite, quite amazing to us that those upon your surface have devised so many different ways of removing from themselves all indications of the reality or even the possibility of understanding. However, you are, although in the physical environment, not of it.

Your choice is completely free. You may seek for this understanding even within the dense illusion which occupies your physical senses. We offer you only simple help. We offer you only simple understanding. For there is only one understanding, only one truth, only one entity: the Creator, my friends. Any attempt to work through any other understanding will be an attempt which is working within an extremely transient illusion.

Confidence

> "I, Aph, son of Neph, bewilder all in my presence by the power and magnificence of my work! Who can come so near the power of the Almighty? Who hath attained beyond the power of my soul? Who hath wisdom like unto me, save the great Creator? I have stretched a line beyond the moon, and by my spoken word hath moved the world …"
> —Oahspe

Comment

There are always times when a person will feel somewhat low on self-confidence. The following was an answer to a request from a group member for some words to help build up one's confidence.

Channeling Selections

February 3, 1974
There is no necessity to establish within one's thinking an appreciation of self. For this presupposes that it is possible to

separate self from the entire creation. If one appreciates any part of the creation, then one appreciates self, for they are one and the same thing. The elimination of the concept of self is an important one in your spiritual seeking. It is necessary only to appreciate the Creator and His product, the creation. In appreciating any part of the Creation, one must appreciate all parts, for they are inseparable.

It is therefore important to act in unison with the creation rather than out of harmony due to a lack of confidence in a state of oneness. It is possible to achieve this understanding of oneness with all by availing yourself of this knowledge and understanding through the process of daily meditation.

April 17, 1974
We are aware that there are disappointments you feel. We can only tell you that there is no need ever to feel disappointment in yourselves. You must have heard us say many times that there is no time but the present. Regret has to do only with the past.

We are not saying that it is not your business to live as correctly as you know how, but the time to live correctly is the present moment. A mistake made or a missed step or a simple misunderstanding later corrected is simply a corrected error. What matters is not that you have made the error, but that you have become aware of it and corrected it. The present, with the awareness that you have known, is all that you need to consider. Waste no more time on what is gone forever than you need to learn from it. Then carry on with the life that you are living now, for, my friends, there is a great deal of each present moment that most of those upon your planet miss completely.

The ability to live with complete awareness of the creation of the Father about you and of the possibilities of that Creation within you, is most rare and most valuable.

Chapter 7: The Original Creation

Space Travel

> "When his voice called the legions in high heaven, from every side, and below and above the earth, there moved myriads of shapely stars, which were beacons of fire, coursing the firmament, wherein came the Gods and Goddesses called by Jehovih for the labor of Earth!"
> —Oahspe

Comment

If the UFOnauts can come here, why can't Earthmen fly to other star systems, or even to other planets of our own system, with equal ease?

Channeling Selections

January 25, 1974

There are vast distances between stars in all systems, and therefore distance between planetary systems. There are vast distances between individual planets of a system. These distances are made to be navigated by peoples of the creation who have gained the ability to navigate them. If people have reached this state of evolution, then they are able to transverse the distances between planets, between planetary systems, and even between galaxies. However, if people have not evolved to this ability, then they are limited to their own planet. If people are limited to their own planet, then there is no contact made by those who can travel from planet to planet, or from system to system. We do not in any instance enter a house uninvited.

This may seem a strange way of thinking to those of your planet, but it is the plan of the Creator. It was planned that only those of sufficient spiritual evolution should travel from system to system or from planet to planet. However, vast numbers of people in this creation are so evolved, and have this ability.

Chapter 7: The Original Creation

Some of the people of planet Earth have this ability, and do it in a spiritual form, leaving their physical bodies behind. Each of you has this ability. All that is necessary is that you realize it by demonstrating in your daily life a complete understanding of the principles that we give to you, the principles of love and total brotherhood for all who exist throughout the creation.

It is unfortunate that it is necessary to limit a [group of] people to a planet, but it is the wisdom of the Creator that has done this. Fortunately, the people of a planet so limited are not aware of their limitations, and therefore do not reach a state of mental frustration due to the knowledge of their limitations. If they were to understand their limitations fully, then they would reach a state that would not be pleasing to the plan of the Creator. He does not wish anything bad for any of His children. When His children reach a state of understanding, and may then move from one planet or system to another of their own abilities, He welcomes them with open arms.

January 27, 1974
The dimensions of the creation that you experience in your present form and understanding seem to be of such a magnitude that it would be impossible for you to travel through any great distance. We do not have these limitations. The reason for our lack of these limitations is simply our understanding of the truth of the concept of total oneness. This oneness is the original Thought that was provided all of the children of the Creator. Return to this Thought. Have no other thought but this thought, a thought of total and complete love. This will enable you to know all of the fruits of our infinite Creator.

Chapter 8: The World in Which We Live

The Physical Illusion

> "All in the golden afternoon
> Full leisurely we glide:
> For both our oars, with little skill,
> By little arms are plied,
> While little hands make vain pretence
> Our wanderings to guide."
> Lewis Carroll, *Alice in Wonderland*

Comment

This chapter is a kind of catalog of topics of aspects regarding the physical illusion. It lists many misconceptions and misunderstandings which surround us. The chapter also can be considered as a further explanation of the spiritual impulse which is the seed, in the Master Jesus' parable of the sower.

Channeling Selections

January 23, 1974
We of the Confederation of Planets in the Service of the Infinite Creator have used this method of contact in many, many places, with many, many people. Upon your planet at present, there are people in almost all areas that are receiving our communications. There are many of these people who do not understand what is happening to them. They do not understand who we are, as do you. They simply receive communications. The reason they have no idea who we are is that they have no concept of people coming to them from the stars.

Chapter 8: The World in Which We Live

This is unimportant. The only thing that is important is that they understand the message that we give to them: the message of love and brotherhood. There are many other people who receive our messages who do understand our identification. In this case, it is also only important that they understand the message that we bring to them. This is what we are here for: to bring this simple, single message. This is what is necessary for the people of your planet to learn at this time.

We of the Confederation have lived an example of this knowledge for many, many of your years. We are totally aware of the results of living the type of life that results from the understanding of the principle of love. We are not unwise in our attempt to give these principles to you; for we have experienced the effect of using these for quite some time.

I am aware that these principles are not understood by the people of your planet, not even the people who have been given them directly through channels such as this one. There seems to be a barrier to this understanding that has been generated through thousands of years of an ignorance of the truth. This barrier is so solid at this time that it is very difficult, even for those who desire this knowledge, to accept it and put it to use. They are able to hear the words and understand them, and even though they agree totally with the concepts that we present, they are still unable to assimilate them into their own thinking.

We have suggested many times that in order to assimilate this knowledge into your thinking it is necessary that you meditate. But this is something that is also misunderstood.

It is extremely difficult for the people of this planet to remove their thinking from the hypnotic state that has been created. Everything that they experience is created by their own thinking. You cannot experience something that you cannot think, because this is all that there is; there is nothing but

Chapter 8: The World in Which We Live

thought. It is found in many forms and expressions, but thought is the source of all that there is—the Thought of the Creator.

And this is what you are. And you are able, like the Creator, to generate thought. The thought that you generate is your responsibility. The people of this planet each generate thoughts, and communicate these thoughts to others. If the thoughts that are generated are of a low quality, then they will in turn generate low-quality thoughts in others. This is a self-perpetuating action. And this is the reason for the strife and confusion that is so abundant with the people of this planet.

It is erroneous to say that you cannot do anything about a situation as complex as this one which has been created by millions and millions of minds through thousands and thousands of years. It is only necessary that the individual remove himself in thought from this sea of confusion and express himself in the true love and light of the infinite Creator. This may be done at any time. It is up to the individual. If he desires to do this, then it is only necessary that he do it

This has been demonstrated to the people of this planet many times in the past by the teachers who were here to demonstrate to the people of Earth life and the expressions of the Creator as they were intended. It is a very simple lesson, but man on Earth desires to ignore this. Very few accept these teachings, and stand in the light and express only the love and understanding of the Creator of us all.

This is unfortunate. It is a situation that we who are in the service of our infinite Creator are attempting to remedy, by giving instructions which are not only verbal, and which have difficulty in penetrating the barrier which the mind has erected, but instructions of a nature that will bypass this intellectual barrier and reach the spiritual self directly. This is done, of course, during the process of meditation. This is why

Chapter 8: The World in Which We Live

we have stated for so many years that meditation is extremely important. It is only necessary that the individual avail himself of these concepts for these concepts to begin to cause the individual to realize once more his proper stature and position in the Creator's scheme of things,

It was stated by your last great teacher, "Know ye not that ye are gods?" This man understood the true, created purpose of all of mankind. Why is it necessary for people, especially people who have been made aware of truth through their seeking, to stop short of achieving the knowledge of their true, created purpose and being?

We have been puzzled at times by the inability of the people of this planet in general to be awakened to this simple truth. We suggest that it is necessary to maintain a continual awareness of your objective. We suggest that that objective is to realize your true position in the creation, and then to act in a manner intended by the Creator.

In order to do this, it will be necessary that a considerable effort be put forth. We find that the state of hypnosis brought about by the evolution of thought of the people of this planet is so great that if an individual is to free himself from it, it is necessary for him to maintain a constant awareness of his spiritual nature and purpose, and to augment this awareness with meditation. The effort put forth to do this will be much more rewarding than any other activity in which the individual can engage.

This step must successfully be made by each individual of this planet at some time or other. Wouldn't it be reasonable to do it at the earliest possible time? For it is an extremely beneficial step. We would suggest that if progress is seemingly slow, then additional meditation may be necessary, for only in this way can the people of planet Earth free themselves from the erroneous thoughts that have been impressed upon them for so very long.

Chapter 8: The World in Which We Live

February 9, 1974
Each part is a portion of the creation. Each holds equal rank. I am aware that there are many upon your planet who would not understand this concept. They feel pain, if it is within their individual being, but they do not feel the pain of others.

This is not so with the Confederation of Planets in the Service of the Infinite Creator. We feel your pain, and this brings us to you at this time, to serve you. For in doing so, we serve ourselves, since you and we are one. Your pain is felt throughout all of the creation, and for this reason there are many, many here to serve you at this time. We serve you in the very best way that we can, to eliminate this pain. We give to you the information that you need in order to eliminate this pain. It is something that may be done in the twinkling of an eye. It is the way that the Creator planned. We did not, however, anticipate that His children would create from their own desires the pain that we now feel emanating from your planet.

This is a result of the desire of the people of this planet. Unfortunately, these desires affect not only the ones generating the desire, but also others who live on the surface. It is what you call a contagion. It requires an extreme degree of understanding to live upon your surface and not experience this contagion.

It can be done, my friends. It is only necessary that you know and demonstrate the Creator's truth in every thought and deed. And then you will be freed from the effect of the desires of your brothers who live about you on the surface of your planet.

February 13, 1974
Your people on this planet seek many things. However, they seek these things in what we would consider to be a very strange way. They seek the result of their desires almost

exclusively within what they know as the physical illusion that they now enjoy. Since they are unable to experience in their waking state anything but this physical illusion, they then think that this is all that exists, and they attempt to find expression of their desires strictly within this illusion. This results in the fulfillment of false desires.

The people who fulfill these false desires wonder why, having fulfilled them, they do not find happiness. This has been demonstrated upon your planet many times, but little heed has been taken of it. The desires still remain very strong, and the people about you strive with much energy to fulfill them. Having fulfilled them they then, as I have said, wonder. They wonder why they still have desires, for as soon as they have fulfilled one, they have generated another.

February 18, 1974
At this time, very few of the people upon this planet are seeking anything outside of the physical illusion that so constantly busies their minds with trivialities. We of the Confederation of Planets are aware of the trivial nature of the things that involve most of the people of your planet. These things seem of great importance to them. However, the importance of their activities is a function of their inability to still their active minds, and to return to the awareness of reality that is possible through meditation.

The activities that seem so important to the people of this planet at this time are so very transient as to be in reality negligible, as are all activities within the physical, except for that activity of service to one's fellow man. For through service, one builds one's awareness of truth. This is the reason for life, as you know it, in the physical.

February 21, 1974
Desire is a thing that dwells within each of the Creator's children. The desire of each of them, however, is different.

Chapter 8: The World in Which We Live

What this desire is, is dependent upon the vibratory level of the individual. The lower the vibration, the more basic the desire. The higher the vibration, the higher the desire. You will find, as you increase your vibration through meditation and seeking and service, that your desire will change. The things that are desired by those that are tightly locked within the physical illusion are not those desired by those on the verge of freedom.

March 10, 1974

Truth is all about you, very obvious to those who have stilled themselves for the very short time that is required to become aware of it. It is very obvious to those of us who view the creation of the Father in its original form. All of its parts act to support all of its other parts. All that sustains each of us is a gift of our Creator. All of the joys and experiences that come to us are gifts of our Creator.

It is only those upon this planet who have become lost in a complex creation of their own, with many thoughts of a complex but trivial nature that keep them very busy, in an effort to reach that which is of no value. [It is] a minor creation which will last only the shortest period of time and which has no value, once it is attained, for they will lose it, and once again return to the creation.

March 11, 1974

Man on Earth has very little understanding of his life. The life of an individual is not what he thinks that it is. Very few of those who dwell upon your planet have any understanding of life. Man upon Planet Earth is concerned with a life that is limited by his waking hours, during a present physical lifetime. His plans, his desires, and his activities are governed by his awareness of this extremely limited portion of experience, which he considers his physical life.

Chapter 8: The World in Which We Live

For this reason, the plans and the objectives of those who dwell upon Earth are extremely limited, and for the most part of no value whatsoever. In order to make plans intelligently, it is necessary that one have information about future objectives. Man on Earth, for the most part, has none of this information, for he has not sought it. He is simply existing in a very limited state of awareness, and reacting to what he is able to determine about this limited awareness. These reactions result in his activities, which are from our point of view ridiculous.

We of the Confederation of Planets in the Service of the Infinite Creator are aware of a much longer span of life than is man on Earth. The span of life of which we are aware is of infinite length. For this reason, our plans, our objectives and our activities are much different from those who dwell upon this planet.

Man upon Earth is not trying to understand how to live. He is not trying to understand how to live because he is not trying to understand life. Life is extremely simple, and an understanding of life requires an extremely simple approach. Presently, man in your society upon Earth is attempting to approach what he considers to be life in an extremely complex manner. In doing this, he is making numerous plans and numerous deductions, based upon observations that are so limited that they are almost totally false.

Some of the people of your planet have some awareness of the principles that affect an individual in his true infinite state, and they are aware of the necessity to make plans for objectives that are totally outside of the very limited state that you call the physical life.

We are here to attempt to help those who are seeking a greater awareness to find it. We are attempting to bring a simple teaching that will allow you to become able to make your own

Chapter 8: The World in Which We Live

decisions as a result of a much greater awareness of truth than is presently available upon your planet.

March 11, 1974
We of the Confederation are aware, more since we have spent much time with your planet, that those of your planet find it very difficult to understand simplicity. It is more to the nature of this illusion here manifesting on the surface of your planet to have a complicated and carefully controlled series of tests to perform in order to reach a goal.

But, my friends, truth is in the opposite direction of this. As we have said earlier tonight, meditation brings to you this realization in a non-intellectual manner. But to arise from your meditation, my friends, and to demonstrate the truth that you have learned is indeed a challenge to your spirits.

For how does one demonstrate the absolutely simple? Picture if you will, my friends, a prison, deep in the ground. There is old metal, and many rusty keys and, inside the old metal cells in this dungeon deep underground, there are many, many ghosts that can barely be seen. And yet they are trapped. My friends, you are holding yourselves prisoner. Meditation allies you with the truth of daylight, with the truth of freedom, with the truth of infinity.

Unlock your own spirits from these dungeons simply by realizing that each intellectual thought process is a mere shade, only a ghost, and cannot harm, hurt or cause you pain. As these shades disappear, you rise from this earthly, rusty frame of mind, and you are aware perhaps of a feeling of parting that was even painful, for it is difficult to let those things that trouble you go. And yet, my friends, once you are up in the sunlight, and the sun is warming you, and you can lift yourself to the infinite grace and listen for the waters of truth, you have found an avenue from meditation to demonstration.

Chapter 8: The World in Which We Live

At most times, my friends, the illusion presses most strongly upon you, and in your desire for spiritual growth you ask what is the truth of this. My friends, ask yourself, does this problem have to do with my spiritual growth? And does it have to do with a service to aid another in spiritual growth? My friends, if the answer is, "yes," this problem is in the area I have described as the dungeon. It need only be let go, and then you need only become aware of the real creation, in its infinity, all around you, for you to have demonstrated at that moment a spiritual growth.

April 4, 1974
What you do within your situation, spiritually speaking, we would suggest, will be a function of one thing only and that is your understanding of the lesson which you are to learn. In general, each situation with which you surround yourself is a part of a lesson for you. We are not referring to daily details which occur under the simple laws of chance. We are referring to the overall trend or generalized direction or general dimension of your situation.

Whatever the difficulty is in this situation, the approach we would suggest spiritually is to take it, as we may predictably say, to meditation. Out of meditation, come with some understanding, not in your life, but simply in you [right now], of the lesson or the job to be done within that situation. In doing the job in as workmanlike and cheerful a manner as your meditation has given you the ability to maintain, as you accomplish your work within that lesson, the circumstances about you will alter of their own accord.

The constant feeling of pressure from outside is an illusion, my friends, sometimes an extremely heavy one, but only an illusion. Your lessons will be learned from within.

Chapter 8: The World in Which We Live

April 16, 1974
We are aware that many of those in this group are experiencing perplexities and while conditions are not serious physically for you, they are somewhat perplexing to you. And we wish today for you to consider that there is a duality of ways to look at the spiritual point of view.

One way is the way of taking a life-or-death attitude towards your understanding and going after spiritual understanding as the life-and-death matter that indeed it is. There is, however, a perfect opposite to this, which is equally valid and equally helpful and too little practiced, my friends, upon Planet Earth. And that is simply not to worry about the meaning behind the illusionary experiences that fill each day. This seems, in a way, very shallow. However, once you have aimed yourself towards the spiritual path and have begun to discipline yourself with regular meditation, patiently and carefully kept up, the ability to take the all-important step backwards towards detachment from that which is about you in your daily life is extremely important.

It may mean the difference between having a great many perplexing situations and having instead a feeling that the rhythm of the universe is resounding recognizably in your life. When your worried mind is still and when all the ripples of worry of your daily life have stopped, then and only then, may you discern the slow and stately movement of the universal rhythms.

April 24, 1974
There is an everlasting experience that's cycled again and again with the physical illusion that you now enjoy. This experience is one of perplexity. Events that happen are always events that are essentially unexplained. My friends, the unexplained sets up with your human intellect a great frustration and you seek the explanation with your intellect.

Chapter 8: The World in Which We Live

But, my friends, the explanation for the cycle of experience within the physical is never within the physical.

The answer, my friends, is to be found within the spiritual consciousness. The flimsy craft of your physical, intellectual ability is not designed to sail the deep seas of spiritual reasons. Do not attempt to take it into the depths of reason or else, I assure you, your flimsy craft will break apart and you will think that you are surely lost.

My friends, there is no loss. There is only unity. The great storm that is within this illusion is forever stilled by the consciousness that you may obtain through your meditation. As the master known as Jesus has been quoted as saying, "Peace, be still." This statement is a statement of faith. When applied to the storm in any illusory existence, the illusory storm is bound to respond and express this "Peace, be still." This concept that the consciousness of the Creator has dominion over the consciousness of the physical illusion is truth and is, we hope, a helpful truth.

May 16, 1974

We would like to give you a thought upon the nature of the spiritual path. Consider for yourself, my friends, the nature of your interior universe. How much of your thinking is involved with striving, attaining and grasping at things within the physical illusion? What fire consumes you? What greed or envy or base desire have you allowed to continue to have power over your thinking?

And then, my friends, what portion of your thinking is clear, calm, motionless, humble, unassuming and content?

I do not need to tell you which portion of your interior universe is more correctly called the spiritual part. The truth of the universe is a very simple truth. Correctly understood and practiced, it eliminates the striving for selfhood within the physical illusion. It eliminates it because it offers a more rewarding reality along the spiritual path.

The reason, my friends, that you have not completely become one with the spiritual path is not because you have not been trying. Do not cause yourself anxiety. It is simply, my friends, that the illusion under which you labor is extremely strong upon your planet, and there is a good deal of constant and faithful meditation and discipline to be achieved before the final breakthrough can come, and you may be free of your selfhood within the illusion.

Without that selfhood, my friends, without that which upon the part of the planet which you live is termed ego, you may achieve all things in the name of the Creator. For having no limitation of self, you may give for all men, and to all men.

It is a matter of knowing whom you serve, my friends.

As you go through your daily existence, therefore, we suggest to you, when it may serve you to do so, that you contemplate that which is called water. Water, my friends, is the humblest and the weakest of all substances. It abides in the lowest places. It constantly seeks a level. It is ashamed to go nowhere, but flows where every opportunity takes it. Water may wear away the hardest substances, for it is far stronger in its weakness than rigid substances can ever be.

Be like the water, my friends. Upon the spiritual path that you are seeking to follow, seek the nature of water.

The Physical Illusion II:

Normalcy

> "If a man sleeps in a damp place, he will wake up with an aching back, and feeling half-dead; but is this true of an eel? If men tried to live in trees, they would be scared out of their wits, but are monkeys? Of the three, which knows the right place to live?"

Chapter 8: The World in Which We Live

—Chuang Tzu

Comment

(This comment was written in 2009.)

I am convinced that normalcy is a myth, a figment of statistics. When you zero in on any of us, we are all unique and special.

Channeling Selection

May 17, 1974
My friends, it is very interesting to us who have come here to aid those of you upon the surface of your planet who seek, to notice the constant and widespread misapprehensions under which your people labor, with regard to the idea of normalcy.

There are many things which are looked upon within your physical illusion as being quite normal, which to us, my friends, look quite abnormal. And as we patiently search among the people of your planet, we find very few whose actions we would call normal. It is as though the people of planet Earth are all mysteriously prey to some widespread emotional disorder.

We did not understand this when we first came, and our first attempts to communicate with your people suffered much because of this misunderstanding. We have come to understand much more. And now, we can see the strong and ever-present cause of this wide-spread aberration of the peoples of this planet.

There is an abnormality which has been developing and building through many, many of your generations, until now what is in truth normal has become unheard of, and its place completely overtaken by that which is complete illusion.

Chapter 8: The World in Which We Live

You, my friends, having accepted the illusion, have simply reacted to what seems to be reality. The fault is certainly not your own, within this particular physical experience. However, it has happened. But, my friends, were there not hope that you might be able to reestablish contact with reality, and thereby return to a normal state of awareness with regard to the creation, we would not be here. We have come because those who have the potential for using our aid have desired our aid. We are here to serve you. We are here to encourage you. And we are here to attempt to give you our understanding of the creation of the Father.

You must realize, my friends, that although we cannot lay any blame at the feet of those people of your planet who do not understand, we can lay the blame at our own feet. For, my friends, we are each of you, and we have, through our free will, created this illusion. Your pain has been created by us, and we feel that pain very deeply. It is our strong desire to enable you to become able to have clear sight of what is real.

The very few people upon your planet who see reality are often thought to be quite insane. My friends, one must not attempt to understand what we are saying on the level of language. Go within, my friends, and meditate. For knowledge of reality will come only from within. Accept nothing, on blind faith, but accept everything that is of good report. Allow all paradoxes to remain so. Accept much, and reject nothing.

Go within, my friends, for within you lies reality.

Dream/Reality

> "Life is but a dream within a dream, within a dream."
> —Yada di shi'ite

Chapter 8: The World in Which We Live

Comment

The sense of reality is sometimes an elusive thing. Some feel most "real" when they are in danger, or are experiencing violent emotional states. Others find reality in their assumed roles, their jobs. These following messages suggest some reasons for these seeming variations in reality around us.

Channeling Selections

December 18, 1973

We of the Confederation of Planets in the Service of the Infinite Father are with you, my friends, and you are with us, in a single effort. Our effort, as I have said before, is to awaken the people of this planet to truth. This has been tried many, many times. They are sleeping very, very soundly. Yes, my friends, they are asleep, dreaming a dream that is fantastic. It is beyond the belief of those who know truth that such a dream could be a dream, but this is the case. Many of your people have dormant within them the memory of truth. Many others have a less accurate memory. And a few have no memory at all. The truth, however, is within them, for it is within all men, in all places.

For those of the first category, it is relatively easy to awaken them from their slumber. The second category is much, much more difficult, and the third, for the present, will be impossible for you to awaken. Do not concern yourself if an individual rejects an attempt you might make to awaken him. This simply means he is not yet ready for this truth to be given unto him. Concern yourselves with those who would seek the truth, and make it available to them in any way that you can.

February 15, 1974

All of the people of this planet should not be where they are at this time. Unfortunately, they are in a state of trance. I have

Chapter 8: The World in Which We Live

spoken of this before and at this time will reiterate that they are truly in a state of trance. They have been hypnotized by suggestions of social systems which have been built up by erroneous thinking through many centuries. The only way to break the chain of foolishness that reigns upon your planet is to awaken your people with proper information.

March 6, 1974
My friends, we come across the deeps of dimensions you know not to speak with you and yet you are asleep. And though you hear us you do not hear us. My friends, what you hear is truth and yet not truth. What you take in with your physical senses is only true for the illusion and, my friends, this illusion is a very small part of the creation.

My friends, you come here, you come to each meeting and you sit at each meditation in an attempt to awaken from the slumber only knowing the illusion of truth. Meditation, my friends, is the great bridge to the total creation of the Father.

All of us together are the creation. Through meditation we can begin to become more aware of it. This is true of us, also. And this is our service to you. We encourage you to continue meditation and, my friends, we encourage you to stop yourself at each point in the illusion at which you think a thought and ask yourself how much of the truth of that thought applies to the real creation of the Father.

March 8, 1974
For seeds in the ground, my friends, there is darkness. There is darkness also in the conscious and waking reality of those people of your planet who are beginning to seek, as they feel that they are awake, yet they are asleep, and in darkness.

And just as people who are asleep and dreaming while their real bodies are in their beds and safe, they may well imagine themselves killed. Such a thing does not happen; they awaken and discover that reality was other than they thought.

My friends, true understanding of the true reality is like this. And how do those of us who wish to serve begin to sow the seed? We of the Confederation of Planets in the Service of the Infinite Creator can only come to you to urge you to meditate, to seek, to turn to the Creator of us all for His love and His light. That is all you can do, my friends.

Evil

> "Why do we never get an answer
> When we're knocking at the door
> With a thousand million questions
> About hate and death and war?"
> —The Moody Blues

Comment

Any search for spiritual truth must needs include the attempt to come to grips with the subject of the evil which we can see about us.

Channeling Selections

February 18, 1974
There are people in this universe. They are infinite. They do many things. They speak to you. You listen. They come to you. Into your consciousness come thoughts. What comes into your consciousness is what you desire. You are limited because of your desire to be limited. Everything that you think is possible, if you desire it. Many things have occurred.

I am attempting to tell you that there are things that have occurred in your past, as you call it. There are many of the Creator's children who experienced what they desired. These desires are varied. There are activities which you would like to call evil. Is this possible, [that] a creation that was formed of love supports what you consider evil? Is this in the creation, or

Chapter 8: The World in Which We Live

is this in your consciousness, or are these two things one thing?

Questioner: It's as much a part of creation as any other duality?

There are many activities that occur upon the surface of the planet at this time that are considered to be evil. There are groups who express themselves in ways that were never conceived by the original Thought. The original Thought, however, provided for no limits on expression. It is possible, therefore, for any of the Creator's children to express themselves in any manner that they desire. For this reason, throughout the creation, there are individuals and groups expressing themselves in infinite numbers of ways.

You, at your present state of understanding, consider some of the expressions to be evil. We consider them to be expressions. We find that for our purpose, certain expressions are of a more beneficial nature to our own enjoyment than others. There are, however, expressions of an infinite quality and an infinite quantity occurring throughout the creation. We attempt to serve those within the creation who desire our service. They desire our service because they are interested in our concept of truth. We believe that our concept of truth is correct. In our understanding, we know that our concept is correct. There are many who would disagree with what we understand. This is their privilege. They do not desire our service. We would freely serve them in any way that we could. However, they do not desire this. Therefore, we do not serve.

May 14, 1974

There are many, many myriads of populations throughout the cosmos. Many of them are extremely advanced, and a few of them are not only advanced but also of a nature which you might call evil.

Chapter 8: The World in Which We Live

The Creator is at the end of your path. Your faith is far stronger, if you indeed realize it, than any evil. Remember this, my friends. It is completely within your powers, through meditation, to gain the love of the Creator that conquers all lack, limitation and pain. But, my friends, be aware that the only true nature of evil is separation from the Creator. It cannot touch you if you maintain your contact with the one who is all , Nothing from the outside may come in to harm. From the universe of truth and understanding you may show love and light upon all who come into your view.

Do not fear, my friends. There is nothing to fear but fear. This has been said before upon your planet, and it is quite true. Never waste time in fear, or in hatred, or in anger, for it is only another opportunity at such a time to experience and to demonstrate the love and the light of the infinite Creator.

Lack and Limitation

> "… early in life an impenetrable barrier is erected within the psyche itself. A barrier of inhibition is built up between the unconscious and the conscious thinking self—a barrier of prejudices, false moral concepts, infantile notions, pride and egotism. So profound is this armored barrier that our best attempts to get past it, around it, or through it are utterly impotent. We become cut off from our roots …"
> —Israel Regardie

Channeling Selection

April 24, 1974

You are aware upon your planet of night. This darkness is real to you within the illusion that you know as life. There is a simple, physical way in which you can intellectually imagine that darkness to be only a local phenomenon. The method of that understanding is to imagine that you are observing the solar system from the standpoint of the object that you call

Chapter 8: The World in Which We Live

your sun. From the standpoint of your sun, there is no night. There is no darkness. There is no lack. There is no limitation. There is only light, an enormously wasteful amount of energy, infinite, self-perpetuating, a type of light that expresses itself in all directions with all of its heart and strength.

The concept of darkness, lack, limitation or any petty restriction of any kind is quite foreign to the point of view of the inhabitant of the sun. It is for this reason, my friends, that we often describe to you the love and the light as being like sunlight or some form of light. This light, this phenomenon called light, is a spiritual phenomenon. It is one of the two building blocks of your entire universe.

Light, with no limitation of any kind, vastly energetic and infinite in its capacity, is the basis for all that is in a physical sense. The shaping, the creating, the molding force is the consciousness, the Thought which we call love. Love shapes light into the vibrations that we know as the physical world. The Creator's love is completely, down to the vary smallest detail, a spiritual thing. The lack, the limitation, the darkness, and the want are the creation of that most chief of the Father's creations, that being mankind.

Mankind is a creator, even as his Father wished for him to be. He has created. And those things which he desires are things which he does not truly desire. He has invented a great many different ways to experience lack, limitation and want. This, my friends, is only true thought from the point of view of the dweller within the illusion who rotates with the planet and sees the sun go down and disappear. A simple shift in point of view, from the point of view of the planet to the point of view of the source of light, for the planet, will enable the understanding of the conditions of the planet upon which you now enjoy the physical existence to come into much clearer focus.

Chapter 8: The World in Which We Live

We are aware that this is a far more generalized statement than requested. However, there are many things which do not have the spiritual answers for ourselves, but deal only with the illusion. The ability to change one's point of view will often banish a question and replace the question with understanding simply by the realization of a shift in point of view.

The Antichrist

> "Another prophet shall arise,
> And bring fresh fever from the skies;
> Another woman shall awake
> The lust and worship of the Snake;
> Another soul of God and beast
> Shall mingle in the globed priest;
> Another sacrifice shall stain the tomb;
> Another king shall reign;
> And blessing no longer be poured
> To the Hawk-headed mystical Lord!"
> —Aleister Crowley

Comment

(This comment was written in 2009.)

The dictionary defines the antichrist as an opponent of Christ, or one who is antagonistic to Christ. If there is but one antichrist, then that would be Satan. In a larger sense, however, all of those who have lost their faith in the power of unconditional love can be said to begin to take on the tinge of anti-christ-hood.

Channeling Selection

February 18, 1974
You have spoken of the term, Antichrist. What then is the meaning of this term? It is simply the ignorance of the

knowledge of this truth. This ignorance is widespread upon this planet. This is what is known as the Antichrist. It is the ignorance of truth. We speak to you, through instruments such as this one. We do this because it would be a mistake to speak to the people of this planet in a more direct manner. It is necessary that the ignorance of truth be eliminated from within, for this is the only possibility available to the individual, if he is to achieve a true awareness of truth.

The concept of Antichrist is with you but it is a false concept. If there exists an individual who would be called the Antichrist, then there exists an extremely ignorant individual. Should this be a threat to any of the Creator's children? I think not!

Satan

> "Cleopatra: Thou shalt be whipp'd with wine
> and stewed in brine,
> Smarting in ling'ring pickle.
> Messenger: Gracious madam,
> I that do bring the news made not the match."
> —William Shakespeare

Comment

(This comment was written in 2009.)

There is a mythic sweep of lore in the story of Satan. It is said that he was an angel who tired of following the Creator. So he started a war in heaven and was cast down to a lake of fire in his new precinct, Earth, taking with him, in one whip of his great tail a full third of the angelic host.

However, another name for Satan is Lucifer which, translated from the Latin, means light-bringer. The Confederation entities would appreciate this second naming. For although the suffering of humankind is dark, yet it brings eventual realization, knowledge and freedom to those who go boldly into that lake of fire, to wrest from the suffering the spiritual maturity and tempering of consciousness which are its fruits.

Channeling Selection

February 18, 1974
The one known as Satan was interested in experiencing the result of a desire, a desire of individualization; a desire for isolation. There are many of the Creator's children who are at present desiring isolation. To our understanding, this is not possible. The creation is full of the expressions of the Creator. Isolation is only possible through the creation of illusion.

In creating the illusion of isolation and intense individuality, the one known as Satan has experienced his desire. He has attempted to serve others in giving to them the experience of isolation. And many have sought this experience. For this reason, there are many groups who actively seek to experience isolation. This, then, is occurring, and has occurred, within the creation. This is a part of the original Thought of the creation, that each of the parts might fulfill its desires.

Death

> "Old Lazarus, why come you're not dead?"
> —Eldridge Cleaver

Comment

(This comment was written in 2009.)

The great gift of spiritual and religious faith alike is the changes made in the seeker's view of death. "Ashes to ashes and dust to dust" is undisputed, in terms of there being a decisive and final end to our physical bodies at death. Yet to the religious person, death is only a door into a larger life. And the Confederation, with their views on reincarnation and the grand procession of densities, describes what is beyond

Chapter 8: The World in Which We Live

that door. Thusly death loses its sting, and becomes merely the dropping of the physical body. We who occupy these bodies at this time are seen as citizens of eternity.

Channeling Selection

February 25, 1974

Hatonn: I have said that there will be the destruction of physical bodies upon your planet. This is a necessary consequence of the physical change. We of the Confederation of Planets in the Service of the Infinite Creator are aware that within your illusion much attachment is in evidence with respect to the physical. The body that you know as your physical body it as much a part of the illusion that you now experience as the illusion created by the people upon this planet. It is only necessary to avail yourself of the knowledge of reality to understand the reason for what you consider the physical body.

It has been stated earlier this evening that it is necessary to understand the words written in one of the holy books that have been given to your people. These stated that even though you should walk through the valley of the shadow of death that you would fear no evil. These words have reference to that which you consider as the destruction of the physical body.

R: So, what you're saying is that regardless of whether or not people raise their vibration their physical body is going to be destroyed.

Hatonn: Your physical body will be destroyed. You are aware of this. There is not a single physical body upon the surface of this planet that will not be destroyed at some time in what you consider to be the future. You have an awareness of this and expect it, as do all of the people of your planet. This is what you know as death. It is a natural cycle for the physical body to be destroyed. It is alarming to most of the people who inhabit this planet to assume that their physical body will be destroyed before they expect it to be destroyed. However, it is possible at your present level of awareness in the physical to expect this destruction at any particular time.

R: Will all the bodies of all the people of this planet be destroyed during the changes that you have stated or will some people be taken with their bodies in your craft off the planet?

Hatonn: There will be a change of density of vibration. The physical body as you now know it will not be in evidence in the fourth density of vibration. You would have no need for this dense a body. If you were to retain it, you would not pass into the fourth density. Do you wish to retain this and remain in the third density of vibration? I think not. Do you know what you desire? What is death? What is the physical body?

R: What's the process of translation that you have spoken of? Is it what we call death, or is it something else?

Hatonn: There is no death. The reason that you presently have the concept of death is that you are unable to communicate in your present state of awareness with these whom you consider dead. There will be no inability to communicate between levels of awareness when the planet has moved into what is considered the fourth density. Therefore, there will be one awareness of the concept of death. All physical bodies that now exist upon this planet will in the future not exist. This would occur even if there was no change of density, for it has occurred in a cyclical manner throughout all of the history of this planet.

Chapter 8: The World in Which We Live

Wealth

> "Sweet will be our days, and bright,
> And happy will our nature be,
> When love is an unerring light,
> And joy its own security."
> —William Wordsworth

Comment

(This comment was written in 2009.)

There are several ways of calculating wealth. The first is to count up all the assets a person has on this earth – money, stocks, bonds, real estate and so forth. The second is to consider wealth the accretion of worldly power, influence and connections. And the third, which the Confederation as well as most world religions embrace, calculates wealth as the "treasures in heaven" of contentment, joy, presence, realization and devotion to the service of the Creator and one's fellow human beings. It's all in your point of view!

Channeling Selection

March 24, 1974

There was a man upon your planet who had great wealth and in this wealth, he saw much power. For his fellow men would eagerly do his bidding to share part of this wealth. And, for this reason, many of those who dwell upon this planet, known to you as Earth, require vast quantities of material wealth and therefore acquire what they consider to be much power. What is not understood by those men is that in acquiring this wealth and in attempting to possess much power through this wealth they are giving up an infinite amount of power for that which is in actuality no power at all.

The man of which I spoke, who had much wealth, used it to satisfy his desires. And his desires were for things which he

Chapter 8: The World in Which We Live

thought that he wanted and needed. For he saw in this wealth not a only a great happiness which would come from possessing those things that he desired and having dominion over all of his fellow men about him, but also great security in that he would need not want for the rest of his days. And, therefore, he coveted greatly his accumulation of wealth. And had at his command everything that he desired and great status.

But he lacked one thing. He lacked love. For it was not given to him by those about him. And this he did not understand. And he became aware of his need for this experience that he called love end he set about to discover how to obtain it. And he questioned those about him, and asked them why he was not given love. And they could not answer for they did not know.

And he went to a wise man and offered to pay him much of his wealth if he would but tell him how to obtain love. And the wise man gave unto the rich men all that he possessed, for all that he possessed was but a pitiful, small amount. And the man of great wealth accepted it. For he had long ago resolved never to turn down a gift. And he left the wise man and went to his home and pondered this gift, leaving the wise man penniless. For he had not paid the wise man. For the wise men had not told him how to find love.

And as the days passed, he returned to the wise man, for he could not understand why he had been given all that was possessed by the one who was said to be so wise. And when he asked him he was answered by the wise man who said, "It is because I have a great love for you and you desire wealth. Therefore, I give you that which I have to add to your riches, for this is what you desire."

And at that moment, the man of great wealth looked at the wise man and said, "And in turn, I, for the first time, know love."

And he gave to the wise man great wealth. And in doing so, he felt an even greater love. For, for the first time, he had learned the truth of the Creator's gifts to His children. And this man was very fortunate, for he had been able to discover a way of generating love.

And yet, man on earth continues to seek within his material illusion; continues to seek that which is of no real value. For he lacks faith. He stands upon the surface of this planet and experiences all of the gifts of his Creator. He breathes the air and smells the fragrance of the flowers and is in the company of his fellow man and finds many things provided for him. And yet, he does not understand. He does not have faith that within this Creation, he is supplied, and due to this lack of faith, he finds hardships, for he does not understand faith. Therefore, man, in many instances, does not seek the knowledge of the wise man. But he seeks a security and a power that is not secure and is not power.

Time

> "All dogs, past, present, and future, are equally happy. … The enormous price of knowledge is the power to imagine, and the consequent power to compare."
> —John Fowles

Comment

(This comment was written in 2009.)

The concept of time has baffled, fascinated and provoked discussion as long as written history shows us the writings of philosophers, poets and artists. We have a tight grasp on the passage of time here on Earth, with our atomic clocks and our various calendars. Yet time slips away from happy souls and drags for those with woe and trouble in their hearts. According to the Confederation, time is a part of the grand illusion of this third-density environment. Also, according to the same source, third density itself is running out of time, as we welcome the dawn of fourth density.

Channeling Selection

January 26, 1974

You see the future as something that will come to you. We see the future as an event that is presently here. This is a difficult thing to translate into your language, but I will attempt to give you an understanding of what you know as time.

Time, my friends, is an illusion. The creation is, in fact, timeless. You are at a particular point in the evolution of the creation. There seems to be a progression of time. But there is actually a continuing stream of consciousness. It is only necessary to displace yourself along this stream of consciousness to be at any point along the stream that you call time.

In other words, it is possible to move through time as you understand movement through space. Each of these concepts is as real as the other. We have stated to you previously that there is one place and there is one time. This place and this time are the creation. We are able to move through space. We are also able to move through time, for in actuality these things are the same thing: they are the creation.

Sleep

> "In the evening, before sleeping, thou shalt say: Whilst my corporeal body sleepeth, O Jehovih, help my less encumbered spirit to see the ways of thy righteous judgment."
> —Oahspe

Comment

(This comment was written in 2009.)

Chapter 8: The World in Which We Live

Sleep is a blessing and a rest to the weary human. It is also a voyage into mystery, as we dream of things impossible to explain in any rational sense. Seldom do our dreams speak clearly to us. Yet we sense that our dreams give us valuable clues about what is most deeply on our minds and hearts. It is fascinating to consider that in the short burst of REM sleep, such detailed, rich stories are spun, stories that take us a long time to tell and even longer to consider.

To the Confederation, however, we all seem to be asleep within the illusion of physical life. Their recommendation is caught in the little nursery song,

Row, row, row your boat gently down the stream.

Merrily, merrily, merrily, merrily, life is but a dream.

Channeling Selections

February 9, 1974

We were, for quite some time, confused about the conditions that are manifested upon your surface, and the reason for the turmoil. It took us some time to understand the state of total ignorance that is in evidence among your peoples. This is not a condition that is often found in this creation, for the Father has given to each of his children an understanding that is within them.

This understanding is within all of the peoples throughout all of space, and it is within the people of this planet. However, since they have not sought this understanding that is theirs, that is a part of them, they have continued in directions brought about by desires that have nothing to do with truth; desires created by intellectual games played in their sleeping state.

And if they did not come in contact with their innermost thoughts at this time, they would long since have ceased to exist, for a being cannot long exist in a condition of total lack of the Creator's truth. For this reason you find it necessary to sleep. Sleep, my friends, is not a normal condition. It is something that the people of your planet do out of necessity.

Unfortunately, this condition of sleep does not totally satisfy the requirements that are necessary if the truth of the creation is to be revealed in its totality. It is therefore necessary, if they are to return to this truth, to avail themselves to it in daily meditation.

May 14, 1974
Questioner: What is sleep?

Hatonn: I am Hatonn. I am aware of your question. At night, my friends, you truly come alive. Many, many upon your planet only rise to consciousness in their sleep. There is a desperate starvation upon your planet. It is the starvation of the spirits that have forgotten how to contact their Creator. During sleep, my friends, your spirit involuntarily goes directly into the real universe, and breathes and lives and radiates the joy of the Creator.

Were it not for this unconscious activity of the spirit of many of those upon the surface of the planet, they would be unable to continue their existence in the physical body.

In fact, this is the reason for the amount of sleep that is needed upon this planet. It is necessary in order to give enough food to the spirit. In the case of those who through meditation have found a conscious contact with the Creator, they may find that less sleep may be adequate.

Questioner: Can this sleep activity be remembered, [when we have] awakened?

Hatonn: All is remembered, my friends. Nothing is forgotten. There will be much remembering of much that we seem to have forgotten when we leave this chemical vehicle and this heavy illusion.

Sex

> "The length of our passions no more rests with us than the length of our lives."
> —La Rochefoucauld

Comment

(This comment was written in 2009.)

Our sexuality is one of the most magical things about us. Although in the wrong hands, used for the wrong reasons, it can make us miserable and cause us untold pain, in the right hands, used for the right reasons, it can make us sacred dancers in the fields of the Lord, playing and gamboling with the Creator and offering a new understanding of unity as two people of flesh and blood become one in spirit and in body. Sex gives us all the chance to explore the right use of power.

Channeling Selection

May 14, 1974

Questioner: What about sex? Is it better to be a monk if you are on the spiritual path?

Hatonn: My friends, the subject of the physical illusion has always been a difficult one, and your question about what you call sex is an area which has a great deal of trauma associated with it.

We can only tell you that you are a free agent. You have incarnated into a physical vehicle. This physical vehicle is designed in order to offer you various experiences which you need for you to progress spiritually. Due to the fact that each one is sovereign unto himself, being a free child of the Creator, each man therefore will have come to this incarnation with a peculiar and unique set of needs, which his excursion into the physical illusion will satisfy. To some

Chapter 8: The World in Which We Live

people, the experience of sexuality is extremely important. To some people, there is little or no need for this particular type of activity. The rather large number of people who have lined up on one side or another of this question, and others like unto it, are reasoning about an infinite situation. There is only one answer for each person.

My friends, sexuality is neither good nor evil. Your physical body is neither good nor evil. Sexual activity, as such, is neither good nor evil. The natural activities upon your planet are part of the Creator's plan. Were it not part of the Creator's plan that man should have sexuality then man would not have sexuality. It exists simply as an opportunity. It is completely under the control of each individual as to the use to which he puts this opportunity.

There is a simple progression for those on your plane. We have noticed that you are aware that many of your Earthly masters on your planet were not particularly interested in the experience gained within the province of human desire. This is due to the fact that the earthly plane is experienced first in a relatively gross or material state, a state which yields great strength, great sexuality, and a great deal of aggressive emotion.

The progression towards the next density of experience is one which more and more experiences an abiding within spirit, and a detachment from the needs of the material part of the self. In extreme cases, this has meant that there will be no activity of a physical nature at all, for a certain person.

However, we must point out to you that this state is not arrived at by a person who decides to become holy by imposing such restrictions upon himself. This state is properly attained as a natural result and an involuntary occurrence upon achieving a completely transcendent state.

There are many, many seekers. Many of these seekers are in many, many different places. We are aware that much good may be accomplished by the correct mating of two individuals in mind, body, and soul. Again, this is not a necessary path to take. There are a thousand paths to take. Each individual finds what is proper for him. To find a proper path, one may meditate, as we have said so many times. Simply, meditate.

We are aware that this is a subject of confusion. But my friends, it is simple. There are opportunities, and you are a discerning entity who seeks to understand.

Seek, and ye shall find. These are true words. Seek through meditation.

Drugs

> "Lucy in the sky with diamonds.
> Follow her down to a bridge by a fountain
> Where rocking horse people eat marshmallow pies,
> Everyone smiles as you drift past the flowers
> That grow so incredibly high."
> —The Beatles

Comment

Drugs have been with us since the dawn of civilization as we know it, but seldom have they been as generally well-regarded by as many sincere seekers after truth. Timothy Leary, Richard Alpert (before transition to his new self as Baba Ram Dass) and John Lilly have all helped put the spiritual possibilities of various psychedelic drugs before our eyes. In the face of this sometimes unreserved enthusiasm, it is well to have a balance, a moderator for enthusiasm. Without undue concern, the Confederation seems in the following answer to provide some balancing thought on the subject.

Chapter 8: The World in Which We Live

Channeling Selection

May 16, 1974

Questioner: I want to know whether it is harmful or helpful to use drugs, especially for intellectual purposes.

Hatonn: The use of any outside or external stimulus has no appreciable effect upon your internal spirit. The center of the problem of which you speak is not the fact that these foreign substances do or do not transfer parts of your vibratory makeup into novel spaces. Various external influences have various effects. By the use of these, the type of awareness that may be achieved through meditation can be achieved. The difficulty, as we have said, lies in the fact that these substances are external, and do not come under the will of you, the individual who is seeking.

It may be an acceptable therapeutic measure, to increase one's faith in the reality of the spiritual path, to experience such a state by means of such an outside stimulus. However, the use of internalizing effects, such as meditation and service, wherein your will makes its own contact with the Creator and the creation offer far more realistic ways of entering upon the spiritual path.

It is important in the extreme that you be living within yourself, at the center of your being, in order that you may experience the reality of the Father's creation. It is important that you be able to achieve the awareness of that creation from within your own spirit. The use of outside agents simply puts you in places which you are not ready to comprehend or make use of. True seeking is inner seeking. To be able to give, it is best to refrain from taking. It is far better to achieve an awareness of the creation through meditation than through the use of any external agent.

There is not any more harm or acceptability for the use of any drug or material over any other. We have observed simply that they all lie outside the control of your inner self, and are therefore not a part of your spiritual world.

Chapter 9: The Place of the Intellect

The Intellect

> "My nature is in itself sufficient. To search for principles in affairs and things was an error."
> —Wang Yang-Ming

Comment

In some aspects, what the Confederation expresses as their philosophy is fairly easy to understand. Their vision of the original creation and of the illusion which replaces reality for us on the physical level is fairly easy to grasp.

But the placing of this information out of reach of the intellect, in a way, is much more difficult to understand, since we all attempt to understand first with our intellectual faculties.

As obscure as this concept may seem to some who prize their intellects, it does reward consideration with a growing sense of understanding, on a deeper level. This growing understanding can aid greatly in enhancing a sense of peace and wholeness.

Channeling Selections

January 15, 1974
My friends, truth is very, very simple. The Creator's plan is very, very simple. It is not necessary that we weave a complex web of circumstance to lead you to the Creator. He is within you, and you are He. It is only necessary that you realize this in its fullest sense for you to be aware of all the Creator's wisdom. The people of this planet have blocked their minds

Chapter 9: The Place of the Intellect

from this knowledge. We are attempting to teach the people of this planet how to remove this blockage.

It is a very simple process. Unfortunately, the people of this planet are more accustomed to complexity, and would therefore desire intellectual juggling of various propositions and theories. This, my friends, is not necessary. To get from where you are to where you should be requires an understanding that has nothing to do with the intellect. It requires, simply, a knowing of truth.

This truth is extremely simple. What I am trying to say is that when you become totally aware of this simple truth, then you will not use intellectual processes to understand anything that you wish to know. This knowledge will be yours, for all knowledge is linked in the Creator's universe. There is no separation. This separation occurs only when man desires it, through use of the freedom of choice that has been given him by his Creator. Return, therefore, to the Creator. Return to the knowledge and the wisdom and the power that is yours. Do this by giving forth only His light and His love. This is what was intended. Acting otherwise, and knowing otherwise, results only in the isolation and blockage to which I referred.

Consider very carefully these simple teachings that I offer to you, for these simple teachings are all that is required. There is nothing of a complex nature that is needed.

March 2, 1974
Unfortunately, there has been much misinformation about us, and much misunderstanding, even of the ones who are aware of us, of our real message. We have attempted to maintain a simple message, for man on Earth has confused himself for many generations with complexities. We have attempted to maintain a simplicity in our teachings in order to remove man on Earth from the web of his entangled complexities. What we here present to those of the peoples of this planet who

would desire it is the simplicity of truth itself, the truth of this creation and the truth of man's part in it.

It is, my friends, very, very simple. It is not necessary to get lost in the complex web of intellectual seeking of which man on Earth seems to be so fond. It is only necessary that he avail himself to an understanding that is not of an intellectual nature. And this he may do in daily meditation. It is only necessary that he raise his awareness, so that he grasps the understanding of his unity and oneness with the creation and the Creator. This we bring to man of Earth. This we offer in hopes that he will accept it.

Allow your mind to stop. Think of nothing. It is difficult to change quickly, in the confusion that you meet during your daily activities and the intense use of the intellect that you experience. This is one of the great problems on your planet.

It is not necessary for man to use his intellect in such a manner. Everything that man desires is provided. It is only necessary that he realize his true relationship to the Creation. It is only necessary that he realize that he is the creation.

And this is not done by intellectual complexities. This is done through a simple process, a very simple process of becoming aware. We call this process meditation, but it is not necessary that it be so formalized. It is only necessary that man realize that this may be done at any time. Relax, and allow this awareness to be with you, and my brothers will help you. We are here for that purpose.

April 14, 1974
It is very often that these words are misunderstood for one reason or another. The difficulty, my friends, is the constant use of the intellect taught to all people who have been at all educated. There is very little spiritual teaching for growth upon your planet, and that has not ever been the type of spiritual training that would be most helpful in supplying a

Chapter 9: The Place of the Intellect

spiritual development in a growing entity. As the physical body grows, the entity within is educated upon those portions of your planet which are now receiving the aid of technological advances. This enables his intellect to grow and his body to grow. There is much lacking after these two items have become matured.

April 15, 1974
We would like you to consider, my friends, an island in an ocean channel far out at sea. There is no land in sight and this small rock, washed by waves, bleached by the sun, with small flora and fauna growing upon it, looks out upon the world, and its limited consciousness attempts to grasp the reality as it eddies and swirls about it.

The little island detects many strange things as they enter its purview. It lives through differences in climate and feeling and mood. It experiences the seasons of its flora and its fauna and it attempts to piece together a reasonable and holistic view of its reality. It is fixed in position, my friends, a poor, small rock. The far limits wherefrom come the waves, and the far limits to which they return, will be forever unknown to the island. The island can never know or fully understand that which appears at its doorstep, so to speak. This, my friends, is a very rough and perhaps shallow example of the type of instrument the intellect is.

The intellect upon your planet is very useful within the imagery for which it was made. But the attempt, my friends, to use the intellect to understand the far limits of your origin or the far limits of where you shall return again is impossible. For in the image upon which your intellect works, you are a rock chained to one mooring. This is not reality, nor can your intellect give you a picture of reality. Rather, my friends, in meditation seek to be the water. Seek the consciousness, the oneness, the unity and the adventure of the water. All water is inseparable. There is no separation. Water flows, it is as one.

Chapter 9: The Place of the Intellect

And each wave that breaks upon this shore may have broken anywhere and may move to anywhere. Let your consciousness flow like the water, not like an island, inwardly.

May 15, 1974
My friends, your minds are stayed far, far too strongly upon those illusory goals of the intellect of which your conscious awareness makes such advanced company. These intellectual pretensions, my friends, are no kind of advanced company in which to be. Their group name is complexity and, my friends, understanding is simple.

Let us examine this concept. Understanding, my friends, is simple. It is unitary. It is not logical. It is not intellectual. It is not necessary that you understand understanding. It is not necessary that anyone around you understand what you are understanding.

It is necessary only for you to seek the understanding of the true creation within, and this we will attempt to give you in a simple way. With the intellect and with words, my friends, we can only approximate understanding to you. And your attempts to examine it on an intellectual level can only be a type of subterfuge, camouflage and misdirection. You must not depend upon the tools of the physical illusion in order to build for yourself your bridge to eternity, for that which is of the illusion will vanish and be no more before you are able to cross that bridge.

Let go of the preconceptions which are embedded deep in your intellectual mind. Allow yourself simply to seek, and then to have faith in the seeking. What you seek is simple. The creation is simple. There is only one understanding which we can offer you, my friends, and that is that the creation is one great being. The creation is you; the creation is me; the creation is all that ever was and ever will be. The creation, my friends, is the Creator. As you look into the eyes of another upon your planet, you are looking at the Creator. As he looks at you, my friends, he also is looking at the Creator.

If you may achieve this simple understanding, then and only then may you live in harmony with the understanding of the Creator, who created each portion of His creation in order that it may be of service to every other portion of the creation.

This is our understanding. This is our simple understanding. All is one. We cannot speak to you in any complex manner, for we do not have a complex statement. We sincerely hope that you may heed our caution, and allow that portion of yourself which is stored with the knowledge of all of the creation to come into life within you. Allow it to do so by exposing it to the love and the light of the Creator through meditation.

Seek, my friends. Seek understanding, and through meditation, understanding will be given.

Free Will

> "The highest wisdom is to suffer all men to have full liberty to think on all subjects in their own way."
> —Oahspe

Comment

As the Confederation presents the concept of free will, it emerges as one of the great and unassailable laws of the Creator.

Channeling Selections

January 17, 1974
Those of the people of your planet who do not desire the thoughts of those of us who now surround your planet are not obliged to receive them. This would be a great error on our

Chapter 9: The Place of the Intellect

part. Those of the people of your planet who desire these thoughts receive them. Whether they may be translated into a verbal form or not is of no particular consequence.

January 26, 1974

The illusion that is now impressed upon you because of your limitations in a physical condition, as you call it, are limitations that are not at all ordinary. They are limitations that are impressed upon those who desire them for certain experiences. Each individual in this creation is able to select precisely what he desires. This is exactly the plan of the Creator. He not only gave man free will, but he also gave man the ability to select exactly what he desired. There are many, many paths to take through this creation—in actuality, an infinite number—and the choice is always left up to the individual.

Some of those who have explored have explored in a direction that led them away from the all-knowing One, the all-loving One, the Creator. In wandering away, there were conditions encountered that were at that time desired by the individuals who were wandering. But as they wandered farther and farther, they became more and more immersed in an illusion that they created. This illusion is at present so very strong that many of the children of the Creator find themselves confused and unable to easily find the pathway back to the infinite light.

It is necessary that they realize for themselves how to do this, for the principle given to them by their Creator is still totally in effect. It allows them to do precisely what they desire. It is therefore necessary that they realize for themselves what they desire, and then it is necessary that they seek this realization. In order to do this, it is necessary that they become aware of the techniques of bringing about this understanding. This is our purpose, at the present time: to help those who are presently seeking the pathway that will return them to the love and the light that they now desire. It is necessary for us to help those who desire this, in order to act within the plan of the creation. It is necessary also that we do not overly disturb those who do not overly desire at this time such activity.

March 23, 1974

Our gift and our service to you is simply our understanding of the truth. We are still seeking. We are not of the ultimate authority, nor would we ever insist upon anyone listening to what we have to say if another mode of thinking seemed more profitable. So, my friends, understanding is possible only for one person at one time. Each person is completely free at any time to choose. This is why we are indirect. We may say things to you that you may consider in the privacy of your own thoughts, but what you choose to do is completely your own idea. This is as it should be, my friends.

The Mind

> "He who created thee alive, gave to thee of His Own Being. Be thou steadfast unto Him, and thou shalt not err, but eliminate thyself from the chance of error."
> —Oahspe

Comment

The Transcendentalists of the nineteenth century had a sure and certain feel for the concept of the unitary mind. And the idea that the Creator is alive within each of His creatures is as old as our known history. This concept of mind is an alternative to the concept of individual intellectual striving which has created our society as we know it.

Chapter 9: The Place of the Intellect

Channeling Selections

January 13, 1974

You may have some question about how we are always so available to your contact. We are aware of your thinking because it is also our thinking. When you have, shall I say, tuned your mind so that it will operate at the same vibration as ours, then, if you think something, it is a mutual thought between your mind and ours. This is the way that it should be. It is not as it was intended for minds to be individualized as they are upon your planet. This results in much confusion and difficulty in communication.

Individualization of mind is something that we do not desire. Many of the people of your planet desire to separate themselves and their thinking from all others. This is their choice. It is a choice given to them by their Creator. However, those of our planet are not so individualized. We are always able to contact those who avail themselves because we are always availing ourselves, for that is our mission and purpose at this time. There are always a great number of our people ready and willing to send to you that which you desire.

January 14, 1974

It has been the practice of the people of this planet to separate their thinking from the thinking of others. This is not a common situation. It is not a necessary situation. It is a false illusion. It is very simple, my friends, to rid yourselves of the illusion that your mind is a separate and unique entity. It is very easy to establish contact with us in the same way that this instrument has. It is only necessary that you first become aware of the creation in its true essence. This causes a variation in the attunement of your mind.

January 14, 1974

I and my brothers are aware of your thinking. We are aware of your thinking because it is also our thinking, for our minds

Chapter 9: The Place of the Intellect

are as one. However, we are not aware of everything in your mind, because at times your thoughts are disrupted or cut off from us by the individualization that I earlier spoke of that is so common with your peoples.

January 17, 1974
When I say to you that I am with you, it has more than one meaning. I am with this instrument in a direct sense with respect to his ability to understand an intellectual communication. I am with each of you in an equivalent way. It is not necessary for you to be able to receive my thoughts in an intellectual way. This is only convenient if they are to be passed in a verbal fashion to others, as I am doing now. However, the same thoughts are also yours, for they are everyone's. It is only a matter of whether or not you desire the thoughts.

January 17, 1974
We have actually only one thing to present to your people. This is truth, and it is very simple. If they would simply learn to accept this truth and utilize it they would be free of their limitations. We have stated many times in our communications this truth, in many different ways. It is all that is needed. There is nothing more that is required.

January 17, 1974
When I say to you that I am with you, it has more than one meaning. I am with this instrument in a direct sense with respect to his ability to understand an intellectual communication. I am with each of you in an equivalent way. It is not necessary for you to be able to receive my thoughts in an intellectual way. This is only convenient if they are to be passed in a verbal fashion to others, as I am doing now. However, the same thoughts are also yours, for they are everyone's. It is only a matter of whether or not you desire the thoughts.

Chapter 9: The Place of the Intellect

January 17, 1974
We have actually only one thing to present to your people. This is truth, and it is very simple. If they would simply learn to accept this truth and utilize it, they would be free of their limitations. We have stated many times in our communication this is truth, in many different ways. It is all that is needed. There is nothing more that is required. For once you are able to assimilate this knowledge, you are then in a position to know all things, for you are then in communion with all of the creation. This is the way that you were created. Only through, shall I say, errors in experimentation with free will, has man limited his thinking, and cut himself off from total knowledge.

The mind of man is not created so that it is isolated. It is created to be in contact with all consciousness at all times. It is possible through understanding, which is not intellectual in form, to realize the single truth that allows man of Earth to remove this limitation or separation from the infinite mind. It is only necessary that the individual avail himself to this infinite mind through the practice of daily meditation. It has been found by some of the people dwelling upon your planet. However, it was necessary for them to seek this mind through meditation.

February 1, 1974
Everything that you experience has been created by mind. It is in some instances obvious that this is true. In others, it is less obvious. If you consider the creations of man, whatever they may be—his cities, his homes or factories, or vehicles for conveyance—all of these things are expressions of his thought. They have been brought into existence through a physical manipulation of his physical body. However, they are no less a direct manifestation of thought. We have stated that the entire creation is an expression of thought, the original

Thought of the Creator. It is possible for you to appreciate this statement by considering what is in evidence about you.

About you, find the expressions and manifestations of the creations of man. This preoccupies most of the people of this planet. In addition to these creations, you find the expressions and creations of the Creator. However, upon considering this, it should be noted that man is an expression and a creation of the Creator; therefore, his creations are simply an extension of the original Thought and the original creation of the Creator.

Chapter 10: Complete Messages

> "We shall not cease from exploration
> And the end of all our exploring
> Will be to arrive where we started
> And know the place for the first time."
> —T. S. Eliot

Comment

Up until this last charter, what you read were parts of messages which were received by telepathic contact. Here we have placed for you a sampling of complete messages. You may see the typical format of their contacts, and the periodical difficulties which are encountered, but you may also perhaps note an appeal which the complete messages hold by their very format. For although it seems loose and scattered at times, the style and content of the messages seems also to be very clear and easy to follow.

The content of the messages varies according to the desires of those meditating and seeking knowledge. Many times, after a message, someone in the meeting will indicate that he had this question in his mind before the meeting. At other times, the Confederation brother who is speaking will simply open the meeting to questions, either spoken or unspoken. They are very happy to answer questions, and it is due to this service-centered attitude that messages often seem to wander in their subject. Various questions, or parts of questions, are being answered.

The most-received entity in the Louisville group has always been Hatonn[13], which is the name not of a single individual

---

[13] Editor's note in 2009: Since 1985, our most common contact has been Q'uo, which is a principle made up of the Hatonn, Latui and Ra groups acting as one.

but of an entire community of like-minded people who wish no individualization in their service to the Creator. Hatonn seems to guide several other groups of entities in their combined efforts to serve those of Earth. These other entities include Latui, Laitos, Oxal and several others. These are all names of groups of individuals, rather than personal names, which makes it easier for us to understand how the Confederation always seems able to respond to a call for a contact, regardless of the time or circumstance.

Channeling Selections

December 18, 1973

I am Hatonn. I am very pleased to be with you this evening. It is always a great pleasure to be with you. I greet you, my friends, in the love and the light of our infinite Creator. I and my brother, Laitos, are here. We will condition you as I speak to you. It is very important, my friends, to spend time in meditation—very important.

We of the Confederation of Planets in the Service of the Infinite Father are with you, my friends, and you are with us, in a single effort. Our effort, as I have said before, is to awaken the people of this planet to truth. This has been tried, many, many times. They are sleeping very, very soundly. Yes, my friends, they are asleep, dreaming a dream that is fantastic. It is beyond the belief of those who know truth that such a dream could be a dream, but this is the case. Many of your people have dormant within them the memory of truth. Many others have a less accurate memory. And a few have no memory at all. The truth, however, is within them, for it is within all men, in all places.

For those of the first category, it is relatively easy to awaken them from their slumber. The second category is much, much more difficult, and the third, for the present, will be impossible for you to awaken. Do not concern yourself if an individual rejects an attempt you might make to awaken him. This simply means he is not yet ready for this truth to be given unto him. Concern yourselves with those who would seek the truth, and make it available to them in any way that you can.

There are many people upon your planet at this time who are attempting to cloud the memory of this truth. They are not aware of what they are doing. This is not their fault. But it is unfortunately the condition. It is not a simple task that we have outlined, and I am afraid it will require a great deal of effort. We have not been as successful as we had hoped to be when we initiated this project some years ago. The people of your planet do not actually wish to be awakened, for the most part. Those who are sleeping very, very lightly are all too few. However, you will know them, as you find them, and you will recognize their lightness of slumber by their activities, for they will not be as enmeshed in the insanity, if we can call it that, that is so prevalent on your world today. These people are already seeking. In this case, it will be but a simple matter for you to convey to them that which they need.

It is, however, very important that you be able to give them what they need. For this reason, we suggest that you continue to meditate, for only in this way can you be prepared to serve them. I speak not only of the preparation to act as does this instrument, as a vocal channel, but also a preparation of your own thinking, so that you will know the truth with no doubt or hesitation in speaking it. It is within you, my friends, and we will reawaken it within you, for your slumber is but very, very light. It is only necessary that you avail yourself to us through meditation. There are many wondrous things that we would freely give you, if you would simply avail yourself to us. These gifts are freely given.

It is not only our pleasure and our privilege to do this but our duty, as it is your duty to pass them on to others, for this is the plan of the creation. The creation is a single entity. Each part of it is designed to aid and help all the other parts. This is the original plan. It is a very simple thing for you to understand if you will relax and look at the original true creation, and forget that which was created by your fellow man, upon the surface of your planet that you now enjoy, and think of the plan and the working of the Father's original creation. It is quite obvious that each part was designed to aid and benefit each other part.

Unfortunately, due to the action of the free will that He gave to its parts, there have been some errors, shall I say, made by some of the parts, and they have strayed from the original plan, confusing themselves and confounding the workings of this plan. It is only necessary to realize the truth of this plan to know its workings. It is only necessary that you meditate to have all of these things given to you, or reawakened within you for all of this knowledge was originally given to all of the parts of this creation. It dwells within every living thing, and everything in this creation lives.

We of the Confederation of Planets in the Service of the Infinite Creator are living as closely to the plan as we possibly can. We do this because we know it to be the only logical and rational way of living. To divorce yourself from the plan is only to confound the true workings of nature. Your people at present are totally unaware of such a plan. Your scientists ignore it. They are extremely interested in plans of their own. Unfortunately, their plans do not follow the plan of the Creator. Therefore, they waste much of their time and energy, and build devices that have no real valuable purpose. [Their purposes] are transient, I can assure you.

Your scientists should realize that there is a purpose to the creation that far surpasses what they suspect. They should avail themselves to the purpose in meditation. Then they would find that they would begin to understand the plan, and

Chapter 10: Complete Messages

thereby, they would be able to use their knowledge to build within the plan, not, as they do now, with no heed at all to the truth, and with plans of their own which have no relationship to truth.

Your governments make the same error. They do not work within the plan. They are not aware of the plan. They attempt to make laws, but their laws do not work. They appear to have some value, but very shortly, much strife is generated, and the result is war. They do not understand that the reason for this strife is that they have ignored the natural plan of creation, the natural order of things, and the law of the Creator that devised this. Your leaders should avail themselves in meditation to truth, as we do.

We are aware that at this particular time it is impossible for your scientists and your leaders to do such a thing, for they are in the vast depths of slumber, and cannot at this time be awakened, for the most part. There are only a few, many, many too few, who are very lightly slumbering. It will be necessary, therefore, to concern yourself with those whom you contact in any and all walks of life, the ones who are lightly slumbering, the ones who will seek on their own, after they have been made aware of the possibility of seeking.

It is our plan to alert as many of these people as possible, so that, when it becomes obvious to your leaders and to your scientists that we are real and we are what they suspect that we might be, there will be a sufficient number of awakened entities on your planet for some form of communication to take place between those who are already awake, and those who are lightly slumbering in the future. For as time passes, those who are in the depths of slumber now will begin to awaken. Those whom you cannot contact at all now will begin to awaken. It will be a self-generating process, so that large numbers of your people will be given the truth. It is a very, very big task.

It will be up to you, and those like you, to help us in carrying this out. We have said before that we would very much like to land upon your surface and contact your peoples directly, but we have explained that this is not at all feasible.

I am aware of many planets such as this one that have gone through a cycle of awakening. Many planets made this transition with considerable ease, because they were following the plan. Unfortunately, this planet has lagged in the natural scheme of things. This is what you night refer to as a borderline case. There will be those of your people who make the graduation, and those who don't.

This is not always the case with all planets. In some instances, all individuals are ready for the graduation that you now approach. In some unfortunate instances, none are ready. In your particular place, it is a combination of both instances. Therefore, do not be dismayed if your ideas are totally rejected by some, for this is to be expected. And this is the major reason that we cannot come among you, for it would be a direct violation of one of the laws of which I earlier spoke. Due to these conditions, it is necessary for those of you who would help us, who are on the surface of your planet, to help us. We request that you meditate. This is all that is necessary. This is all the help that we need, because if you meditate, then you will know what to do. And this is all the help that we need, or all the help that we would desire, for this is also part of the plan.

It has been a privilege to be with you this evening. I am Hatonn. I will leave you in His love and in His light. Adonai. Adonai vasu.

January 7, 1974

I am Hatonn. I greet you, my friends, in the love and the light of the infinite Creator. It is a very great privilege to be with you this evening. My brothers and I are here. We have been

Chapter 10: Complete Messages

here for many years. And we have given freely to your people that which we had to give, our knowledge of truth. Unfortunately, there has been too little dissemination. Most of your people are unaware of [our] contacts, and if they are aware of them, they have been misled. They do not understand what we have for them.

Your people are somewhat unique. We have visited other planets and made contacts such as this one, and we are listened to, for they recognize truth when they hear it. The people of your planet do not seem to recognize truth as easily as the other peoples of which I just spoke. The peoples of your planet are quite hypnotized by a false illusion created by themselves. At an earlier period in your history, many more of your people would have paid attention to our words, for they were, as you might say, more superstitious at that time.

It is only necessary that our words be made available to your people. Those who will recognize them as truth will do so. Those who cannot recognize them as truth will not. It is as simple as that. There is no need to impress this information any further upon your people than simply exposing them to it. This, however, has not been carried on in sufficient quantity. It is for this reason that we are now attempting to impress upon channels such as this one the need for greater dissemination of that information that we have to present to your people.

We of the Confederation of Planets are here, and have a job to do. We have been working diligently at this job for many of your years. We are aware of the problems that you face in attempting to make more of the people of your planet aware of our communications, but we assure you that we will aid you in doing this. As time progresses, more and more aid can be given.

You will have noticed that, in the past twenty years, attitudes have changed considerably. Things that were very difficult to

Chapter 10: Complete Messages

talk about with the general population are now relatively easy to talk about. Their acceptance of our presence is much greater than it was in the past. Your own expeditions into space, however slight, have aided greatly in the acceptance of your general public's attitudes a toward possibilities of extraterrestrial contact.

We of the Confederation of Planets in the Service of our Infinite Creator are here to contact you now. We must emphasize this: we are here to do this. This is our purpose. We must, however, make this contact very, very carefully, in a predetermined way. That is what is happening in this room at this instant. There can be no variation from this technique at this time. We have had many experiences in contacting peoples. It has always been found that it must be done with extreme caution. There are grave consequences when an alien society is impressed directly upon another society, especially when the technological separation is as vast as is ours.

Your people would not understand at all. They would not accept us for what we are. We could not walk among them and be accepted, and this is what we wish to do: be accepted. For, my friends, we are all exactly the same. We could not speak directly to your people and have them gain benefit from our teachings, for they would feel that they must accept, without question, what we say. This is of no benefit, my friends.

You are here, at this time, as we are where we are, primarily, to seek: to seek in our own way that which is the path back toward the Creator of us all. An interruption that is too great in this personal seeking is not a very good thing. For this reason, we are unable to contact your people directly. We must provide them, however, with that which they need. And this we are doing to the best of our ability. However, it is of extreme importance that those of you who are available to help us do so.

You will find that, at first, you may have considerable difficulty in doing this, because, as this instrument has stated, it is a tricky business. You must always remember that the individual must seek. If you provide information, then do it so that it is understandable, simple and in no way forced upon the recipient.

We of the Confederation of Planets in the Service of the Infinite Creator are always with you. We are constantly serving you. It is only necessary that you avail yourself to us and we will be there. In the future, in the very, very near future, you may expect much, much more support from us in a physical way, for time now grows very, very short. Reach out to your brothers in space, as we do to you.

I will leave you now. I am Hatonn. I leave you in the love and in the light of our infinite Creator. Adonai vasu.

I am Oxal. I greet you, my friends, in the love and the light of our infinite Creator. It is a great privilege to be with you. I and my brothers are here. This you have heard, and it is true. We are here, and we will remain here, until the entire program on your Earth is complete.

We are here for a special purpose. We are here to serve. Think of this. We are here to serve. This is important. As you now near the end of a master cycle, there will be changes in your physical world. These changes should not be feared. They should be welcomed. For they are signals to you that a new age is dawning. If you understand it and walk among your people unafraid, then you, too, will serve. For they will see in you an inner knowledge, which we will provide you. We will also serve you to the absolute limits of our ability.

There are cycles in time, and cycles in space, and all things operate in cycles. Your planet now approaches the end of a great, great cycle of time. This has been a learning time, an evolving time, a time of growing. And many of the people of your planet are now ready for a transition to a much more glorious existence.

But they will not understand this transition unless they are told. There have been many contacts speaking of this transition, but too few of your people are presently aware of what is shortly to take place. It will be necessary to provide them with the reasons for what they experience. It is only necessary that you avail yourself in meditation for you to be able to understand and therefore serve.

This is your call. This is why you are here, where you are.

We of the Confederation of Planets are aware of all of the problems which confront you, for we are in contact with you at all times. It is not an easy place to exist, your world. But pay it no attention, for it is not a lasting world. Everything that is happening and will happen is not really of any importance. It will shortly be gone. We speak of a lasting creation, an unchanging but infinite creation.

We will at all times serve you. This is our duty. If you will meditate and avail yourself to the truth, you will understand your true position, and you will know your duty. I am Oxal. I will leave you now. I leave you in the love and the light of our infinite Creator. Adonai vasu borragus.

January 12, 1974
I am Hatonn. I greet you, my friends, in the love and in the light of our infinite Creator. I am with this instrument. It is a great privilege to be with you this evening. I am at this time in a craft high above your house. You could not see me if you looked, for I am much too high. I am aware of your eagerness to meet with us. We will attempt to arrange this at some time in the future, but for now you must be patient, for we cannot at this time greet you openly.

We are sorry that this is the situation. It is at this time impossible. But in the relatively near future, we will be glad to

Chapter 10: Complete Messages

greet you directly. We of the Confederation of Planets in the Service of the Infinite Creator are waiting to meet as many of the people of your planet as would wish to meet us.

The reaction of the people of your planet is quite varied as to their realization of our presence. Some of them are convinced that we are here now. Some of them do not believe in us at all. That is exactly the condition for which we have strived. It is a condition which will produce a maximum effort on the part of the individual to seek--to seek the truth of our existence, or of our nonexistence. This seeking will lead him upon other ideas. These ideas have been presented in many forms in your literature in the past many hundreds of years. In his seeking he will, if things are correctly progressing, discover certain truths that have been available throughout all time. He will also, if he is fortunate, come in contact with some of the material that we make available through channels such as this one to the peoples of your planet.

This condition of questioning, seeking and thinking about things is precisely the condition that we have attempted to generate by our rather nebulous contact. It is always much more satisfactory if the individual finds out something by his own efforts than it is if he is taught a principle. The mental activity required for the individual to seek out and find the basic truths of the creation allows him time to reflect and examine with his own point of view each one of the propositions offered to him. This results in an understanding of the propositions that surpasses any understanding that he could achieve if these propositions were made to him in a relatively short period of time. This, of course, would have been necessary if we had landed upon your surface and directly communicated with the people of your planet.

The ways of the Confederation in establishing contact with a planet that has no knowledge of their presence, or the galactic Confederation, or any of our peoples, is now quite

Chapter 10: Complete Messages

standardized. For this reason, we have chosen to limit our contacts severely. There is, however, only a certain amount of time available to make and establish a contact which will disseminate to as many of your people as possible the truth of this infinite creation, and the true workings of man in it.

We will, therefore, be much more in evidence in your skies in the very near future. As I have stated earlier, many, many more of your people are ready for the truth that we bring than were ready a few years ago. We therefore increase our activity in hopes that it will increase the seeking of individuals in an attempt to understand us. We must emphasize that this understanding can come only through an effort put forth by the individual to do so. Without this, there will be very little progress in his development of understanding.

I hope that I have been of some service in helping each of you to understand our purpose and motives with respect to our relatively unusual form of contacting the people of your planet. It has been a great privilege to give you these thoughts, and we are in hopes that it will aid you in understanding the importance of your own seeking, for this, my friends, is a great truth: that it is necessary to seek in order to find. It is necessary to seek, my friends, in order to grow. Do not be neglectful of your personal seeking. It is the most important thing that you do.

I hope that I have been of service. I will leave you now, and will allow this instrument to be used for contact by one of my brothers. I am Hatonn. Adonai vasu.

(Pause)

I am Latui. I am with this instrument. I greet you, my friends, in the love and the light of our infinite Creator. It is a very great privilege to be with you, my friends, for I have not been with you before. I have been with this instrument before but

Chapter 10: Complete Messages

not with you, in the sense that I have not spoken with you. We of course cannot be separated in our totality.

I am Latui. We of the Confederation of Planets in the Service of the Infinite Creator are always privileged to speak with the people of your planet. We are sorry that we have to use this method, but the reason for this method has been adequately explained by my brother. I will, therefore, continue using this instrument to give you certain thoughts, which I truly hope will help you in your seeking.

This planet, my friends, is a ball in space. It is a ball of light. But it does not appear to you as what it really is. The reason, my friends, that it is a ball of light is that all things in the entire creation are comprised of nothing but light. This is the basic building block of all of the material creation. When we greet you in His love and His light, we greet you in the only existing ingredients of the creation: love, the formative force, and light, the building block.

I am aware that it is difficult for you to conceive of light as matter, but this, my friends, is the actual situation. Light is one of the two things that we always mention at the beginning of a contact. There is a good reason for this. There is a good reason for us to greet you in His love and His light. The reason is that this encompasses everything. And that is what we wish to do: include within this greeting everything and everyone in the creation. For, as we have told you, it is true that all of these parts are one single thing.

Imagine, if you can, an infinitely large sphere of pure light. Impressed upon this is absolute love. Out of this, then, condenses the unimaginably vast number of created parts, each of these parts connected by this original force, the love of our infinite Creator. Each of us, my friends, and everything else is made up of this single fabric: light.

Chapter 10: Complete Messages

It is only necessary to learn the truth of what I say in its totality to be able to return to that place and stature that was designed for you by the Creator.

Light, my friends, is the substance of which you are made. Light is the substance of which I am made. Light is the substance of which everything is made. Love is the substance which forms light into the forms that you know as living beings, as planets, as trees, as stars, as air. It is all one substance. This substance, my friends, can be affected only by love.

Love, my friends, is not what you think it is. The word in your language has a meaning that has various interpretations. But it is none of these things. We use the word when we speak to you, because it is as close as we can come to the concept, using your language. Love, my friends, is that force which does all of the things that are done in the entire creation. All of the things, my friends, even those that you would interpret as being without love. If it were not for that love, my friends, then the freedom of choice to do these things would not exist. It is only necessary that the individual realize the truth of what I am saying in order to be able to do those things that he was originally intended to be able to do by the Creator of us all.

The things that he was intended to be able to do are quite surprising. They extend so far beyond your present limitations that I could not possibly convey to you the scope and magnitude of these abilities. However, it is possible, let me assure you, through proper methods of advancing your understanding with respect to its present limitations, to regain what is rightfully yours: the knowledge that you have buried within you, the knowledge of the use of our Creator's light through love.

It is very, very important, my friends, that you seek an understanding of love. Do not be satisfied with your first

Chapter 10: Complete Messages

interpretation of this concept, for it is much, much broader in scope than you might imagine. It covers everything that there is.

I am going to instruct the people of your planet in the use of love. This will be done in an unusual way, but please bear with me. We have found that it is necessary to do things in unusual ways, as far as you are concerned. It is necessary to teach to you a way of thinking that is not common to the people of your planet, if you are rapidly to gain understanding of the concepts that are of utmost importance in your present progression.

There are three ways to achieve a knowledge of love. The first way is to relax, and let your mind become at rest. This is the method of meditation. If this is done on a daily basis, then it is not possible to shut out the love that is ever-present. You will become aware of the true creation and its meaning.

The second way is to go forth among the people of your planet and serve them. They will return to you love, and you will absorb this love and store it within your being. I must at this time caution that this service to your people must be done in such a way that it is a service that they wish. Do not make a mistake, as so many of your people have done, in trying to impress an unwanted or unsolicited service upon your neighbor. To go forth and to serve your fellow man at this time upon your planet requires much care and planning, for it is at this time rather difficult to accomplish. For interpretations of service vary greatly, and it is necessary that you understand what service is in order for you to be effective. This can only be done by following the first step, or plan, which is meditation.

The third technique is to give all that you have to your fellow man. If this is done, then you will not be encumbered by material possessions. You will no longer give part of your love to material possessions. Giving love to material possessions is

Chapter 10: Complete Messages

an extreme waste of your abilities. This is a mistake that is made by most of the people of this planet. It is necessary, if one is to attempt this method of gaining love, to divorce oneself from the desire for material things.

Each one of these three avenues may be used. Each one will produce results. At present, it is very difficult to work and live within a society such as yours and to follow each of these programs for knowing love. It is therefore suggested by those of us of the Confederation of Planets in His Service that you employ the first method. Meditation, my friends, will allow you to decide to what extent you may employ the other two methods. For it is sometimes impractical to attempt to follow these two suggestions literally, in that those whom you attempt to serve will not understand. It is, however, recommended that you keep each of these methods in mind, for they are all important.

Much of the strife that has occurred upon your planet in its history is due to the attachment of the people of this planet to material possessions. They have a false concept, which is the concept of ownership of possessions. Everything is made of light. All of these possessions, everything that exists, is the property of our Creator. He provided ample materials for all people in all space. It is not necessary to covet any of these materials, for all of them are part of you.

At present, there is much strife upon your planet. There is much coveting of properties, but this is of no avail to those who covet these properties, for even though they may acquire these properties, as they think, their apparent possession is very, very short-lived.

I am Latui. I hope that I have been of service. Adonai vasu.

(Pause)

I am Oxal. I am with this instrument. I greet you, my friends, in the love and in the light of our infinite Creator. It is a privilege to speak with you, my friends. I am at present in a craft which is very high in your sky. It is several hundred of your miles high. I am, as you say, one of those who dwells within a flying saucer. I am trying to impress upon you this fact for a definite reason, so please bear with me.

I, Oxal, of the Confederation of Planets in the Service of the Infinite Creator, have for many of your years lived in a craft that orbits your planet. This has been my service and my duty. I am attempting to give to the people of your planet something that they need more than any other thing. I am attempting to give them love.

This is not an easy thing to do on your planet. What do you think would be the reaction if I met, on the street, a group of your people and told them this? I am afraid that it would be not at all effective. To give your people love is quite a problem. All of us in the Confederation are attempting to do this. Your people just do not seem to want our love. Oh, yes, some people are accepting us, but the vast majority is not interested in accepting our love. They are interested in us, but not in our love. What can we do to remedy this situation? What can we do to arouse within the people of your planet a desire to receive our love? Why is it necessary to bring to your people this love?

My friends, it has just been explained to you: this is what you need. This is the only thing that you need. The Creator has amply provided everything for you. We are just simply trying to redistribute the love that He originally planned for you, and that many of your people have rejected.

It is a long and difficult task, but we will be successful, for we will not tolerate a lack of diligence for ourselves. We will continue to bring to you the Creator's love. When you are fully able to accept this, then and only then can we land and contact the people of this planet in general. It is a very simple thing, and could have been accomplished in a few minutes' time, if your people would simply accept this love. However, as you know, this is extremely improbable.

We must accelerate our program of bringing this to the people of this planet. There will be a greater attempt in the future to arouse those who would wish to know of our purpose. So please bear with us, as we continue in our efforts to bring to you the only gift that is possible, for there is nothing else of value to give.

I am Oxal. I am going to leave you at this time. I leave you in the love and in the light of our infinite Creator. Adonai vasu.

January 15, 1974
I am Hatonn. I am with this instrument. I greet you, my friends, in the love and the light of our infinite Creator. It is again a great privilege to be with you. I and my brothers are here. I have said this to you before. This is truth. We are here.

We are here to serve you. We will be here to serve you. We have been here to serve you. We are here to serve all of the people who wish our service. We cannot presume that our service is of value to all people in all places. Therefore, we can only offer what we have. You must accept or reject. Sometimes, you wonder why we give you what you might consider to be relatively elementary material, or material that is repeated. We do this because this is what is needed. In actuality, this is all that is needed. It is only necessary to learn to think in the original way planned by the Creator of us all to benefit totally from all of His gifts. This is why we would prefer to continue speaking in what you might consider to be relatively elementary or simple terms.

My friends, truth is very, very simple. The Creator's plan is very, very simple. It is not necessary that we weave a complex web of circumstance to lead you to the Creator. He is within you, and you are He. It is only necessary that you realize this in its fullest sense for you to be aware of all of the Creator's wisdom. The people of this planet have blocked their minds from this knowledge. We are attempting to teach the people of this planet how to remove this blockage.

It is a very simple process. Unfortunately, the people of this planet are more accustomed to complexity, and would therefore desire intellectual juggling of various propositions and theories. This, my friends, is not necessary. To get from where you are to where you should be requires an understanding that has nothing to do with the intellect. It requires, simply, a knowing of truth.

This truth is extremely simple. What I am trying to say is that when you become totally aware of this simple truth, then you will not use intellectual processes to understand anything that you wish to know. This knowledge will be yours, for all knowledge is linked in the Creator's universe. There is no separation. This separation occurs only when man desires it, through use of the freedom of choice that has been given him by his Creator.

Return, therefore, to the Creator. Return to the knowledge and the wisdom and the power that is yours. Do this by giving forth only His light and His love. This is what was intended. Acting and knowing otherwise results only in the isolation and blockage to which I referred.

Consider very carefully these simple teachings that I offer to you, for these simple teachings are all that are required. There is nothing of a complex nature that is needed. We will continue in a program designed to bring the thinking of the people of this planet back to that which they desire. Those that avail themselves of these teachings will benefit greatly, I assure you.

I hope that I have been able to clarify certain things. It has been a great privilege to speak with you. Adonai vasu.

(A question concerning personal business decisions is asked.)

Chapter 10: Complete Messages

I am Hatonn. I am with this instrument and I am using control. It is a great privilege to have a question asked. I shall answer it in the love and the light of our infinite Creator. It is a very great privilege, and we welcome all questions. I am afraid, however, that it is impossible for us to interfere in the plans of the people of your planet. This is our policy. We would request that questions involving your understanding of the nature of truth be asked, for it is impossible for us to do anything to change what will occur upon your surface at this time. Each time we do anything, each time we are seen, each time something is written about us in your periodicals, anything that we do to cause your people to change their attitudes, is an infringement. We are attempting to balance our service so that the infringement that does occur will be at least balanced by the good that is created.

This is why we can only accelerate our help for our teachings for the awareness of your people as they desire it.

I hope that I have answered to your satisfaction. I will gladly give to this instrument all that I can with respect to answers to questions that you might bring to me. But questions involving changes of your activities, especially of a physical nature, are completely beyond that that we desire to do. Please allow me to apologize for my lack of ability to act in this area, but this has been agreed upon by those of us in the service of the Confederation of Planets in the Service of the Infinite Creator. I am Hatonn.

(Pause)

I am Latui. I greet you, my friends, in the love and the light of our infinite Creator. It is a great privilege to be with you this evening. I am Latui. I have not been with you except for one previous time. It is a great privilege to speak with you. This instrument is not as familiar with my contact as he is with some others. Therefore, please bear with us.

Chapter 10: Complete Messages

My friends, I am what you call a space man. But so are you. For where do you dwell but in space? From our point of view, you are as much in space as are we. The only difference is that you are limited in your ability to travel to different points in space: you are at one place in space at this particular time.

Therefore, you are also a space man. You see, my friends, there is very little difference between yourselves and us. Our system of transportation is simply a little more refined. We enjoy certain other abilities which are much more useful than a simple conveyances. They are available to all men in all places. All men are in space. They are all space men. For what you call space is infinite, and surrounds all of the creation.

We are no different. We are just slightly separated, not by distances, my friends, but by thinking. You have learned to think in a way that isolates you. It is not necessary that you remain in isolation. To do this, it is only necessary that you think in a slightly different manner.

It is not a difficult thing to do. It is a simple thing to do. Do not use the intellectual processes that you have used in the past. Learn totally to rebuke arriving at conclusions in what you consider a logical manner, for these conclusions will be based on suppositions that are made with very weak fabric, the fabric of the creation of man of Earth. If you wish an answer to any question, it is only necessary to base your knowledge on truth. This you can do through meditation. It is always available. It is not necessary to make a complex analysis.

There is a correct solution for every problem. Analyses based on the false fabric of your material world are short-lived, and the intellectual process that is so prevalent among the peoples of your planet is invariably based upon this falsity. It has been stated: Know the truth, and the truth shall make you free.

Free from what? Free from many things, my friends. Free from many, many things. For cutting yourselves off from truth begins to put more and more limitations upon you. It is a difficult thing to relay to you, because you have been accustomed to another way of thinking. You have been accustomed to the proposition of cause and effect.

The cause, my friends, is the Creator. The effect is love. This is all that there is. This is the simplicity of the truth. Hear my words and understand them. Man was created with this truth within him. It is available to all men throughout all time. It is available through meditation.

It is not necessary to try to understand in an intellectual way. It is only necessary to know. It is stated that you should know the truth, to be free. The word that is used is "know." Know what the truth is, my friends. Know it. Meditation will provide this knowledge.

I will leave you now. I am Latui. Adonai vasu borragus.

January 21, 1974
I am Hatonn. I greet you, my friends, in the love and in the light of our infinite Creator. It is a great privilege to be with you again this evening. It is always a very great privilege to speak.

We of the Confederation of Planets in the Service of the Infinite Creator are here for the purpose of speaking with you and giving you directly our thoughts as you meditate. These thoughts are yours to accept or reject. They are constantly available to you. It is only necessary that you desire them, if you wish them. This is our service to people of the planet Earth at this time. This is not our only service, but it is our most important service.

Why are your people at this time not very interested in these thoughts? We have said, time and time again, that thoughts of this nature are what the people of this planet need. And yet they show very little interest. This puzzled us at first, until we became more familiar with the reasons for the thinking of the

Chapter 10: Complete Messages

population of this planet in general. We are now aware of some of the problems involved in bringing truth and understanding to a people so very long in the darkness that has been generated by those that have gone before them in the history of this planet.

It is a very difficult thing to change thousands of years of erroneous thinking in a very short time. It is something that we will not be totally successful in doing. However we will be, and we have been, partially successful in bringing certain information to those who would desire it. This is the key, my friends: desire. If the individual does not desire what we have to bring to him, then he will not receive it. This is exactly how the creation is designed, so that each entity, no matter where he is or who he is or what he is, will get exactly what he desires.

Unfortunately, in some places, certain actions of one entity with respect to another cause an infringement that was never designed by our Creator. This results in a discrepancy in the plan of the creation, and creates unfortunate situations, as it has upon your planet. It is necessary for man on Planet Earth to realize this, and individually to correct his understanding of himself, in order to bring himself back into alignment with the plan and design of our Creator.

Each individual must make up his mind, and he must do it now. He must decide whether he is going to attempt to understand and to serve in the light of the infinite, or whether he is going to seek for himself, and follow a pathway that has been laid down for him by man on Earth, rather than that provided by the Creator of us all.

It is very necessary that the people of this planet at this time be made aware of the plan and the design of their Creator. Without this awareness, they may continue in their erroneous and unintelligent ways of acting. Each individual will interpret information given to him in a slightly different way, if it is of an intellectual nature. Some individuals will not be able to interpret information of this type at all.

This is why it is so necessary that man of Earth at this time meditate and go within. For that which he obtains in this fashion will be information which is not of an intellectual nature. It will be the truth, the understanding, of the original creation. Within every individual in the universe is this knowledge. It is only necessary to seek it out through meditation. If this is done, there will be no question in the mind of the individual. There will be no need for interpretation of information, for this is not of an intellectual nature.

Man on Earth considers that he has many problems. But these problems are not reality. They are an illusion, developed by his thinking. Nothing in this universe follows the laws man on Earth considers the laws of the generation of events. I have stated before that the only cause is the Creator. Man on Earth interprets cause and effect in a very illusory manner. This is not the way that the creation is designed; it is not the way the Creation works. It is only necessary that an individual give forth love and light. If this is done, this is what will be returned to him. It is not necessary to consider complex propositions and plans in order to reach an objective that is assumed to be of great benefit. It is only necessary that you generate the love that is amply provided by the Creator of us all.

This is how we were meant to live. Man on Earth has forgotten this very simple principle. He believed that he can generate, through plans and activities, great pleasure that will come to him as a result of these plans and activities. And then he goes forth and does these things in great complexity. And very seldom does he glory in their product. But he does not learn. For he does not meditate. For within him is the truth, the truth of the pathway to the ecstasy that awaits him. It is not a complex pathway. It is not a product of his intellect, of or of his ability to act in the physical, producing great changes in the many things that he desired for his pleasure.

The pathway, my friends, is simply love, a total and universal love, expressed for all things and all peoples and demonstrated daily in his activities and thoughts. And then, my friends, everything is returned. And this love that he generates is reflected to him a thousand-fold. For this is the plan. This is the design. This is the gift of the Father. It is so very simple. For the Father is very simple. He did not mean for his children to find it necessary to generate complexities in order to achieve the state of ecstasy that he designed for them.

It is only man on this planet that has become confused, and drifted away from this knowledge. This knowledge is deep within you. It is part of you. It is part of everything that exists. Seek this knowledge within yourself. And then, go forth in your daily activities, demonstrating to your fellow man this knowledge, and it will be reflected one thousand-fold.

It has been a very great privilege to be with you this evening, and I hope that I have been able to give to you some understanding of that which man on planet Earth so badly wants and needs, an understanding of the principle of love. I am Hatonn. Adonai vasu.

January 26, 1974
I am Laitos. I greet you in the love and in the light of our infinite Creator. I will condition each of you. I will speak through the instrument known as R.

(R channeling)

I am Laitos. I would speak to you at this time regarding your personal daily meditations. This is becoming increasingly necessary as we near the coming events upon your planet. I will be with you upon request, for this is our purpose: to

Chapter 10: Complete Messages

serve. There is some difficulty with this channel's receiving my thoughts.

(Pause)

(Unknown channeling)

I am again with this instrument. I am sorry for the difficulty, but it will be remedied.

Please bear with me.

(Pause)

(R channeling)

I am again with this channel. Your daily meditation is necessary in order that the veil might be lifted, and all things which you have been promised will be shown. This higher vibration will enable you to perform such things as healing with little difficulty. Again there is some difficulty with this channel.

(Don channeling)

I am Hatonn. I am with this instrument. I am Hatonn. I greet you, my friends, in the love and the light of the infinite Creator. It is a great privilege to be with you this evening. We are very happy to see that one more channel is being developed. My brother Laitos will continue to work with the one called R until he receives our thoughts as clearly as this channel. It is actually a very simple process, and requires only that you continue in your meditation, availing yourself of our contact.

We of the Confederation of Planets in the Service of the Infinite Creator are experienced with this form of communication, and we can say at this time that each of you in this room will be able to receive our thoughts with little difficulty in the near future.

Chapter 10: Complete Messages

I would like to speak with you today about a subject that concerns your very near future. I would first like to speak to you about the definition of this term, "future." You see the future as something that will come to you. We see the future as an event that is presently here. This is a difficult thing to translate into your language, but I will attempt to give you an understanding of what you know as time.

Time, my friends, is an illusion. The creation is, in fact, timeless. You are at a particular point in the evolution of the creation. There seems to be a progression of time. But there is actually a continuing stream of consciousness. It is only necessary to displace yourself along this stream of consciousness to be at any point along the stream that you call time.

In other words, it is possible to move through time as you understand movement through space. Each of these concepts is as real as the other. We have stated to you previously that there is one place and there is one time. This place and this time are the creation. We are able to move through space. We are also able to move through time. For in actuality, these things are the same thing: they are the creation.

The illusion that is now impressed upon you because of your limitations in a physical condition, as you call it, are limitations that are not at all ordinary. They are limitations that are impressed upon those who desire them for certain experiences. Each individual in this creation is able to select precisely what he desires. This is exactly the plan of the Creator. He not only gave man free will, but he also gave man the ability to select exactly what he desired. There are many, many paths to take through this creation, in actuality an infinite number, and the choice is always left up to the individual.

Some of those who have explored have explored in a direction that led them away from the all-knowing One, the all-loving

Chapter 10: Complete Messages

One, the Creator. In wandering away, there were conditions encountered that were at that time desired by the individual who was wandering. But as he wandered farther and farther, he became more and more immersed in an illusion that he created. This illusion is at present so very strong that many of the children of the Creator find themselves confused and unable easily to find the pathway back to the infinite Light.

It is necessary that they realize for themselves how to do this, for the principle given to them by their Creator is still totally in effect. It allows them to do precisely what they desire. It is therefore necessary that they realize for themselves what they desire, and then it is necessary that they seek this realization. In order to do this, it is necessary that they become aware of the techniques of bringing about this understanding. This is our purpose at the present time: to help those who are presently seeking the pathway that will return them to the love and the light that they now desire. It is necessary for us to help those who desire this, in order to act within the plan of the creation. It is necessary also that we do not disturb those who do not overly desire at this time such activity.

For this reason, we are somewhat limited in our abilities to reach out to the people of this planet at this time. It is possible for you to eliminate certain conditions that you are now experiencing, and it is possible for us to help you do this. We are acquainted with certain aspects of what you would call the future, because of an ability to move not only in space, but in time. However, due to the action of the freedom of desire that was given to each of the Creator's children, it is possible for them to cause alterations in the stream of consciousness, and therefore, as events change due to these desires in what you know as the present, so do they change in what you know as the future.

Therefore it is not possible to travel through time in exactly the same sense that you travel in space, for it has properties that are dependent on the action of free will, just as special properties are dependent upon this action. Time and space are in many ways very similar in their properties, and we are aware of the nature of action not only in space but also in time. We would attempt to give you aid in understanding how to free yourself from the illusion of being trapped in a continuous and unchanging stream of time, for this is an illusion: an illusion that has been sought by a large number of individuals.

It is difficult to relay to you these concepts, for they are not at all familiar within the illusion that you now enjoy. I have spoken of this at this time to give you some clue to the problem of living as you do. The illusion is so strong that you become accustomed to understanding events in a way that is not at all real. You become accustomed to a relationship between the illusion of past, present and future that is not actually real.

Many of your people have in the past traveled in the dimension of time. Many are experiencing this dimension now in what you know as dreams. We who are aware of the possibility of traveling in both space and time find that an additional understanding allows for an instantaneous or immediate transportation from one portion of the creation to any other. This is how you were created: with total freedom.

I am going to leave you at this time, and allow another of my brothers to speak using either instrument. I hope that I have been of some service in attempting to bring to you some understanding of a subject that is quite difficult for you at this time to realize. I am Hatonn. I leave you in the love and light of our infinite Creator. Adonai vasu.

(Pause)

(Don channeling)

Chapter 10: Complete Messages

I am Hatonn. I am with this instrument. I greet you once more, my friends, in the love and the light of our infinite Creator. It is a privilege to speak with you once more. My brother Laitos was attempting to use the instrument known as R. However, there were certain difficulties.

I am going to speak with you at this time on another subject. I am at this time in a craft that is high above your planet. You may ask why we utilize craft, if we are able to travel through space and time. My friends, there are many things to be experienced in this creation. There are things of different natures, and we, as you, enjoy experiences of different natures.

We are able to move in space, as do you, using craft. We are able to move in time, as I have just spoken to you, using nothing but our understanding. Both of these concepts or realms were meant to be utilized by the children of the Father. This is why there are so many of our craft near your planet at this time. It is possible to get here from elsewhere by moving through that dimension you know as time. This is why we state that there is only one place, and that is the creation. For you may move from one place in the creation to any other place using the dimension you know as time. In actuality, you are in the same place. Also, in actuality, you are in two different places. It depends upon your awareness.

There is much about this creation about which the people of your planet are not aware. I have stated that the principles are extremely simple. Everything is provided for the individual. All knowledge is yours. It is only necessary that you seek it out within you. Everything that we do is within the abilities of everyone else. All of the people of your planet are also able to do all of these things. It is only necessary that they return to an awareness of these abilities. This awareness is an awareness of the love and understanding with which they were originally created. This is the only thing that blocks them from their abilities and their knowledge.

It is recommended, therefore, that through meditation it is possible to regain this knowledge and these abilities. For this reason, we continually impress upon you the need for meditation, and the need for understanding your fellow man. For only through this process can you return to your rightful position.

The people of your planet are not aware of the simplicity of this process. If they could learn how very simple it is, and not forget this, then they would not any longer have the difficulties that they experience. I must be very emphatic about this: that the entire process is of an extremely simple nature. It is only necessary that the individual realize that he is a part of the creation, and that the creation is one single thing, and that in so being, he and all of his brothers and sisters throughout all space are one being. This realization will result in an ability to demonstrate only one reaction to anything. That reaction will be love.

It is extremely simple. First it is necessary to realize your relationship with everything that exists. It is then impossible to realize anything but love. This is the realization of the Creator. This is the principle upon which everything was created. It is that orientation of mind that is necessary to know all knowledge and to demonstrate all of the things that were intended for you to demonstrate through the expression of the Creator's love.

Do these simple things. Do not sway from this understanding and this love. Do this and only this, and you will reach a state of ecstasy that is enjoyed by all of those of the Creator's children that are living in His light.

I cannot overemphasize this simple truth. It is easy for an individual to forget this truth in his daily activities, especially in an environment such as the one you experience at this time. However, it is possible to overcome the illusions that are impressed upon you by your present environment. And when this is done, you will know and feel the intense love of the Creator, and then you will know that you have found the pathway that leads to Him.

This has been stated to you many, many times. This has been given to the people of this planet by many, many teachers. It has been stated in many, many ways. And yet it is so easily forgotten! Do not forget this. It is what you desire. We are in a position to know what you desire. If you did not desire this, we could not tell you this. We could not say to you that you should do these things, for this would be against the will of the Creator.

Remember these simple teachings. Remember them throughout each instant of your daily activities and express the principle of love. This is all that is necessary. This can be done if you remain constantly aware of the need for doing it. In order to remain aware of this need, it is necessary to meditate. Do this, and join us in the kingdom of heaven, for this was what was meant for you. This is your destiny. It is what you desire.

There is a strong illusion, which is in a way a test of your abilities, and this test was designed by you. For you are always the recipient of that which you desire. Do not falter and do not reject that which you desire. Remain aware of your true desire. And express it through love.

I hope that I have been of some assistance in reminding you of that which each of you is seeking. I will leave this instrument at this time. I am Hatonn. Adonai vasu.

February 3, 1974
I am Hatonn. I greet you, my friends, in the love and the light of our infinite Creator. It is once more a great privilege to be with you.

I am aware of the subject of which you have requested that I speak tonight. We of the Confederation of Planets in the

Chapter 10: Complete Messages

Service of the Infinite Creator are always available to you for information and guidance on subjects of this and other natures. It is a great privilege to be of service in attempting to give you our viewpoints. We hope that these viewpoints will be of benefit in your understanding of the truth that is in you.

This is where we obtain the answer to questions such as the one you have asked. It is possible for you, like us, to find these answers directly, for they are within you, as they are within everyone. However, we realize that conditions on your planet sometimes make it difficult readily to accomplish this understanding of the truth that is abundant for all of us.

For this reason we endeavor to use instruments such as this one to help in guiding you so that you may, using the information that we present, find similar truths within your own consciousness. For these truths are the ones that are of great value. We only hope to remind you that you have these within you. We only hope to help guide you to a remembrance of what you seek.

There is no necessity to establish within one's thinking an appreciation of self. For this presupposes that it is possible to separate self from the entire creation. If one appreciates any part of the creation, then one appreciates self, for they are one and the same thing. The elimination of the concept of self is an important one in your spiritual seeking. It is necessary only to appreciate the Creator and His product, the creation. In appreciating any part of the creation, one must appreciate all parts, for they are inseparable.

It is therefore important to act in unison with the creation rather than out of harmony due to a lack of confidence in a state of oneness. It is possible to achieve this understanding of oneness with all by availing yourself of this knowledge and understanding through the process of daily meditation.

We of the Confederation of Planets in the Service of the Infinite Creator extend our hand to the people of this planet.

It is not necessary that we appreciate ourselves in our attempts to serve. It is only necessary that we serve. This will be appreciated by the Creator. For, my friends, the Creator is all that there is. It is as impossible to separate the Creator from the creation as it is impossible to separate yourself from the creation.

Appreciate, then, this unity. Appreciate your oneness with the Creator and the creation. If this is done, then other objectives will be of very little value. For this is what the Creator meant for all of the parts of the creation to do: to act in such a way as to serve. He did not specify this service, and he did not demand it. He simply provided the opportunity.

It is not necessary that you seek out opportunities to serve. It is only necessary that you serve as best you can as the opportunities present themselves. It is impossible to serve if one is not knowledgeable as to how to serve, and it is not possible in your particular state of awareness to know how to serve unless this knowledge is sought through daily meditation.

The process, therefore, is quite simple. It is only necessary that an individual become aware of how to serve through meditation. It is then only necessary that he serve as the opportunities for service present themselves. If these simple tasks are performed, he is fulfilling all of the requirements that were specified by our Creator.

I hope that I have been of service tonight. I hope that I have been able to act as the opportunity presented itself. I am Hatonn. I leave you in the love and in the light of our infinite Creator. Adonai vasu.

(Pause)

(Don channeling)

I am Hatonn. I am again with this instrument. I greet you once more in the love and the light of our infinite Creator. It is always a very great privilege to be with you. Do not hesitate to call on me and my brothers for service, for this is why we are here. We are here to serve you. This is our only purpose.

In the fields of your planet grow many things that are edible. These things are given you by your Creator. They are given to you to sustain life in your present physical form. There is much wisdom in this arrangement. It is necessary for you, if you are to exist in a physical way as you know it, to sustain the body with food. However, the food that you select is up to you. There are some things in your environment that are impossible to eat. There is a very large variety of things that can be eaten, however. What is eaten is up to the individual. Selections may be made dependent upon his desire. The Creator provided for the fulfillment of desire. And it was his plan that each individual should have exactly what he would desire.

We have said to you that it is necessary to meditate in order to understand. This understanding includes the understanding of desire.

I hope that I have been of service. It is only possible for me to say that with an understanding achieved through daily meditation. It is possible to understand desire fully. I will leave this instrument at this time. I am Hatonn. Adonai vasu.

Unknown date in 1974

(Editor's note: this is apparently a channeling session that was never saved in our archives, as I can find no matching session there. We lost several channeling sessions because of our habit, when we first began recording sessions of channeling, of re-using tapes once the transcription of the original text was done. Therefore this is the only version of this particular session which is extant.)

Chapter 10: Complete Messages

I am Hatonn. I am with this instrument. I greet you, my friends, in the love and in the light of our infinite Creator. It is once more a great privilege to be with you.

I am aware that it is difficult to understand each nuance in this program of self-development. However, there will be an attempt made to clarify several points.

We of the Confederation of Planets in the Service of the Infinite Creator are just that: in the service of the infinite Creator. The service that we perform now in helping others to understand how to go about their seeking is the most important aspect of our service.

I am aware that there will be some difficulties communicating certain concepts when we are limited to a language that was not formed from these concepts. However, it is possible to communicate, using your language, much of what you would desire to know.

There are many ways and many paths to ultimate truth and understanding. We have said many times that meditation is the most important of these paths, and this is true. However, it is sometimes helpful to have direct communication in an intellectual sense for use in augmenting the awareness that you achieve through meditation. There are several points that I can cover at this time regarding the development of spirit.

The first of these is the development of spirit through self-knowledge. This is of extreme importance, and can be done in an intellectual way in addition to gaining this knowledge through meditation. Each thought that you have, and each reaction that you experience as a result of an action in your daily experience is important.

If an individual is to make rapid progress in his spiritual seeking, it is important that he analyze each of his thoughts and each of his reactions to experience. There is a test that may be given to each thought that you have. There have been

Chapter 10: Complete Messages

many teachers upon this planet. The one whose works are best known to you at this time is the teacher known to you as Jesus. This man demonstrated a way of thinking that is necessary if one is to evolve to the desired state of spiritual evolution.

The demonstration for the people of this planet made by this teacher was meant to be used by each of them. It may be used by yourself as a guide to understanding your thinking. If you will maintain an awareness of your thoughts, and then compare each of your thoughts to your understanding of the way that the man called Jesus thought, you will then make great progress in developing your thinking toward the state that you desire. If you experience a reaction in your thinking as a result of any activity during your daily involvement with the people of this planet, then you should compare this with the understanding of the one known to you as Jesus.

In this way, it is possible for you to eliminate thoughts that you do not desire to generate. It is possible for you to eliminate reactions of thinking that you do not desire to have. This was his service: to present an example of thinking so that those who might desire to follow this example could do so simply by comparing their thinking with his.

This has not been done by many of the people of this planet. But his teachings are nonetheless valuable, for the demonstration that he performed was a demonstration of truth; the simple truth that there is one governing force. That governing force is love.

Use this man's example of thinking in order to evaluate your own. It is simplicity itself, and was provided for this purpose. Do this with every thought. Maintain a constant awareness of this, and you shall truly make rapid progress towards the goal that you desire. This progress will be quite obvious to you.

There are additional techniques for increasing your spiritual awareness. I have given to you the first, and possibly the

Chapter 10: Complete Messages

easiest, and possibly the most important at this time. It is up to you to put it into use.

We of the Confederation of Planets in the Service of the Infinite Creator can suggest how your desires may be fulfilled. However, it is always up to the individual to implement this activity, and reach the goal that he has chosen.

I shall now speak of another way that you may use in order to achieve that which you desire. This is the production of the condition of awareness of reality. This is done by availing yourself to truth through meditation, and then observing the creation that is reality. You at this time are experiencing two separate creations. [You are experiencing] the creation of the Father, the original creation which is all about you. You are also experiencing the creation of man on Earth, which is camouflaging, to some extent, the creation of the Father. This camouflage is extremely effective for many of the peoples of this planet. However, it is possible to see through it, and identify the creation that is the original creation.

It is very helpful to become aware of this true creation. It consists of all of those things that you experience in your existence that are not creations of man on Earth. If you will maintain an awareness of the original creation as you experience it in your daily activities, and remove from your thinking the consequences and effect of the creations of man on Earth, all of his creations, both of a mental and a physical nature, you will, through this awareness of the natural or original creation, become at one, as you really are, with it. For then, instead of being misled by that which disguises it, you will recognize the creation as it is and always will be.

Man on this planet has become intensely involved in creations of his own, both physical creations and creations of the conceptual sense. These occupy his thinking to such an extent that he has lost an awareness of the creation of the Father.

Chapter 10: Complete Messages

It is helpful to return to the awareness of this original creation if one desires to increase his spiritual awareness.

There is one more way that I will discuss at this time for achieving that goal which you seek. This way is also very simple. It is the way of service. The man known to you as Jesus set an example, as did many other teachers who have lived upon this planet. This example included not only a demonstration of love by his actions and thinking, but also a service, given freely to his fellow man.

Service is possible in many forms. It is up to the individual to select his form of service. Each individual may serve. In order to do this, it is suggested that he meditate, for he has within him the knowledge of how to go about the service that he desires to perform. Each individual has this within him.

We of the Confederation of Planets in the Service of the Infinite Creator identify ourselves as being in the service of the infinite Creator. For that is our mission, to serve in His love and in His light. It is possible for you who dwell upon the surface of this planet to serve in even a greater way than we, for we are limited by the knowledge of the ways of the Creator to what we can do to serve. You are less limited than we in many senses.

However, service must always be performed with understanding, and understanding can be achieved through meditation. Do not be concerned that your service at the present is inadequate. It is only necessary that you have the desire to serve, for as we have stated before, the creation is so designed that desire is always fulfilled.

You will serve exactly as much as you desire to serve, and the effect of your service will be exactly as much as you desire the effect to be. This will occur, but patience and understanding, which may be achieved through meditation, are necessary if this service is to be effective. For your desire must be effective,

Chapter 10: Complete Messages

and this desire is generated through understanding, and this understanding is generated through meditation.

Go, then, within, for here lies all of that that you desire. We have stated this many times, for it is truth. It is reality.

At this time I will ask if there are any questions that I can answer using this instrument.

(Pause)

If there are no questions, I will leave this instrument. But I will be with each of you at all times, as we are one. Adonai vasu.

January 12, 1974

(Editor's Note: there are discrepancies between the text of this message and the text of the message dated January 12, 1974 in L/L Research's archives. I assume that this has happened because there are two sessions which were held on this date, one of which was not preserved beyond the making of this manuscript in 1975.)

I am Hatonn. I greet you, my friends, in the love and in the light of our infinite Creator. It is once more a great privilege to be with you. We of the Confederation of Planets in the Service of the Creator are always extremely privileged to speak directly to those who dwell upon the surface of this planet.

We would prefer to speak with all of the people of this planet. However, there are many who would not wish to hear us. They would not wish to know us. And they would not understand anything that we said, even though, my friends, we are able at this time to use any of your languages fluently. It takes a considerable amount of time, as you know it, to establish a base for communication when the concept from which we generate ideas is as largely displaced from yours as is ours. When I say yours, I am speaking of the general basis for concepts of the majority of the people of your planet.

Chapter 10: Complete Messages

The bases for our concepts are what we consider universal truths, truths that are unchanging, that are the reason for the creation that is all about us and is us and is you. Unfortunately, the people of the planet upon which you presently dwell are not aware of the truth behind the functioning of the creation in which they find themselves. This is not an abnormal situation, but it is not normal either. There are many other peoples throughout the creation who are not aware of these truths. However there are a very, very large number who are.

There are a certain percentage of the people within your population who are ready to be instructed, for they have reached a state of understanding so that they may easily assimilate the little more knowledge that they need in order to understand the truth of the functioning of this creation.

This is what we are attempting to do at this time, and this evening we will endeavor to do this so that each of you will be able to make one more step in your journey towards a complete understanding of truth. Most of the problems that you encounter in understanding this truth have to do with false impressions given to you by the society in which you now find yourselves. If you had been living in a society that had always been aware of truth and of the true nature of the creation, you would have no difficulty in applying the truths, since they would be a part of your life. It is difficult to do this when living in a society that continues to focus its attention on things that are very far from the Creator's plan.

The society as you know it at present has focused its attention on many things. Very, very few of these things in which it is interested have anything at all to do with the basic truth of the functioning of the creation in all of its ways and all of its parts.

Your people on this planet seek many things. However, they seek these things in what we would consider to be a very

Chapter 10: Complete Messages

strange way. They seek the result of their desires almost exclusively within what they know as the physical illusion that they now enjoy. Since they are unable to experience in their waking state anything but this physical illusion, they then think that this is all that exists, and they attempt to find expression of their desires strictly within this illusion.

This results in the fulfillment of false desires. The people who fulfill these false desires wonder why, having fulfilled them, they do not find happiness. This has been demonstrated upon your planet many times, but little heed has been taken of it. The desires still remain very strong, and the people about you strive with much energy to fulfill them. Having fulfilled them they then, as I have said, wonder. They wonder why they still have desires, for as soon as they have fulfilled one, they have generated another.

We are going to attempt to give you instruction at this time on the proper use of desire, so that you may work within the truth of the creation and become once more knowledgeable about its function.

There are certain desires that every individual has within him. These desires are a natural state, and they should be fulfilled. The reason the individual has these natural desires is that he is a part of the creation, and the Creator had an original desire, which continues throughout all of time and all of space.

This desire of the Creator was to provide an experience for all of His parts that would fulfill in totality the desire of all of His parts. But since all of His parts have this same desire, then it should be evident that this desire is to serve the other parts. This is how we have interpreted the functioning of creation. This is why within each individual throughout all of the creation there dwells a desire to serve the creation in any way that he can. This dwells within each of the people, all of the entities of this planet, for all of them are a portion of the Creator.

Chapter 10: Complete Messages

It is possible to fulfill this desire. As we have said, the Creator has attempted to provide only good for all of His children, but since all of his children are a part of the Creator, and since all of us and everything is in actuality one thing, then we have this necessity occurring within each individual in all of the parts of the creation: an attempt to serve. This is natural. The planet upon which you now stand serves you. The growth that comes from the planet serves you. Its atmosphere serves you. Its water serves you. The entire creation serves you. You feel the energy from your sun. It serves you.

This principle is simply the original concept of the Creator being expressed through all of its parts, for this concept remains undiminished. For this reason, you will find that you will achieve what you actually desire only if you are to serve the rest of the creation. This is a law that is natural. This law is [of] the creation.

The people of the Confederation of the Planets in the Service of the Infinite Creator are just that: we are in service. But we are in our service, and we are in your service, and we are in the creation's service, for we have recognized that, in being a part of the Creator, and having within us the expression that was originally generated, it is only possible to fulfill desire through service. For this reason we are here now, to give to you our service. This fulfills our desire. This fulfills the Creator's desire. The entire process is simplicity itself.

My friends, this is the creation: simplicity. It is only necessary that you understand this, and then act in such a way as to carry out your desire in its true sense for you to unite once more in totality with the original and true creation.

We have stated many times that meditation is very necessary. If you are to understand what and how to serve at this time, it is necessary that you find this through meditation, for this is the only process that will allow you to understand in its totality this information. So, it is necessary that you spend time each day in meditation, and become aware of the technique of fulfilling your desire to serve. When you have done this, you will find that you are experiencing something that is phenomenal. It will be an event that is beyond your wildest dreams. It will be of a nature that you might consider impossible at this time. But it will take place. Many of the people of this planet are serving at this time. They serve in many different ways. However, only a small percentage of them are actually fulfilling their desire to serve. For what I will call "blind" service is not as effective as service that is performed as a result of the knowledge gained in meditation.

It is important, then, to learn how to serve and who should be served. As I have said, it would seem that we would perform a service by coming among your people and helping. Our meditation reveals to us that this is erroneous. For this reason, we contact you in this way. We request that you do as we do, if you are to know how to serve and who should be served at this time.

Meditate, for this knowledge is within all people throughout the creation. For they are the Creator, and this is His desire, to serve; to serve all of His parts, so that each experiences the ecstasy that He originally created, and that exists all about you.

I hope that I have been of service this evening, for that is my objective.

I will leave this instrument now for a short period. If there are any questions I shall return shortly. I leave in the love and the light of our infinite Creator. Adonai vasu.

(A question is asked silently, telepathically, directly to Hatonn.)

I am Hatonn. I greet you again in the love and the light of our infinite Creator. I would attempt to speak on a subject of interest. The subject is love.

Chapter 10: Complete Messages

This is a subject that is necessary to understand if you are to be effective in fulfilling your desire of service. In serving your fellow man upon Earth, it is necessary to give him love. This is sometimes difficult to do in your present society, for these expressions are often misunderstood.

Love is very misunderstood among your people. We express total love for all of your people. We cannot help doing this, for we express total love for all the creation. It is impossible to do otherwise, when you are aware of the love expressed by the creation. In order to achieve this awareness it is only necessary to meditate, and then to serve, for with each service effectively performed, love will be reflected. This will generate within you more love, and the process will be repeated, or recycled.

This process will be self-generating and will continue to build. This is what occurred with the teacher with whom you are most familiar, the one known as Jesus. Why was this man much more effective in generating this love than others who have attempted this recently? The reason, my friends, is that he was able to fulfill his desire for service intelligently. He was able to do this in an intelligent manner because he sought answers to the questions of how to fulfill his desire for service through meditation.

Many of those upon your planet who seek to serve their fellow man at present, seek to serve him in ways that they have learned intellectually, from others, or from readings. And they find, in many cases, difficulties in performing the service that they so much desire to give. And the love that they desire and expect as a return for their service is not reflected, for the service that they have attempted is not desired, and is therefore not a service.

A service is only a service if it is desired. Man has free will. He is free to choose anything that he desires. It is necessary, if you are to serve, that you understand the desire of those served, not in an intellectual sense, but in a sense that you gain through meditation; a knowledge that transcends the intellect; a knowledge that results in effective service.

I hope that I have been of assistance in explaining this particular point. I will leave this instrument. I am Hatonn. Adonai vasu.

The Channel: Was that an answer to your question?

Questioner: Yes, that was a specific answer to my question.

Unknown date in 1974
(I was unable to find this transcript in the L/L Research archives. Therefore this is the only occurrence of this session. It is likely that the tape which was used to record this session was re-used to tape another session, and therefore this session was lost until now.)

I am Hatonn. I greet you, my friends, in the love and the light of our infinite Creator. It is a great privilege to be with you this evening. It is always a great privilege to be of service to those who seek the service of the Confederation of Planets in the Service of the infinite Creator. I am going to condition this instrument for a short period of time. If you will please be patient, we will shortly continue this contact.

I am Hatonn. I am with the instrument. I am very happy to be with you. I greet you once more in the love and the light of our infinite Creator. It is always a great privilege to be with you. We in the Confederation of Planets in the Service of the Infinite Creator are here to aid you in any way that we can.

I am aware that there are some questions, and that these questions should be answered. We will answer them to the best of our ability. However, there are certain limitations. This instrument is not aware of the questions. However, I will use him to transmit to you our opinions of what reality is.

Reality is exactly what you think it is. Our reality is varied. Our reality is what we desire it to be. Your reality is not necessarily what you desire it to be. Conditions on your

Chapter 10: Complete Messages

planet are not correct for reality to result as a function of desire.

However, we who are in the service of the infinite Creator are able to appreciate any reality that we desire. This may seem strange. But this is true. This is how it was planned for the children of the Creator, for them to experience the reality that they desire.

You are experiencing a result of your desire at this time. You will continue to experience this until you leave what you call your physical life. We are attempting to show to you how to alter reality so that it conforms within your present limitations to exactly what you desire. This is your birthright. It is a simple thing to do. And is meant to be mastered by everyone.

The reason for the lack of mastery of this simple principle upon the planet upon which [you] now dwell, is that its occupants have forgotten the principle. We have attempted during these past weeks to state the principle to you in many ways. However, it is so very simple that it is difficult to dwell upon it in many different ways for any length of time.

It is difficult for the people of your planet at this time to understand that they are locked within an illusion created by their desires, and that they can unlock this self-inflicted illusion, at any time they desire, simply by altering the form of their desire.

My friends, most of the individuals upon the planet at this time actually continue to desire that which they are presently experiencing. This has been, you might say, programmed, as you express it, into their consciousness, and they continue in their present methods of expressing themselves and experiencing the illusion in which they now find themselves. It has been pointed out to the people of this planet many times in the past that it is possible to unlock the door to this illusion at any time. It is only necessary that the individual learn to think.

Chapter 10: Complete Messages

There are many institutions upon your planet that profess the teaching of thinking. However, we find that very few of them teach anything to do with actual thinking. The thinking that is taught in these institutions of higher learning is a thinking that is limited by the illusion in which you presently exist. This is what we are trying to break. This is what we are trying to help you extract yourself from. This is our only real service.

There are ways to think to reach a goal that you actually desire, and there are ways to think to reach a goal that is within the limits of your present illusion. If you are to reach that goal that you actually desire, it will be necessary for you to begin to think in a way that will accomplish this. It will also be necessary for you to reject all forms of thinking that are associated with the illusion.

This will be, primarily, manifested through dismissing the complexities and intellectual appraisal of the various manifestations and consequences that occur in your daily life. All that is necessary in order to reach the stratum of thinking that you actually desire to reach is to reject all of these intellectual games and presupposed values, and to return to a simple understanding of the unity of the creation and your part as part of it.

This does not require any complex, intellectual appraisal or understanding. It requires only that you become aware, through each instant of your waking life, that you are a portion of all that there is, that all that there is, [is] the Creation, and that the Creation is love.

Is this possible? This is possible. We have answered this question because we have seen this done many times. We of the Confederation of Planets in the Service of the Infinite Creator are here to help you realize this possibility and then to demonstrate it. There is nothing else that is of any value. There are many things that seem to be of value within your illusion. However, they are of no value.

Chapter 10: Complete Messages

You might ask why these things are of no value. My friends, they are of no value because they do not exist. They exist in illusion, not reality. Your illusion is a very, very small part of the creation, and it lasts for a time that is not even worth consideration.

Your illusion is created by you and for you for your expression in a certain way. It is also a necessary illusion for you to produce the growth of the spirit that you desire. However, this may be accelerated at will, if you so will it. We are here to help you produce this acceleration. It is only necessary for you to look about you. There are certain ones in the illusion who express this knowledge, and certain ones who do not. Which do you choose - to express this understanding of love and unity, or to reject it and remain within the illusion?

We know the answer. This is the reason that we are here. We are here to help you reject the illusion and join us of the Confederation of Planets in the Service of the Infinite Creator in our enjoyment of the entire creation of the Father, not one small illusion.

There are individuals scattered throughout this infinite creation that have created small and finite illusions for themselves. The reason for individuals falling into conditions of illusion are many and varied. However, we find that the actual desire of every portion of creation is the unity of which I have spoken many times.

We are here to help you re-find this. We have done this in other places in this creation, and we will continue to do it, for service in this manner is the greatest reward that we could ask in the service of the Creator. We realize that it is very difficult, when continually hypnotized by the illusion that so constantly surrounds you, to break from this state and reach the understanding that you desire. However, it is quite possible to do this in a short period of time. What is the route, my friends? It has been stated to you time and time again:

Chapter 10: Complete Messages

meditation. Meditation is the route between you and the unity that you seek.

It is difficult for many of those who are trapped within this illusion to understand the importance of meditation, and why this should be the route that unlocks the door to their present entrapment. But, my friends, the illusion is an illusion of the mind. Meditation is an exercise of the mind, an exercise in reverse from what you normally consider mental exercise in the illusion. This is what is necessary to erase the illusion that you have created, to reverse the mental exercise that has created this illusion, and back out of your entrapment. Turn off your mind, your intellectual mind. Let it once more absorb the knowledge of the Creator which is deep within it. Let this be your thought, rather than that given to you by the multitudes who continue within the illusion. This simple process will bring you to what you desire, what is desired by all of the Creator's children throughout all of the universe: love and light.

Many of the Creator's children have gone far from this love and this light. They have burrowed deeply into their self-made illusion, and wrapped themselves tightly within the robes of that which their mind has manifested. They have done this until they are so deeply locked within this manifestation that we cannot even communicate with them. If we were to land upon your surface, and grasp them by the shoulders, and speak to them directly, they would not hear us. Their illusion is so strong that they would attempt to kill us.

This is extremely unfortunate. For these individuals at present, we find no avenue for aid, and this saddens us. It will take a longer period of time for them to return to the fold, for they will have to experience the product of their illusion for some time before it finally drives them back out to the point where they can begin to re-communicate with the one Intelligence.

Chapter 10: Complete Messages

Those such as yourselves are very fortunate in that you now have the opportunity to communicate directly with those of the Confederation who would bring you the aid that you desire. Our craft are in your skies. We are about your planet in swarms. But we stand off at great distances.

And why is this necessary? Why cannot we come among you as we so desire? The illusion, my friends, that you have created, is too strong. It must be weakened. Each one of our craft that is seen by one or more of your peoples has its slight effect, in our program to help you in weakening your illusion. Each message such as this one, listened to or read by your peoples, has its slight effect in weakening this illusion. But only you, only the individual, can actually reduce it to what it is: an insane and unwanted manifestation of the mind of those who exist upon your planet. Its strength holds within its grip almost all those who dwell upon this surface. The last great teacher who came to you was plucked from his life at an early age by its strength, for the illusion manifests with physical power; power within the illusion.

But, my friends, it is so very limited: limited to one small speck in an infinite Creation. And why, my friends, is it so limited? It is limited by itself. For in this creation, illusions of this type are always limited. For that is their nature.

Reject these limitations. Rejoin your brothers, who are one with the entire creation. Look into your night sky. There are billions and billions of suns and planetary systems, in all directions from you. And yet the strength of the illusion that surrounds you limits you to seeing them as tiny dots of light.

The Creator never intended for his children to see the Creation that is theirs as tiny dots of light in blackness. He meant for them to experience the total love and light that is the Creation. Erase this from your consciousness. You are not limited. You are the same as we, and we are all the same as each other, and we are all the creation, and all of the creation is we, and it is all meant for us, and we are all meant for it. Erase the illusion. This is our service to you: to teach you to reach out for what you desire.

You are very fortunate. Many of your brothers on this Planet cannot and will not hear us. And if they hear us, they cannot understand us. Take this opportunity to regain what is rightfully yours: an infinite creation, filled with love and light.

I am Hatonn. Adonai vasu.

www.ingramcontent.com/pod-product-compliance
Lightning Source LLC
Chambersburg PA
CBHW062152080426
42734CB00010B/1656